LIFE OF SISTER MARY OF ST. PETER

L' ABBE JANVIER

SENSUS FIDELIUM PRESS

Gastonia, North Carolina

CONTENTS

PREFACE

The life which we are now about to offer the public, will undoubtedly be acknowledged to be one of the most remarkable that has appeared in our century. A poor, simple seamstress chosen as the mediator between the anger of a justly offended God and the sins of a guilty, ungrateful people: — the heavenly ambassadress to one of the mighty courts of the world:—the recipient of the most astonishing revelations:—and all this in our days! Is it possible that visions, ecstasies and revelations are the lot of mortals of the nineteenth century? Do these not rather belong to the days of the prophets, of the apostles? *Sit Nomen Domini benedictum!* May the Name of the Lord be blessed! His arm is not shortened, nor his holy spirit mute in our day more than in times gone by. The life of this generous spouse of Christ is only one of the many proofs that his Church is now, as it ever has been, holy: holy in her doctrine, holy in her ministers and holy in her children.

In obedience to her superiors, Sister Mary St. Peter writes her own life, the charm of which lies in its childlike simplicity. Her humility and her obedience shine forth in every line, producing the most wonderful fruits of generosity and zeal for the salvation of souls. What a heroic mission was hers! To establish Reparation in the Church; to vindicate the honor due to the most Holy Name of God. And with what admirable generosity, untiring zeal and devotedness without reserve, has she not delivered herself to the Spirit of the Most High, to be a docile instrument in his hand for the glory of his Name, and the consolation of his Holy Face!

It is to you, O children of Erin, whom the iron heart of the usurper has driven from your green hills and fertile valleys, to you who have braved the perils of the deep, the dreary exile in the midst of a strange people, to you who, in the midst of trials and dangers, of difficulties and hardships whose name is legion, you who have gloriously surmounted every obstacle and have succeeded in planting the faith from ocean to ocean, from the ice-bound shores of the Canadas, to the zephyr-fanned plains of Mexico, it is to you to uphold the glory of the Name of the Most High; to teach your children to honor this most Holy Name, to perform all things *in the name of God,* the hallowed expression of your ancestors: *In the Name of God.* It is to you, the Irish American people, worthy children of a St. Patrick and a St. Bridget, to you is this little book affectionately dedicated. May its perusal produce fruit a hundred fold to the glory of the most Holy Name of God!

May 1, 1884.

INTRODUCTION

Our Lady of the Holy Name of God, pray for us.

St. Michael, pray for us.

St. Martin, pray for us.

St. Louis, pray for us.

P robably the most underestimated Catholic person in the last two centuries, Sr. Marie de St. Pierre, received the revelations that now make up the Archconfraternity of the Holy Face, the devotion destined to save society. The volume the reader holds most likely was read by St. Thérèse of the Little Child and of the Holy Face and helped to transform her life into one of the most popular saints of all time. In logic, the cause is greater than the fact. It may be argued that the current autobiography caused St. Thérèse to experience an intense growth in her interior life. One can see the vast interior depth of this most humble of Carmelites in Tours, France. A summary of this autobiography, arranged by that great promoter of the Holy Face, Fr. Janvier, will show the depth this holy nun lived and the potential to bring about one of the greatest movements by God, one that is prophesied to defeat the future World Revolution. Although, "...the malice of man in open rebellion against itself," 1 meets us in every sector of modern man, Jesus has given us a remedy, a blue-print to re-establish Christendom which seems to have been lost decades ago.

Sister Marie de St. Pierre was permitted to make a private vow early in life. She exhibited her faith by the healing through the Miraculous Medal. St. Martin played a role in her life so many times on November 11th . On that date St. Martin interceded for Sister and opened the Carmel in Tours, 2 she left the world on his feast, and met Ven. Leo Dupont, native of Martinique. 3

As heaven continues to give us clues how to wage mystical combat, it is worth noting how private revelations are connected to each other. But they come in parables, a code which needs to be cracked. This story helps bring pieces together. Sister received two visions were, "...multitudes of souls [were] daily falling into hell...". 4 Our Lady of Fatima warns how "souls are falling into hell like snowflakes." The only thing that matters is that the soul lives with God in heaven. These two revelations, on the Holy Face and in Fatima, give us a clarion call to do all that we can to save our race from falling into the kingdom of hell. Is it a wonder how the Veil of Veronica 5 was brought out on the anniversary of the consecration of the Pantheon into St. Mary of the Martyrs on May 13 th , the date that Our Lady of Fatima began her series of revelations to the three children of Fatima? Let those who have eyes see and those who have ears hear. 6

Sister's heroic humility, for example, allowed her to receive permission from her superior to be sold to God as a mere donkey in order to pay for a new convent. Her humility also granted many favors, not only for her but for posterity. She received the Golden Arrow prayer. She was told the three patrons of the Arch-confraternity of the Holy Face, who are all soldiers; St. Michael, St. Martin and St. Louis, King of France. She was told how Jesus wants valiant soldiers who would be called Defenders of the Holy Name of God and how they would be a secret virtue tow wage ware against evil and Satan. She was told that St. Martin was chosen as one of the three patrons because of his zeal and charity in driving out Satan from Gaul. She was told how Christians can avenge Christ the King by making reparation for blasphemy and profanation of the Lord's Day and Holy Days. She was given that blasphemy is one of the worst of all sins. She was given the sacramental of the "Little Gospel," and how it secured a deathbed conversion, and how she was retaliated by a legion of demons for two hours. She was given the "Chaplet of the Holy Face" a minor exorcism for lay people.

"Demand of my Father," Jesus tells her, "as many souls as I have shed drops of blood in my Passion!" This and other revelations encourage the Church Militant to apply the merits of Jesus to, "...buy millions of souls by presenting the infinite merits of Jesus at the bank of the Divine Majesty." 7

Jesus encouraged her to have pity on poor "Sinners, as clouds of dust borne into the wind, are whirled from this world and precipitated into hell." 8 But the main object of note are the warnings from Jesus on a group of revolutionaries known as Communists 9 who try to blindfold the Catholic Church by stopping the hierarchy from approving this devotion. But alas Pope Leo XIII, made the devotion to the Holy Face in which the revelations of Jesus to Sr. Marie de St. Pierre are derived into an Arch-confraternity that is to exist in perpetuity. Jesus tells her how clients to this spiritual army will be hidden in the secret of His Holy Face and how they must beg for the Blessed Virgin Mary, under the title of Lady of the Holy Name of God to be their general in this work destined to save society. The Blessed Virgin Mary spoke to her how the more this army would be augmented, the more Satan and the enemies of the Church would be weakened. This is a model for exponential growth derived from Leviticus 26: 8, "Five of yours shall pursue a hundred others, and a hundred of you ten thousand: your enemies shall fall before you by the sword." Exponential growth is like a hockey stick. As more people join the ranks of the Archconfraternity of the Holy Face it will be like the top of the blade. But eventually when a critical mass is reached, a pre-ordained number of mystical combatants known by God, the stick will show the curve and the collapse of the plans of the revolutionary men. This book gives us the plan of how God can fight the war for us as mentioned in the Old Testament. 10

Lastly, this book ends with themes of the copies of the Veronica touched to the Veil of Veronica in St. Peter's at Rome and how Ven. Leo DuPont burned an oil lamp day and night before the relic. Eventually this oil was used to anoint sick people and over six thousand certified miracles ensued! Another of them included was the work of Archbishop Colet who rescued the revelations from the secret archives of the chancery and consecrated the house of Ven. Leo DuPont into a public oratory. His Grace also established the Priests of the Holy Face to promote the devotion. It may be the only devotion promoted by diocesan priests, who were taken from the secular canons of the Archepiscopal rectory.

In conclusion, I am grateful for Sensus Fidelium reprinting this spiritual treasure. I hope that it will help augment the remnant who continue to fight the kingdom of darkness. My hope is that this reprint will secure a cultus that will demand the Church to take another look into the cause of Sr. Marie de St. Pierre that was abruptly halted in the late nineteenth century. May she someday be raised to the holy altar. This work will hopefully spark new brigades who will swim against the tide of modernism and receive the highest thrones in heaven and whose faces will shine brighter than many others in eternity.

Ad Iesum per Mariam,

Fr. Lawrence Carney

February 27, 2024 Anno Domini

1 Life of Sister Mary St. Peter, written by herself, arranged and completed by M. L'Abbe Janvier, 1884, p. 286.

2 Tours, France was the See of the great thaumaturgus, the wonder worker St. Martin.

3 Ven. Louis DuPont was sent to Tours as a wish of his dying wife and he found the relics of St. Martin after the French Revolution buried them.

4 Life of Sister Mary St. Peter, written by herself, arranged and completed by M. L'Abbe Janvier, 1884, p. 293.

5 Veil of Veronica was given to St. Clement I and has been owned by the popes up to today. The Veil was taken out on the anniversary of the consecration of St. Mary of the Martyrs, May 13 th for over 100 years beginning in the seventh century as a remedy against pestilence, the elements and revolutionary men. Sr. Marie de St. Pierre was given intellectual visions regarding how the Veil of Veronica and devotion to it through her revelations given by Jesus and Mary would save us from world revolution.

6 See Mark 8:18.

7 Life of Sister Mary St. Peter, written by herself, arranged and completed by M. L'Abbe Janvier, 1884, p. 296.

8 Ibid., p. 309.

9 The revolution changes their name to fit the caprice of the time.

10 See II Paralipomenon (2 Chronicles) 20.

PROMISES MADE BY OUR LORD JESUS CHRIST TO SR. MARY ST. PETER IN FAVOR OF THOSE WHO HONOR HIS MOST HOLY FACE

"By my Holy Face you will work marvels."

"You will obtain from my Holy Face the salvation of a multitude of sinners."

"If you could comprehend how agreeable the sight of my Holy Face is to my Heavenly Father! "

"According to the care you take to repair my countenance disfigured by blasphemy, so shall I be animated in the same degree to transform your soul which has been disfigured by sin; I will imprint thereon my own image, and I will render it as beautiful as when it came forth from the baptismal font."

"My adorable Face is the seal of the Divinity, having the power to imprint itself on the souls of those who apply it to their persons."

"As in an earthly kingdom, the subjects can procure all they desire by being provided with a piece of money stamped with the effigy of the monarch, so also shall you be able to obtain all that you desire in the kingdom of heaven, on presenting the impress of my sacred humanity, which is my Holy Face."

1

OUR LITTLE BRETON

"I weep over my sins."
(Words of the Sister when but a child.)

I t is to Catholic Brittany, that ground so fruitful in virtuous and heroic characters, that we are indebted for Sister Mary of St. Peter. She was born at Hennes, in 1816, of worthy and honest parents of whom but little is known. Her father, whose name was Peter Eluere, was a locksmith by trade, and married Frances Portier, a lady worthy by her piety of such a husband, who, as we shall see, was a Christian of the old school. Some years after their marriage this virtuous woman was carried off by death. Being thus left a widower with twelve children, Peter Eluere had to endure many privations and sufferings, and ta labor assiduously to be able to bring up his children, and provide for them in their sickness which, for the most part, was long and fatal; for he beheld them all, one after the other consigned to the tomb, with the exception of one son and one daughter, who survived him. His glory before God and man was to have given to Carmel and to the Church the child of benediction, whose life we have undertaken to narrate.

When Sister Mary St. Peter had become a religious, she was obliged by obedience to write her own life, even the most minute details of the early years of her childhood. We shall make an extensive use of her letters and other writings during the course of our narrative, preserving as much as possible the simple and unassuming style so natural to her. She thus enters upon the task set before her.

"Notwithstanding the great repugnance I experience in writing of matters concerning myself, I will not hesitate to submit to the orders of obedience. I shall perform what I have been commanded with the assistance of the child Jesus, into whose revered little hand I have placed my pen, entreating him to write an account of the precious graces which he has accorded me, and my malice in so often offending Him, that thereby God the Father may be glorified for having by his almighty power produced such abundant fruit for the glory of his Holy Name, from such sterile ground covered with the brambles and thorns of sin and imperfection. At the feet of the child Jesus in the manger, I now commence my narrative, in obedience to you, reverend Mother."

"I was born on the 4th of October 1816, a day rendered memorable by the death of our holy Mother, St. Theresa; it was also the feast of St. Francis of Assissium, whose name my mother bore. I was baptized in the church of St. Germain, at Rennes, receiving for patrons St. Peter and St. Francis of Assisium. My poor, dear mother received on this, her birthday, a sad bouquet, in presenting to the world a little girl who was to cause her so many anxieties, and such solicitude, by her ill health and her willfulness. She confided me to the care of a nurse, who was a most excellent person. But about a month after my birth, an accident occurred, which would have caused my death, had it not been for the special protection of God. My nurse, having gone out for a moment, left me in my cradle. One of her little girls took me in her arms and carried me to the fireplace to keep me warm; but I fell from her hold into the fire: I have always retained the marks of this accident even to this day. My mother, much grieved at the occurrence, dismissed this woman from her service."

"I will now give an account of one of the first acts of malice which I can remember. When I had grown a little older, someone told me of the accident, which had happened to me. To my surprise, my good old nurse came one day to see me. I received her coldly, remarking with much asperity: "You have already burned one of my cheeks, have you come to-day to disfigure the other?" At four years of age. I was attacked with scarlet fever, which brought me to death's door. My parents have often told me that I had been in great danger for nineteen days, having been unable to take nourishment of any kind, save a small glass of cider. The very recollection of this often made my father laugh, when speaking of my illness, during which, a beverage so contrary to my condition, should have been the means of preserving my life."

"From the moment my reason commenced to develop itself, my virtuous parents gave me the advantage of a pious education ; but I was naturally very disagreeable and obstinate. My pious mother took me often to church with her, but here I was thoughtless and giddy, and kept turning my head in every direction to see what was going on around me. After manifesting such a want of reverence and decorum in the House of God, and failing in fidelity to my mother's counsels, I was severely punished on my return home. When I was a little over six years of age, I was taken to confession to accuse myself of all my faults. I was so jealous of my little sister that my parents were obliged to separate us and send her away for some time. Besides these exterior defects, which rendered me so disagreeable to others, my heart was filled with pride and self-love. On one occasion my mother said to me in the presence of my father, for the purpose of mortifying me: 'Surely, this is not our little girl, if so, she must have been transformed by her nurse; it is impossible that our child could be as perverse as this little one.' Such reflections coming from the lips of my mother, were not very flattering. But I soon gained quite a victory over my pride. Every day a poor, blind, old man, shabbily dressed, passed our door. On approaching the corner of the street, he required the assistance of some kindly hand to conduct him to the right path. My kind-hearted parents frequently requested me to render him this necessary assistance; but I was so excessively proud, and manifested so much repugnance that they did not insist. Finally, one day I determined to overcome my pride. I ran from the house and took the poor old man gently by the hand and led him to the right path. It seemed to me then that I had performed a most heroic act. Whenever I was reprehended for my misbehavior by my parents, I did not rebel against their authority for I perceived that it was for my benefit they corrected me, and my wayward heart was touched at times by the voice of God, which reproached me for my ingratitude."

"I received particular instructions concerning the ever Blessed Virgin; most wonderful examples of her protection and power were related to me;my . heart was touched, and I commenced to pray fervently to this good mother, and I soon became better. I began to love prayer and no longer received admonitions on my return home from High Mass and the other religious services of the Church, for I had become more sedate. When anything repugnant to my inclinations occurred, I offered it to God, saying, 'My God, I offer Thee this in expiation of my sins.'"

Let us for an instant interrupt this artless narrative and insert two incidents which we have learned from another source. These trifling imperfections which she considered as serious faults, were nothing more than the result of that forgetfulness common to childhood, yet which, at so tender an age, had impressed her with the most lively horror. Several times, her eldest sister found her alone, weeping bitterly. When asked the cause of her tears, the dear little one replied, "I am weeping over my sins." She feared even the slightest appearance of sin to such an extent, that at eight years of age, having had some scruples with regard to a book which had been lent her, she repaired to the parish priest before ever opening it, to ask his opinion regarding its perusal; when she learned that the book would do her no injury, yet, that it was only a frivolous story from the reading of which nothing profitable could be gleaned, she returned it to the owner immediately, without even having read the first page.

"My good parents," said she, "sent me to catechism with the other little children of the parish. I enjoyed the instructions greatly, and my conduct soon becoming more edifying, flattery succeeded the reproaches which I had been in the habit of receiving. On one occasion, a lady said to my mother in my presence:'Madam, your little girl conducts herself in church like a person of forty years of age!' But I think that these flattering remarks only increased my pride and self-love. I commenced about this time to practice the devotion of the Holy Way of the Cross. The reflections on the sufferings of our Divine Lord affected my heart in a very sensible manner, for I felt that my sins had been the cause of his sufferings, and full of contrition, I said: 'Oh! my Savior, didst thou not perceive during thy dolorous Passion that one day I would be converted and would belong entirely to Thee?' I kissed the ground and humbled myself to the earth at each station. When I returned home, it often happened that my face was all covered with dust, and our Lord permitted that this act of devotion should draw upon me a humiliation, for whenever my sister was displeased with me she would taunt me with the appellation: 'dirty nose,' which frequently put my feeble virtue to a severe test."

"The grace of God was attracting me strongly, yet, I was inconstant in the practice of virtue, alternately rising and falling. I know not how it happened, but I remember having heard of a sort of prayer called mental, which was much more agreeable to God than vocal prayer. I had an ardent desire to pray in this manner, and I said to myself: I shall recite no more words in saying my prayers;for the future I shall pray mentally. But when I finished my prayers according to my new method, I was seized with doubts and scruples for not having said my morning and evening prayers as had been my custom. Our Lord, beholding my desire, inspired me to contemplate his sufferings caused by my sins and infidelities, over which I wept sincerely;and He permitted, a little later, that I should hear a sermon treating entirely of meditation. I opened both my ears and my heart to receive this beautiful instruction, for I was so anxious to learn how to make so delightful a prayer."

This attraction for prayer in a child of such tender years, prognosticated the winders which would result. When the favored child had attained the age of ten and a half years, she prepared herself for her first Communion, by making a good general confession.

"By the mercy of God," said she, "my heart was truly touched by grace. I received with great devotion this Divine Savior whom I had so often offended in my childhood, and I offered myself entirely to Him On the same day I received the sacrament of Confirmation, and was invested with the scapular, thereby placing myself under the protection of my tender mother, the Blessed Virgin Mary, to whom I owed my conversion. My confessor, observing that I was entirely changed, permitted me to receive holy communion again during the course of the ensuing year. He was surprised at the marvelous change which grace had operated in my soul, and did not hesitate to tell me so; but after saying many fine things on the subject, he commenced to ridicule and humble me. As I was not very humble, I would have much preferred not to have received these flatteries and thus to have avoided the humiliations which followed. Our Lord, who watched over me, sent me at this time spiritual trials, well adapted to humble and purify my soul."

"The devil, seeing that his prey had escaped him, made a last effort to regain an entrance into my soul. Having been driven from his hold he went, as the Gospel relates, to seek seven other spirits morewicked than himself, to aid him to regain his prey. Then I was attacked by a thousand temptations: my mind was enveloped in darkness, my soul tormented with scruples, and I believed that I was committing sin every moment: I had not a minute's peace. If I listened to a sermon the demon whispered imprecations and blasphemies in my ear, and my mind was harassed with evil thoughts. I was then but twelve years old. The sins of my past life returned to my memory with redoubled force; it seemed that I had never confessed them. Confession appeared to be something impossible for I lost myself in lengthy examinations, and never believed myself sufficiently prepared. When my turn came, I entered the confessional with my soul filled with doubts, sorrow and anxiety; I no longer found any consolation in my prayers, for I feared I recited them without the proper dispositions, and I repeatedly commenced over and over again the same prayer.

"This repetition was as absurd as it was fatiguing. My confessor did all in his power to console me; but being so young, and having had no experience in this kind of temptation, I did not make him sufficiently acquainted with the nature and extent of my sufferings;during this time of trial our Heavenly Father was only purifying my soul. I was then far from entertaining notions of pride and self-love."

"Our Lord afflicted me in a most sensible manner, by depriving me of my good mother, whom I loved most dearly. When she expired, I recalled to my mind that St. Theresa was but twelve years of age when she lost her mother, and like this great saint, I also implored the Blessed Virgin Mary to become a mother to me, and to fill the place of my own dear mother who had been just taken from me. Our Blessed Lady, indeed, heard my prayer, for I have always experienced, in a very special manner, the effects of her maternal protection."

"I continued to attend the catechism class for several years. The priest in charge of the Sunday School, was a very competent and worthy person. He is now a most zealous Bishop. I believe he saw clearly the sad condition of my soul, but as he was not my confessor, he could not give me the consolation of which I stood so much in need. However, it was he who taught me the method of making mental prayer by the sermon to which I have already made reference, and later on he rendered me great service."

"The fete-day of the Catechism class was approaching. Three little girls had been chosen to recite a piece in the form of a dialogue. I was one of the numbers; each one received her role to memorize. My two companions were to discuss with me on the pleasures of the world, which they were to laud highly, whilst I was to represent their vanity and nothingness. At the termination of the piece one of the two concluded by saying, that my discourse had convinced her that I had made a vow of poverty, and that perhaps I would become a Carmelite. May our Lord be blessed! for I really received this vocation sometime later: the other two remained in the world and were married."

"Finally, it pleased God to deliver me in the following manner from the torture of my mental sufferings. A pious young companion of mine, aware of my spiritual condition, had the charity to speak of it to my confessor, who was also hers. One day I entered the confessional after her, but feeling that I was not sufficiently prepared, I arose to retire. What was my astonishment, when I heard my confessor open the door of the confessional and order me to return immediately and commence my confession without delay. I excused myself saying, that I was not sufficiently prepared, that I had not finished my examination of conscience, and that I felt no contrition for my sins: but he would not listen to my reasoning. I submitted to obedience, made my confession and received absolution; my confessor then said to me: 'My child, be assured that this confession has been one of the best of your life.' He then expressly forbade me to recite my prayers over and over again ; and he gave me a rule to follow respecting the scruples which tormented me so terribly. Our Blessed Lord granted me the grace to submit to the counsels of my director, and the devil was overcome by obedience. All my disquietudes vanished like smoke, and a holy peace returned to my weary heart. Then approaching our Divine Lord in the sacrament of his love with a humble confidence and a holy peace of mind, I soon experienced its marvelous effects; my soul was inundated with consolation. I also received many graces while assisting at the holy Sacrifice of the Mass. When the moment of consecration approached it was with difficulty I could conceal my transports of joy from the observation of those present. I kept myself in the Divine Presence continually, and my union with God was uninterrupted."

As she lived at home with her father, her brothers and sisters, Perrine, (feminine for Peter, her baptismal name,) cheerfully joined in all their amusements. Having assisted at Mass and the other offices of the Church on Sundays, they assembled in a party and walked to the country. On these occasions they took with them some little refreshments, and each one diverted himself as he thought proper. Our little Perrine knew well how to pass these hours of pleasant recreation piously, and to the edification of all. We have learned these particulars from one of her cousins of the same age, Jennie Benoit, who generally formed one of the numbers on these little fetes. Having arrived at the place where they proposed passing the remainder of the day, Perrine would draw her cousin aside and then they would entertain themselves, conversing on the Blessed Virgin and on the benefits bestowed on them by their heavenly Mother.

The education of our little Breton was exceedingly limited, she having had but two years regular attendance at school: reading, writing, grammar, and arithmetic, such, at that period, was all the instruction considered necessary for persons in her sphere of life. The daughter of the mechanic Eluere, although naturally gifted, received no further educational advantages than those afforded by the times to persons in her position.

Two of her paternal aunts kept a dressmaking establishment of considerable importance, and to them our little Perrine was confided to learn the business.

"My good aunt," said she, "placed me in a corner near her where I worked as if I were in a little cell, separated from the other young persons employed in the establishment. I was not disturbed by them, nor they by me, for they never for a moment perceived the operations of divine grace which were going on in my soul. Nothing could divert me from the intimate conversations which I held with our Divine Lord. I often made spiritual communions, which so enkindled in my soul the fire of divine love, that in the midst of my occupations I was so transported from this earth, that at times it became difficult to control myself. Our Divine Lord granted me the favor of being admitted into the Congregation of our Blessed Lady, of which one of my good aunts was the directress."

This Association had been established by some holy missionaries in 1817, to maintain and preserve piety and the practice of Christian virtue among the youth of the city. At that time the association numbered several hundred members, it continued to flourish for many years and was the means of doing much good at Rennes; it still exists, though not so flourishing. The ordinary reunions take place in the same isolated little chapel where but very recently an image of the Holy Face was installed with -great devotion and solemnity in honor of the former member whose life we are now narrating.

"After the ordinary period of probation," said she, "I was received as a member by the council and made my act of consecration. Oh, what a day of consolation! The ceremony recalled to me my first communion. I was, as on that day, attired in white, with a lighted candle in my hand, and kneeling before the director and another ecclesiastic, and in the presence of over five hundred of my new sisters, I renewed my baptismal vows, and I promised faithfully to observe the rules of the association. I then consecrated myself to the most Blessed Virgin, my good mother. This association had been established for the working classes, who were bound to it by no vow;the rules and regulations were well adapted to preserve a religious spirit and the love of piety in the hearts of the young; every two weeks the director gave an excellent and instructive discourse to the members."

The Divine Master, having nourished his- little servant with the spiritual milk of consolation for a sufficiently long period, now wished to strengthen her soul by more solid and substantial food, that she might be fortified to pass, as she herself expressed it, "from Thabor to Calvary."

"Consolation gave way to aridity and spiritual barrenness, this condition seemed strange to me. What! to feel that I was no longer loving and serving God! Being ignorant of the ways of grace, I imagined that by force of application, I could again taste the ineffable delights of those transports of love with which I had been favored; but these vain efforts only wearied me and made me sick. I spoke of the state of my soul to my confessor, who did not seem to be at all moved by what I related to him. He only said that by degrees I would again enjoy the same consolations. I continued in the same state of aridity, and in my ingratitude to my heavenly benefactor, I relaxed in the path of perfection; my weary, miserable heart turned to creatures for consolation. I had no peace of mind, and although my faults were not grievous, yet they were injurious to my soul, for our blessed Lord demanded of me a greater degree of generosity."

In this painful state of mental suffering, she took a step which might have compromised her whole future. Imagining that her confessor seemed indifferent to her faults, Perrine, docile and confiding as she had ever been, asked permission of her virtuous father to consult another confessor. Being a discreet person, he doubted the prudence of assenting to his daughter's request, and before so doing, consulted the same priest whom she wished to leave. This was the cure of the parish for whom he entertained the greatest esteem. Perrine's father represented to him that perhaps she might feel better under the direction of another confessor, who was then held in great repute by the pious. The good cure readily gave his consent to the desired change; but our little penitent soon had cause to repent of her inconstancy.

"Although," said she, "I received the most excellent counsels from my new director, yet I became no better. At the age of seventeen the vain attractions of the world began to entice me, and growing lukewarm in the service of God, I soon gave myself up to the foolish vanities of the world. But what was most disastrous of all at this time, was my neglect of prayer, a means so necessary to the soul in vanquishing her passions, and in strengthening her against the attacks of the Evil One."

"After the death of my mother, the care of the house devolved upon my eldest sister and proud I was not always disposed to submit to her authority, and was thus, often the cause of much trouble and dissention. My conscience often reproached me for my infidelities:I recalled to mind the happy days of my childhood when, faithful to the God of mercy and love, I was filled with ineffable delights; I longed to return to Him, but my soul was, as it were, enchained by my evil propensities; finally I had recourse to Her who is never invoked in vain, to Mary, my tender mother, to whom I had consecrated myself forever."

The feast of the Purification was approaching, and I prepared myself by a novena. I passed this beautiful day in great devotion, offering a taper to be burned before the altar of the Blessed Virgin. The chains, by which I had been so long bound, were severed, and my heart was entirely changed. Some invisible power seemed to impel me to return to my old confessor. As soon as I beheld him, I exclaimed, 'Oh! my good father, virtue fled from my soul when I left your direction. I implore you to number me once more among your many penitents.' He received me as did the father of the Prodigal son, with great charity. Soon after this, I made a retreat of eight days in a religious house where there were missionaries preaching. It was there that divine mercy awaited me. I had most earnestly besought the Blessed Virgin to obtain a happy result to my retreat, and my prayers were heard. The grace of God, together with the instructions of the good missionaries produced the most salutary effects in my soul. I made a general confession and beholding all my sins and the infinite mercy of God which I had so long despised, and contemplating the wounds of my crucifix, I felt my heart penetrated with contrition, my eyes shed torrents of tears, and I promised for the future ah inviolable fidelity to God."

2

HER VOCATION

"All! my child, your passions have been only wounded, they must be immolated."
(Words of her Confessor.)

O ur little Perrine had just completed her seventeenth year:her retreat "entirely converted her," as she herself said. She always attributed this great grace to the most Blessed Virgin, the mother of Jesus, and from that moment united to her past sentiments of filial affection for this tender Mother, a lifelong debt of gratitude.

"I became devoted to the Blessed Virgin," said she, "in a most particular manner; I admired with what mercy this divine Mother withdrew me from the verge of the abyss whither my infidelities were leading me; my confidence in her daily increased and I felt inspired to beg her to obtain for me the grace of becoming a religious. My good Mother heard my prayer, for I soon felt the desire of abandoning the world grow stronger in my soul. But what was I to do? I was afraid to mention the subject to my confessor. One day, when my sufferings were extreme and the grace of God was strongly agitating me on the subject of my vocation, I hastened to the altar of my cherished Mother, our Blessed Lady, and deposited in her maternal heart all my fears and anxieties. The Blessed Virgin soon soothed my troubled heart and delivered me from my disquietude. There was in this chapel, opposite her beautiful silver statue, the confessional of one of her zealous servants, the vicar, of whom I have already spoken, who had given me the part of a religious in the catechism conference at which I was asked if I would like to be a Carmelite. I was kneeling before the statue of our Blessed Mother, supplicating her to assist me in my interior combat, when I suddenly perceived that this good priest was about to enter his confessional, and it seemed that he made me a sign to enter. I cannot account for how it happened, as I had never spoken to him of the concerns of my soul, and behold, much to my astonishment, he told me all that was passing in my interior, saying : 'You want to be a religious, my child, but to obtain the object of your desire, you imagine there is a mountain in your way. Am I not right?' Delighted with having so unexpectedly found a consoler who understood me perfectly, I spoke to him very frankly of my spiritual affairs. He examined me minutely and declared that I had a good vocation. Much encouraged by his counsels, I went to find my confessor to whom I had not dared broach the subject of my vocation?'

"When I made known to him my desire of entering the religious state, he replied: 'Your sentiments accord perfectly with mine, for I have always thought that you would be a religious.' This assurance from my confessor filled me with joy. Some days after this, he advised me to defer my departure until spring; but, alas! in the meantime, I had to pass through the hands of another spiritual father who was not so quick to decide religious vocations. For five years he labored incessantly at the destruction of the inward wall of my pride and self-love, with the hammer of mortification, before he considered me worthy of inhabiting the solitude of Carmel."

The new director, of whom she now speaks, never sent aspirants to religion until they had given ample proof to hope that once entered the convent, they would never return io the world again. From accidental causes, Perrine was led to place herself under the direction of this wise and prudent confessor.

The parish priest, her former director, threatened with loss of sight, was obliged to go to Paris for medical treatment, and knowing that his spiritual child required the direction of a skillful and experienced guide, he recommended her to this holy and venerable ecclesiastic, who at the time rendered valuable services to the various religious communities of the diocese. He was a man of great enlightenment in the ways of grace, and was gifted with peculiar tact in the discernment of religious vocations; he was so widely known that mothers dreaded to see their daughters going to consult him. This skillful director was l'abbe Panager who, at the time of his death, was pastor of Saint Etienne at Rennes. We have his opinion of our young Perrine, too significant in its brevity to be passed unnoticed: "I have only known her from the time she chose me as her director, and this simply because she wished to become a religious. Her motive prompted me to receive her kindly, and I immediately undertook to aid her. I always found her very exact, and very docile under my direction. I lent her books, and from time to time gave her some advice. She edified me very much, and I decided proposing her as a candidate to the Carmelites."

Perrine, accordingly, presented herself to this man of God, informing him of her desire to become a Carmelite. He received her with great charity and encouraged her to persevere in her holy purpose but was not willing to accept the responsibility of becoming her director without mature reflection. His counsel produced such an effect on our little aspirant that after the return of her previous confessor she entreated l'abbe Panager to continue her direction, but he still insisted on having more time for consideration. Finally, he said to her: "My child, I will undertake your direction for the honor and glory of God, and for the salvation of your soul."

"These words," said the sister, "inspired me with great confidence in this holy man's direction. His first wish was to fathom the depths of my soul, and for this purpose he directed me to give him a written account of the manner in which our Lord had conducted me in the past, and also desired to be informed of my present disposition. I wrote a small notice of these matters and remitted it to him; then he bade me make a rule of life. After some time, I requested him to interest himself in reference to my admission to the convent. 'Ah! my child,' said he, 'your passions have been only wounded, they must be immolated.' I had such an ardent desire of becoming a Carmelite that I would have passed through fire and water, were it necessary, to accomplish my object; bearing this end in view, I commenced with renewed fervor to labor at my perfection."

The counsels and exhortations of her confessor made a great impression on her mind, and she "took great care not to forget them". We shall quote from the sister's own artless narrative.

"His first care was to caution me against the foolish weaknesses but too common to devotees. 'My child,' said he, 'do not go about consulting different directors. If you wish me to be really your spiritual father, you must be really my child be simple then, as a child; it is here you must avow your failings, your doubts and temptations, but make no such disclosures elsewhere for it would avail you nothing. Never speak of your confessor, nor of the penances imposed on you; go straight to God in the spirit of faith; make no uneasy research in your soul for these are but fuel for Purgatory. Study to know yourself and to know God; the more you will know him, the more you will love him; be always cheerful and gay; be not like those sad and pensive beings who seem to bear the yoke of the Lord as if it were a heavy burden. Oh, my child, what a beautiful path the Lord has chosen for you! Consider the reward that awaits you if you prove faithful! Prepare yourself for the great designs God has in view over you."

"Such is a glimpse of the wise counsels which I received from this good father. By the grace of God they became fruitful in my soul. He lent me books which treated of prayer, interior life, and also the Lives of the Saints. All these spiritual aids fortified me and strengthened my desire of embracing the religious life. But when I expressed my earnest wish to leave the world, he would calmly reply: 'My child, the habit does not make the nun.' I saw by this answer that I had still to labor at my perfection. I prayed continually to the Blessed Virgin, my dear protectress, to conduct me as a Carmelite into the house where she was most loved. I also prayed fervently to the glorious St. Joseph, begging him to obtain for me the precious gift of prayer. To obtain this grace, and all the others of which I stood in need, especially that of becoming a religious, I performed a little pilgrimage in his honor. On Wednesdays, I ate nothing but dry bread for my breakfast, and on Saturdays, I did the same in honor of our Blessed Lady. I had a great devotion to the Holy Family: Jesus, Mary and Joseph were constantly in my mind. 'Most Holy family!' I would say to them, 'if I had the happiness of living when you were on this earth I would most surely have gone in quest of you, in whatsoever place you were to be found, that I might have had the honor of serving you as your little domestic.'"

"My director lent me the life of St. Theresa. When I read the promise which our Lord made her at the foundation of her first convent, St. Joseph of Avila, that He would dwell therein, the Holy Virgin and St. Joseph guarding the doors, one on either side, oh! how excessive was my joy! I no longer doubted that I would solicit an entrance to Carmel, the abode of the Holy Family. I tormented my confessor from that moment, begging him to interest himself in my behalf: but to try me still longer he gave me evasive answers, such as these: 'I shall see:—God's time has not yet come.' Once he said to me: 'Do you suppose, my child, that I would suffer you to enter a convent hastily, before your vocation has been well tried, and leave it directly as do so many young persons? No, my child, when I send you, you will be well prepared.'"

This was a sore trial for our young aspirant.

In the meantime, Divine Providence furnished her with an occasion of gratifying, at least in part, her ardent desire. An indigent family came to dwell in the neighborhood of her father's house. This poor family consisted of three members: the father, a laboring man, the mother who was blind, and a little son aged about four or five years. They were so very unfortunate, especially during the winter when the husband had no work, that their miserable little hut really bore the appearance of the stable of Bethlehem. They were found without fire or a morsel of bread. "I could not permit to pass such a precious opportunity of honoring the Holy Family in the persons of these poor people, and I did not rest one moment until I had rendered their situation more comfortable. By the grace of God I entertained a great veneration and affection for them, and lavished on them all the care which their indigence demanded. At that time, just previous to my admission as a Carmelite, my limited means did not permit me to supply all their necessities: but the Holy Family, whom I served in their persons, rendered me so eloquent in pleading their cause among my acquaintances that nothing was ever refused me."

"All my happiness consisted in visiting and instructing them in their religious duties, from which they had been estranged, no doubt by their extreme poverty. I persuaded them to go to confession; and I engaged the husband to make a retreat of eight days in a house destined for that purpose. If I loved this family they reciprocated my affection, and I soon perceived the influence I had acquired over them. When dissentions arose between them, from time to time, I would be called on to settle the difficulty and restore peace."

The Holy Family did not allow their little servant to go unrewarded. Perrine daily progressed in virtue. She was permitted by her director to make the vow of chastity which she renewed on all the feasts of the Blessed Virgin. With the view of preparing herself for the religious life, she endeavored to practice the higher virtues of mortification, humility, obedience, and the love of prayer. She also exercised a charitable zeal towards her young companions, assisting them in their spiritual advancement.

Let us listen to her own account of her pious practices of devotion. "I have always had a special attraction for prayer, and believing that I could not be a child of prayer without at the same time having a great love for mortification, I labored courageously to acquire this latter virtue, and also to destroy all my evil propensities. The better to succeed in my purpose, I took note of my daily failures and of the number of my acts of mortification. I kept by my side two little ribbons, on which were strung small beads such as are used for chaplets; one end served to note my failures, the other, the number of my little sacrifices, or virtuous actions performed during the day. This cord of mortification was composed of fifteen beads in honor of the fifteen mysteries of the Holy Rosary; and I believe that, at night, I often had the blessing of offering the entire chaplet completed to our Blessed Lady. I practiced the mortification of the eyes; whenever anything pleasant or agreeable was presented to my view, I would turn my head away and would not look at it. When I would be just on the point of saying something agreeable or witty. I would remain silent. I made my general and particular examination with the view of overcoming my predominant passion,—pride. But our Blessed Lord himself soon sent me the necessary assistance to vanquish mv enemy."

Almighty God, who never permits himself to be outdone in generosity, beholding this candid and faithful soul thus placing herself unreservedly at his disposal, was pleased to instruct and enlighten her himself.

"Many times." said she, "in the course of my life, I have experienced the extraordinary operations of grace in my soul, during which, if I may thus express it, our Lord showed me a glimpse of the celestial favors with which lie would one day enrich my soul. I had the happiness of receiving holy communion three times a week besides Sundays. It was at this divine banquet that our Blessed Lord united himself intimately to my soul. My director had commanded me to inform him of all that passed in my soul, and I, therefore, rendered him a strict account of these supernatural operations with the simplicity of a child, at which he did not seem to be astonished. 'My child,' said he, 'does not your soul belong to God? Then, permit this Divine Master to do as he will in his own house. These interior communications of our Lord, of which I was so unworthy, continued. Then I began to commit them to writing for the purpose of submitting them to the guide of my soul. I was sure by this means not to fall into illusion. He never made any reference to these communications in my presence: this pleased me very much, for such divine favors covered me with confusion. On one occasion when I bad presented to him one of these writings, it occurred to me that if I had read to him, myself, the account of these testimonies of affection which our divine Lord had given me, that it would be a great mortification, I admitted this to my confessor; and I was indeed, obliged to do excessive violence to myself to read my loiters to him. But our Divine Lord in his mercy made use of this as a means of counterbalancing his extraordinary favors, lest they might produce in my soul the germs of vanity and self-love. One day, after having received holy communion, I perceived in my soul something like a wall which shook violently, threatening me with destruction. At the same time, I heard a voice telling me not to fear, that if would serve to crush out my self-love. I comprehended afterwards that this was a kind warning of a long series of humiliations and mortifications, a path so painful to nature, and through which our Divine Lord caused me to walk shortly after."

"As we can do nothing of ourselves, it was necessary that the Divine Master himself should produce in my soul a great love for suffering and humiliation, in order to destroy my pride completely, for it was a great obstacle to my perfect union with Him. This would also cause the violet of humility to spring forth in my soul, hereby inviting Jesus to dwell in my heart. I prayed most fervently to obtain the love of humiliations, and informed my director of my ardent desire of suffering, entreating him not to spare me. 'Reverend father,' said I, 'do not heed the cries of nature, but immolate my pride.' He was slow to act and waited also on this occasion to see, no doubt, if my desire were only the offspring of a passing fervor so common among young persons. At length, he said to me one day: 'My child, I am convinced that our Lord wills you to attain perfection by some other than the ordinary way. Go then, before the Most Adorable Sacrament, and consider before God what you can do to humble yourself; choose what you judge to be the most perfect in the way of humiliations, and then return and inform me of your decision.'"

From that hour commenced what she playfully termed, her "journey through the path of humiliations" which were never wanting; for each time that she went to see her director, he purposely tried to mortify her as much as possible. One day, for example, he brusquely showed her the door. Another time, Sunday, she was seen walking through the streets carrying an old, tattered umbrella notwithstanding that the sun was shining very brilliantly; and this for no other purpose than to attract public attention and ridicule. On another occasion, she took to the dressmaker a parcel containing material for a dress. She had scarcely unfolded the wrapping paper when a general burst of laughter and merriment at her expense, ensued; for nothing more absurd or ridiculous could have been selected for a dress. All these things had been permitted by her director as practices of humility.

"When I went to my director," said she, "to return the books he lent me, or to ask for others, he had always the charity to offer me a good dish of humiliations; yet, he never anticipated grace. I was obliged to implore him to continue the kind service he was rendering me. 'Well,' he would say, 'what does our Lord desire of you today? Have you nothing to ask me?' As I was naturally very simple and childlike, and that our Lord gave me the grace to walk in this way, a multitude of things came to my mind, the greater part being utterly impracticable; but merely mentioning them to him, and asking his permission to perform them, was a most humiliating mortification. When he noticed that it gave me pain to speak undisguisedly, he would reprehend me quietly but sweetly. 'Be simple as a little child,' he would say. 'See with what simplicity a little child repeats all that passes in its mind without thinking of examining what it has to say!' He would then permit all that was reasonable; and as for that which was unnecessary, he appeared equally willing, until he perceived that I had so far conquered my pride as to consent to perform even the most difficult things, when he would interdict them."

One of the great secrets of this manner of direction arose from the confessor's knowledge of the sincerity of his penitent, who artlessly related to him that which she believed would mortify her the most yet choosing nothing of herself. She would say. to him at times: "Ah, father, how much it costs me to act thus." "My child," he would reply, "if it costs you to be humiliated, believe me, it costs me as much to be obliged to humiliate you, but have courage."

"When I had crushed my pride under my feet, our Lord inundated my soul with heavenly consolations: these were necessary to me, for without the most powerful assistance of God I never could have acted in this way. When I was inspired to practice some act of mortification, I felt such a powerful impulse of grace urging me on, that it would have been impossible for me not to have performed this mortification, I had such a fear of becoming unfaithful to grace. 'Come,' said I, to encourage myself, 'one act of heroism and the victory will be mine. I can accomplish all things in Him who strengthens me!' I felt convinced that grace demanded this fidelity from me; and notwithstanding all the bitterness and repugnance I experienced, I continued to implore my director to nourish my soul with the wholesome bread of mortification, so distasteful to nature. He sent me several times to visit two very discreet and pious young ladies with whom he had previously made his arrangements, and there I found the means of triumphing over my pride and practicing humility. On one occasion, when I was on a visit to these young ladies, one of the sisters complained that a person had addressed some very humiliating remarks to her. 'Oh!' said I, 'you are very fortunate to be able to find humiliations already prepared; others are obliged to seek for them.'"

During this time of trial our little Perrine drew all her fortitude from Jesus in the most Blessed Sacrament. "Ah!" said she, "what consolation I found in visiting this good Savior, particularly during the middle of the day, when he is most forgotten; I then poured forth my soul in his divine presence." Once, as she was praying in the chapel of the Visitation, prostrate before the altar, one of her friends perceiving her, was very careful not to disturb her or make her aware of her presence.

She found Perrine kneeling with clasped hands, her head turned upward and her eyes fixed as if on some invisible being with whom she seemed to be in communion.

Perrine often addressed herself to the Sacred Heart of Jesus. "I often made acts of reparation to the Sacred Heart, to whom I have a great devotion. I conjured the most Sacred Heart of Jesus to break the chains which still bound me to the world that I might take my flight toward Carmel. I went afterwards and cast myself at the feet of the most Holy Virgin, in the same chapel where I had already received so many graces for my vocation; and animated with ardent love, I poured forth my heart in her maternal bosom as would a little child. I importuned her unceasingly, saying, 'Behold, my good Mother, my companions are all married. When wilt thou give me Him for whom my heart sighs? I wish for none other than thy beloved Son for my heavenly spouse.'" At the conclusion of this petition, we find the following note: "This good mother obtained my relief from a malady: for nine days I besought her to cure me, promising to have some masses said in her honor; and in thanksgiving for having granted my request, I had fifteen masses said in honor of the mysteries of the most holy rosary."

3

THE TRIAL

"You will be a Carmelite."
(Words of Our Lord)

P revious to her entering the novitiate of Carmel, Perrine, retained in the world by her confessor, was destined by divine Providence to fill the office of little directress, or rather to be a pious little apostle among her young companions. Let us permit her to explain herself on this subject.

"I continued to work with my pious aunts, who employed many young girls in their service. These latter, observing that by the grace of God, I practiced virtue, and that I always looked cheerful and happy as my director had commanded, placed great confidence in me, and frequently consulted me in their little embarrassments of conscience and on their practices of piety. I taught them the method of mental prayer, and assisted them to advance in virtue: miserable sinner that I was, I had received grace in abundance from God and it was but just that I should be charitable to others. One of these young persons made such rapid progress in virtue, that she very soon surpassed her little directress and entered the religious state before I did. We conversed about our Divine Lord, the Blessed Virgin, and the glorious Patriarch St. Joseph, and also on the practice of virtue. Observing that they thus consulted me, who stood so much in need of counsel myself, I was afraid that I was acting contrary to humility, and I sought the advice of my confessor. He told me to continue, that the piety of these young girls would supply my deficiency: this opinion tranquilized me, and I continued to aid them as before. But during all my intercourse with them I never revealed what was passing in my own soul; I kept my secret to myself. I had no difficulty in teaching them the method of mental prayer, as I myself performed this exercise with the greatest ease, for the presence of my Divine Savior was so familiar, that I seemed to behold Him dwelling in my heart."

We know from the testimony of others, that in order to give greater facility for audience to her young friends, our little directress prepared a small room in her father's house, to which they had private and easy access. Here she received these pious young persons for a pleasant little "chat" as she termed it, dissimulating under this popular expression the role of confidence assigned her.

Those who desired could converse without restraint of their spiritual necessities. She taught them how to meditate, to examine themselves interiorly, and how to walk resolutely in the path of virtue, thus, to be prepared to meet all the possible dangers which might menace their innocence in the midst of the world in which they were destined to live.

"One of my companions was afflicted with a very extraordinary malady. The remedies prescribed by the physician giving her no relief, I had an intimate conviction that if she had recourse to the most Blessed Virgin, her distemper would be cured; and I advised her to wear a miraculous medal. We made a novena together, at the conclusion of which she was entirely cured. The graces which we thus received from our heavenly protectress inflamed us with a tender love for her. I prayed her unceasingly to break the chains which held me captive, and I frequently offered tapers to be burned before her altar. I prepared myself for the celebration of her feasts by novenas; and presented little crowns, bouquets of flowers, and other decorations for her altars. In fine, I tried my best to touch her maternal heart, that she might give me her divine Son for my heavenly spouse. So many offerings, though unworthy of being presented to the august Queen of heaven, were not regarded by her with indifference, for she soon removed one of my greatest difficulties, that of leaving my father."

As we have seen, Perrine lost her mother when only twelve years old. "After the death of my mother," said she, "my good father had no other desire but to serve God and his neighbor. He worked peacefully at his trade of locksmith, without any idea of ever marrying again; his life was modeled on that of St. Joseph. Every morning he assisted at the holy sacrifice of the mass, and at the benediction of the most Blessed Sacrament in the evening, when possible; notwithstanding his hard work he always observed the abstinences and fasts of the Church, and regularly approached the sacraments with the most edifying faith and piety. He was often visited with great tribulations which he bore with Christian-like fortitude and patience."

His eldest son, Prosper, had left home and gone to America with Monseigneur de la Hailandiere, to whom he was much attached. He settled at Vincennes in the United States, where he resumed his trade of locksmith, attending punctually to his business affairs, and giving there as well as when at home, the edifying example of a virtuous and Christian life.

But let us return to Perrine: " My eldest sister, " said she, "who attended to the household duties, was attacked with a long illness and about the same time my father had conceived the idea that I was thinking of leaving him to embrace the religious state. This filled him with alarm and anxiety, for he did not wish to confide his house to the care of a servant. In his perplexity he made me the confident of his troubles hoping thereby to deter me from leaving him. I spoke to him rather ambiguously of my vocation, as I myself did not know when my confessor would permit me to enter the Carmelites, for he continued his evasive answers and gave me very little hope, notwithstanding my earnest desire to quit the world. In the meantime, my dear father was preparing for the emergency; he spoke of his troubles to the parish priest, his confessor; this worthy pastor, held him in the highest esteem, for he often said that he was the best of his parishioners. Already aware of my intention of becoming a Carmelite, he advised my father to get married. My good parent was naturally of a very cold and retiring disposition, and as can be easily imagined, was not a little embarrassed in the execution of this project; but his kind friend, the priest, assured him that he would undertake to find a suitable companion; and at last, through the intercession of the Blessed Virgin, he was married to a most excellent woman whom we kindly welcomed to our home, and my father was happy."

The sister concludes this artless narrative by enumerating the many other obstacles to be surmounted in the pursuit of her vocation.

"I thought I had at last reached the term of my sufferings and disappointments, and that the doors of Carmel were about to be opened to receive me. One of my aunts with whom I worked, decided to go to Mans to assist at the benediction of the new Carmelite monastery, and at the same time to visit one of the religious, an old friend of hers whom she loved very dearly, she told me that I might accompany her. This good news filled me with joy, and I hastened to my confessor, entreating him to allow me to take advantage of this excellent opportunity to accomplish my long-cherished desire. He consented and gave me a letter for the reverend mother prioress, telling me that I could enter the monastery of Mans if she was willing to receive me; he then gave me his benediction, and I set out immediately with my aunt. We arrived on the eve of the ceremony at the monastery where we were most kindly received by the Carmelites: the next day I assisted at the benediction of a new refectory and a new cemetery. On the same day a postulant received the holy habit."

"The cloister being thrown open for the occasion, we visited the interior of the convent. I entered the community room and there beheld those dear sisters, many of whom were from my own native province; nothing could have given me more pleasure than this visit. In the afternoon, I had the honor of speaking privately to the very reverend mother prioress to whom I had presented my confessor's letter the evening previous. I expressed my great desire of becoming a Carmelite. She told me that she had received positive orders from his Lordship the Bishop to admit no more subjects, as the house was then too small, every cell being occupied. Although disheartened by this information, I consulted her respecting my vocation, and spoke to her of my inward dispositions. She evidently saw that, notwithstanding my unworthiness, Our Lord had chosen me to be a child of Carmel, and kindly gave me some information on the rules of the order, expressing her regret at not being able to admit me; nor could she make any application in my behalf, as Monseigneur was at the time absent on a journey. She spoke very highly of the monastery of Orleans from which she had come to found the house at Mans, and promised to apply there for my admission."

Our disappointed little postulant was thus obliged to return home and resume her ordinary duties. She entreated her confessor to make application for her entrance among the Carmelites of Orleans or those of Blois; however, he did not seem to be very sanguine about the matter.

"I was so importunate in my request that he must have been annoyed with me.; his evasive answers were most discouraging. 'We shall see to that;' or 'God's time has not yet come.' One day I went to a chapel dedicated to St. Martin. It being his feast, his relics were exposed for the veneration of the faithful; I kissed them with great devotion, and also received holy communion in honor of this great saint of whom, at the time, I knew nothing; not even in what part of France he had exercised his holy ministry; but that was of little consequence to me then, overwhelmed as I was with grief and desolation. I addressed to him this simple and fervent prayer: 'O holy Saint Martin, look down upon me in my sorrow. I desire to consecrate myself to God, but there is no one to take any interest in me or plead my cause. O holy Saint, I feel convinced that if you were now on this earth your heart would be touched at my distress and you would aid me to obtain the object of all my desires.' I implored him to receive me in his diocese if there were any religious in it. St. Martin heard my prayer, for I am confident that it was through his intercession, I became a Carmelite at Tours. I had neither desired nor asked my confessor to enter the house of Tours, for I did not know that there was a Carmelite monastery' in the city until I had been received there."

In the meantime, Our Lord was preparing her for the life of sacrifice which she was about to embrace, and for this end, had already bestowed upon her supernatural graces of the highest order.

"One day after holy communion," said she, "I had a vision: Our Lord concentrated all the powers of my soul in his Divine Heart, and I seemed to behold therein a number of persons bound together by a golden chain, each, seemingly, bearing a cross. These were, without doubt, religious souls, for I recognized among the number, one of my friends who had embraced the religious life. It seemed that I, too, was enchained with them and I besought Our Lord to give me also a cross. He led me to understand that I must submit to his divine will for the present and await with resignation the accomplishment of his designs over me; insinuating that this was sufficient to bear for the present. 'But,' said He, 'when you shall have entered religion, I shall give you another cross to carry.' This promise remained so much engraved on my mind, that falling sick after I had entered Carmel as a postulant, I thought to myself: 'Perhaps this is the cross which Our Lord promised me.' But poor simpleton that I was! This was but a straw to carry in comparison to the cross which my good Master had in reserve for me after my profession. I am now convinced that the *Work of Reparation* with which the Lord charged me later, was the cross then predicted, for I found it in the Sacred Heart of Jesus. It was from that fountain of divine love that he spoke to me for the first time of this work which was to cost me so many sighs and tears."

Thenceforth, she had a very ardent affection for the most Sacred Heart of Jesus. "This devotion was my chief delight: and I earnestly engaged my companions to love and honor the divine Heart of my Savior. My sister was very ill at the time, and I advised her to have a novena of masses offered in reparation for the outrages committed against the

Sacred Heart of Jesus in the sacrament of his love, with the intention of obtaining her restoration, if it were the divine will. She consented, and the masses were said in the chapel of the Visitation; for it was to a sister of this Order that our Divine Lord made known the devotion to his Sacred Heart. The principal altar of the chapel was dedicated to the Sacred Heart of Jesus. I assisted at these masses, during which I received the most extraordinary graces, a written account of which I gave to my director. I cannot recall them now as my mind was so penetrated with the ineffable love of Our Lord manifested to me in his divine Heart that I have only a confused idea of these heavenly favors, for it seemed that my soul was entirely lost in God. However, I am certain of one thing: that Our Lord showed me a cross, telling me it was on this he crucified his spouses. I think I must have been frightened, for soon after he added these words: 'Be consoled my daughter; you will not be as inhumanly crucified as I was, the nails shall pierce though my flesh before touching yours.' Doubtless, He wished by these words to assure me that He being the first to experience all the tortures and ignominies of the cross, the faithful disciples who followed in his footsteps would now find all its bitterness changed to delight."

For some time Our Lord inspired her with a certain kind of prayer which she describes as "delightful," but he soon gave her to understand that this inspiration would be withdrawn: and, in fact, shortly after she fell into a state of mental aridity. "Our Lord," said she, "caused me to pass from Thabor to Calvary, according to his own good pleasure and the necessities of my soul; but as I was now more enlightened in the ways of God than during the period of my spiritual infancy, I passed through these interior trials without any detriment to my soul."

One grace which she esteemed far above all these extraordinary favors, was that of being able to alleviate the necessities of the indigent sick. "The Lord," writes she, "endowed me with a love for giving alms; I had a small private fund which my dear father allowed me to dispose of as I thought proper. I would sometimes make a little offering to Our Lord, and then again to his holy Mother, in the persons of the poor and afflicted. A young woman came to dwell in our neighborhood, who soon after her marriage, had fallen ill of a long and painful malady which proved fatal: the charitable mission of preparing her for death fell to my lot. I placed a picture of the Blessed Virgin near her bed, that this good mother might come to assist her in her last moments. I was then quite young and had seldom confronted death. The poor, afflicted creature whom I encouraged by consoling words, desired that I should remain always at her side. She sent for me one night to inquire if

she were soon going to die: I replied that in all probability Our Lord would soon call
her to himself; she was then reduced to the last extremity. I do not remember distinctly,
but I think it was that same night that she was suddenly seized with terror at the sight of
something invisible to us; it was the Angel of Darkness who had come to tempt her in this,
her last moment. She suddenly screamed out: 'Look at the large black cat at the foot of
my bed!'—For my part I perceived nothing.—I sprinkled the bed with holy water. 'I see it
again!' she exclaimed; we made a second aspersion and the Evil One was put to flight. We
continued praying for this poor creature, who expired before our eyes. She had received
the last sacraments with the most edifying submission to the holy will of God and died
very happily."

"It so happened, that after her death, I and one of my friends, should be the only ones to
prepare her for burial. I had the greatest repugnance to touch the dead, but as no one
could be found to render this service to the poor deceased, I was obliged to do it myself."

"The Divine Master in his infinite mercy thus offered me an excellent opportunity of
cancelling a multitude of my sins, which were undoubtedly the cause of retarding my
entrance into religion. The hour appointed by God was slowly approaching I besought
all the saints to intercede for me, and had recourse to the assistance of our holy mother
St. Theresa. At home we had a picture of this saint, and when I was at table my eyes were
always fixed on this portrait, so much so, that I was often more occupied in contemplating
the picture than in eating my dinner. My father, who was then fully aware of my intention
of becoming a Carmelite, often conversed with me on this subject. On one occasion,
during dinner, he made me laugh heartily at his anxieties concerning my future bed at the
convent. He had, no doubt, heard of some of the foolish notions entertained by people
of the world regarding the austerities practiced by the Carmelites; he said, not without
evincing great concern, 'If the sheets are nailed to the four corners of the bed, how will
you ever get into a bed thus arranged?' 'Oh!' said I, 'that is the least of my anxieties."

"I was not content merely with praying to our holy mother St. Theresa, I read her
life and made a list of her confessors, and of the holy persons who had assisted her in
establishing the reform. I arranged them in a litany without examining whether they had
been canonized or not. St. John of the Cross was the first on the list; and I added the names
of the saints to whom I had a special devotion, hoping that with the aid of these powerful
advocates the doors of Carmel might at length be opened to me. At last they were not

regardless of this simple act of confidence, for it was on the eve of the feast of All-Saints that I was admitted to that happy asylum, the object of all my desires."

Another trial was still in reserve for her. Her director fell ill and was unable to hear her confession. Observing that she made no progress towards the attainment of her object, and being reluctant to importune her confessor, she made a last effort to interest in her behalf the ever-Blessed Virgin.

"I was inspired," said she, "to undertake a pilgrimage in honor of Notre Dame de la Peiniere, from whom I had already obtained many favors. This chapel was in the parish of St. Didier, six leagues from Hennes. As I was well acquainted with its zealous pastor, and had also a friend residing there, I easily obtained permission to perform my pilgrimage. Full of confidence I set out with the intention of asking our Blessed Lady for the recovery of my confessor as a visible proof of my vocation; praying her at the same time to sever the many chains which held me captive in the world. 'Ah,' said I, 'I am like a bird in a cage. I cannot find the smallest opening from which to make my escape.' There was a good priest travelling in the same car with me, with whom I conversed during the journey. I spoke to him of the Blessed Virgin, and observing that it pleased him, I related many little incidents in her honor; I also spoke to him about the Archconfraternity of the Sacred Heart of Mary. This conversation afforded me much pleasure for I loved to honor and glorify the Blessed Virgin as much as I could. At length we arrived at St. Didier, and I directed my steps toward the church. There I offered my devotions, and Our Lord condescended to speak to me concerning my vocation."

"To render what I am about to narrate more explicit, I must state that one of my reasons for fearing I would not be received by the Carmelites was, that my father was poor and could not give me more than six hundred francs ($100) on my entrance. I had asked assistance of a rich priest of my acquaintance, but he only expressed his regret at his inability to aid me in consequence of having recently met with considerable losses. Perhaps, I was wanting in confidence in the Providence of God. The communication which I had received from Our Lord, and to which I have previously hinted, filled me with consolation. I think that this time also He showed me a cross saying: 'Is not a vocation of higher worth than gold?' Thus, giving me to understand that if in his infinite mercy he granted me the first grace, he could as easily provide the second, which was of minor importance. He then said: 'Pray to my mother, and you shall obtain your request.'"

Full of faith and hope, Perrine continued her pilgrimage. This miraculous statue was in a very spacious chapel, which had been built a quarter of a league from the parish church. She cheerfully gave her little offering towards the completion of the chapel, and performed her visits for nine consecutive days, reciting the first part of the rosary going to the church, the second part in the chapel at the feet of the Blessed Virgin, and the third, on her return.

"Oh, how fervently I implored my Blessed Mother to take an interest in my vocation!

What sweetness and consolation I tasted whilst at the feet of the consoler of the afflicted! She did not remain deaf to my entreaties, for I received from her divine Son the most wonderful graces during my novena. For the honor of the most Holy Virgin, I sincerely regret not having preserved a written account of all those graces. I remember, however, that Our Lord commanded that I should be permitted to follow his will without more delay. I made an exact statement of all that had passed in my soul and carried this important letter to the most Blessed Virgin, begging her to bless it and to touch the heart of him to whom I should remit it. 'O my good Mother,' said I with childlike simplicity, 'I do not wish to spend this winter in sewing, I only desire to be occupied in praising your divine Son, and I therefore remit into your hands my scissors, needles, thimble etc., etc.'" Thus saying, she deposited the contents of her workbasket at the feet of the Blessed Virgin.

On her return to Rennes, she found her director in better health, and presented him her letter, which produced a great impression on him. However, he tried to conceal it, but the effects were soon apparent, for he set to work in earnest to obtain her admission among the Carmelites; yet, in seeming opposition to her wishes, he proposed to her to enter among the religious Hospitalieres of Rennes. "I feel no attraction for them," said she, "yet I would prefer to enter among the Hospitalieres rather than to remain in the world. How embarrassing! I knew of no other Carmelite convent than that of Mans, and there I could not be received. I did not know that there was a convent at Tours and one at Morlaix. I went to my little oratory and said to St. Theresa and to St. John of the Cross, of whom I had a picture: 'Alas, you do not want to receive me then among your sisters!'"

She thought that the question of her portion might prove the greatest difficulty. She resolved to go and see the venerable priest who had directed her for two years and a half, and to whom she had been more than once a subject of edification. He was then in his seventy seventh year, yet he had lost none of his faculties and fulfilled the duties of his ministry with as much activity as a young priest.

"I met him one day in the city; he seemed desirous of knowing if I really wished to be a sister, but as I had no intention of unfolding my plans in the middle of the street, I deferred my answer for a more suitable place; and as he possessed much of this world's goods I proposed interesting his charity in my behalf. With this object in view, I called to visit him one afternoon. It was here that Our Lord awaited me, to crown the long series of trials and humiliations to which I had been subjected. Through respect for this venerable servant of God, I knelt at his feet to speak on the subject of my vocation; but ignoring how well the soil of my poor soul had been ploughed and cultivated during the past five years, he desired to test my virtue in a very unexpected and mortifying manner. He took out his breviary and commenced to read without appearing to notice me, or to listen to what I was saying; after a few moments he arose quite abruptly and ordered me to leave. I respected the will of God manifested by his minister and was not long awaiting my recompense. This trial was about the last I had to undergo during the remainder of my stay in the world. The worthy priest, agreeably to my desire had the goodness to present me a small sum of money."

"But eight days had elapsed since my return from my pilgrimage, and as I have said, the last time I saw my director he seemed quite decided to send me to the Hospitalieres. I was in painful anxiety, for I had such a desire to dwell in the desert of Carmel! The spirit of retirement, silence and prayer, had such an attraction for me, and in the order of the Hospitalieres I would be obliged to take care of the sick, and what was still more repugnant, to prepare, for burial the bodies of the dead, of which I stood in mortal terror. Our Lord, in his goodness, relieved me from this embarrassment. He had promised to hear me through the intercession of his Blessed Mother, and he kept his word. The ninth day after my pilgrimage he revealed himself to me after holy communion, and with infinite condescension said the following words: 'My child, I love you too much to permit that you should any longer be a prey to these perplexities! You shall not be a Hospitaliere. This is only a trial to which you are being subjected. Even now matters are being arranged for your reception. You will be a Carmelite.' This last sentence was repeated several times: 'You will be a Carmelite;' and I think Our Lord added, 'a Carmelite of Tours.' But I knew nothing of Tours, not even that the Carmelites had been established there. I feared that this was but an illusion, for I felt persuaded that my director thought

no more of sending me to Carmel. What shall I do, said I to myself! I must write
down this communication and take it to him according to my custom; but I was not
particularly desirous of presenting this note: Oh, the infinite goodness of God! what was
my astonishment when my confessor said to me: 'My child, you have been received among
the Carmelites of Tours.' What delightful news! What happiness I enjoyed that day! What
grateful thanksgiving I offered to our Blessed Lord and to his most Holy Mother for
having so promptly heard the supplications and entreaties which I had addressed to them
during my pilgrimage!"

"The letter which I had placed at the feet of our Lady de la Peiniere and afterwards
remitted to my director, had been the principal instrument in the accomplishment of
the long-cherished wish of my heart. My confessor had written to the mother prioress
of Tours applying for my admission. This good, charitable mother immediately replied
that she would receive me with pleasure. But how was all this accomplished? Why had
Our Lord made known so manifestly that it was his divine will I should enter at Tours,
sixty leagues from my native place, whilst there were Carmelites at Nantes and at Morlaix
so much nearer home? I asked my confessor if he had held any communication with the
Carmelites of Tours. He informed me that once, when passing through Tours, he had
had the idea of visiting the Carmelites, but that he had not gone and consequently was
not acquainted with them. The reverend mother prioress had still less to do in bringing
about this result, for she was greatly astonished that a priest of whom she knew little more
than his name would apply to her for the admission of a postulant. What then was the
solution of this mystery? Ah, I see it all. St. Martin had not forgotten the prayers offered
in his chapel on the day of his feast, when I confided to him my sorrows and besought
him to procure my entrance to one of the houses of his diocese."

Here again is another remarkable circumstance connected with this affair: "The reverend
mother prioress of Tours had fixed the time of my entrance for the feast of All Saints: a
long delay for my ardent disposition, leaving two months still to be passed in the world.
Nevertheless, this day was not appointed by mere chance, for I left Brittany on the very
feast of St. Martin, who evidently wished to prove that it was he who was my liberator."

"There remained still another question to be solved, my entrance-fee. But that was soon
disposed of. As I have before stated, my father was a mechanic attending regularly to
his business; but God often sent him severe trials. He had to meet the heavy expenses
of the prolonged illness of my eldest sister who was still feeble. My brother had failed in

business, and it cost two thousand francs to re-establish him, towards which my good aunts contributed as much as they could. After all these outlays it was found impossible to give me more than six hundred francs, but Our Lord had given me to understand that he who had bestowed the vocation could also provide the dowry."

"The Blessed Virgin, with a generosity equal to her power, compensated me for the alms I had offered for the construction of her new chapel, and a young lady named Mary with whom my director had made me practice the virtue of mortification, as a preparation for her entrance to a religious congregation, promised to contribute the balance."

"What remained for me to do after such special graces from the most Blessed Virgin! Our Lord had well said: 'Address yourself to my mother, it is through her you shall be heard:' remarkable words, of which I have always preserved a lasting souvenir. There still remained the fulfilment of a sacred duty towards the Blessed Virgin Mary: that of offering her a grateful and earnest act of love. I solicited the permission to return to her holy chapel to offer her thanks for all the benefits granted me. I then bade farewell to my protectress, recommending to her the new state I was going to embrace, in which I would be attached to her divine Son by the sweetest ties of love. In the simplicity of my heart I again asked her for that dear Son as my heavenly spouse; she, at length, consented to give him, notwithstanding my unworthiness; my heart had now no other love and nothing more to desire, save the arrival of the happy day of our spiritual nuptials."

On her return, as if to celebrate in advance what she termed her 'nuptials,' the many relatives of the future Carmelite assembled around her for the last time, and celebrated in her honor a modest little fete, touching demonstration of affection worthy of the Christian sentiments which animated the father of the young aspirant and her virtuous relatives. Each felt the regret natural at parting, but all united in praying for her perseverance, for they beheld therein a happiness for Perrine and a blessing for themselves. Their wishes were fulfilled far beyond their most sanguine expectations.

"For myself I most ardently desired the approach of the day of my departure. We were awaiting the arrival of a religious, travelling in the direction of Tourraine, to whose care I was to be confided for the journey; but as she did not make her appearance, and as I was burning with the desire to set out, my father decided to leave his business for some days that he might present me himself to the Lord. I bade adieu to my home and friends with much joy, although I loved them very tenderly, yet, I had such a longing to go and serve the

Holy Family at Carmel that my natural feelings of sorrow at such a separation were easily stifled. I went also to bid adieu to him who had directed me in my vocation. He vouched for my perseverance. But fearing that the way in which the Lord would conduct me might not be in harmony with the community life, he said, 'My child, endeavor to follow the common way; when a religious is conducted in an extraordinary manner she is obliged to demand an extraordinary confessor, which is not always convenient in a community.' Then as if in a spirit of prophecy, he added: 'Do quickly that which you have to do; hasten to sanctify yourself for your course will not be long.' After some other counsels he gave me his last blessing and I departed."

4

THE CARMELITE MONASTERY OF TOURS

"There I found the child Jesus and the Holy Family."
(Words of our postulant.)

" A ccompanied by my father, I left the town of Rennes on the feast of my dear patron, St. Martin of Tours, the 11th of November 1839, and travelled towards Tourraine, my future home. I reached Tours on the 13th and proceeded immediately to the convent where I arrived at 5 o'clock in the afternoon. What rendered this event remarkable to me was, that it was St. Martin who presented me to 'all the saints of Carmel,' for on the next day their feast was to be celebrated. I felt assured that these good saints would not refuse me admission on the day of their feast, for I had prayed fervently, entreating them to admit me into their company; they could not have given me a better or more striking proof of my perseverance than that of having received me on such a day."

Our little Breton postulant seemed to have had no curiosity to visit the city. "That," said she, "is of little importance to me. Having quitted the travelling coach, my father conducted me to the Carmelites; he gave me his benediction and said with great emotion, while embracing me for the last time: 'The will of God alone, my child, gives me courage to make this sacrifice.' Poor father! May God reward your admirable resignation to His decrees! Very soon the doors were thrown open and my father remitted me to the care of this new family who presented themselves to receive me. If at that moment I offered to God the sacrifice of a fond father, he gave me in return a most excellent mother, who was to render me inestimable services. This was the reverend mother Mary of the Incarnation, prioress and at the same time mistress of novices. When in the world, Our Lord one day gave me to understand that the mother whom he destined for me would have a special grace to conduct me in his ways; and, in fact, the promise was verified as soon as our reverend mother understood my interior dispositions. This knowledge came to her by degrees, and according as God judged it proper for his glory and the salvation of my soul."

"After I had embraced my new sisters, the reverend mother conducted me to the altar of the Most Blessed Virgin Mary, my heavenly mother, to thank her for my admission into the holy house of Carmel, and to place myself under her special protection. The hour of recreation soon drew nigh: I was invited to sing and I did not wait to be importuned, for I had sung the same hymn many times while awaiting the happy day of my entrance into Carmel. It was as follows:

> Oh! Bless'd be God! I've found that peace
> For which I've sighed so long;
>
> For Him my love shall never cease,
> He'll ever be my song.

"There were fifteen stanzas which I sang with such cheerfulness that no one thought of interrupting me."

The new postulant seemed inclined to continue, when suddenly the reverend mother prioress, who had been absent, entered the recreation room. Finding one disposed to sing, the others to listen, and all apparently enjoying themselves, she considered it a splendid occasion to test the postulant. "Well," said she, "you have been in a hurry to display your little talent." A dead silence ensued. After a few seconds, the mother prioress, turning toward the little singer, said: "See if you can entertain us with something better!" "Oh! reverend mother," replied she, "I have sung you the very best thing I know." Such was her simple reply. Not a shadow of disappointment or embarrassment could be observed on her countenance. It was very evident that by virtue as well as by natural disposition, Perrine was not of a melancholy turn of mind.

"This frank gaiety," said she, "was already a proof of my vocation for Carmel; for our holy mother, St. Theresa, would not allow sad or melancholy subjects to remain among her daughters; of this I was fully aware. The following day, I attended the Divine Office, during which I had a very ridiculous temptation, and as it was the only one I remember having had against my vocation, I shall relate it. Observing the officiant, the chantress, the chorists and other sisters going to the middle of the choir, make a genuflexion, say something in Latin, then return for others to take their place,—I was alarmed at the number and variety of these ceremonies. I thought I would never have intelligence enough to know how to do so many things, nor to perceive when my turn would come to do likewise. I concluded that perhaps it would be much more expedient for me to take my little bundle and return to Brittany. But how could I get home! I had only forty francs in my purse; surely that would not meet the expenses of so long a journey. I had forgotten that I had given even this to the good mother prioress. However, I consoled myself by saying: have patience and we shall see what will happen. I was conducted to the confessional:—further dismay. I perceived a small slab of iron painted white, pierced with little round holes, and placed in the wall according to the Carmelite custom. They told me that I should speak through this grating to the confessor:—Patience again, my soul, and we shall soon see how all these things will terminate! From the chapel I was conducted to the novitiate. *There I found the child Jesus and the Holy Family,* the cherished objects of my affection. From this moment the Holy Family, for whom I had quitted the world and entered Carmel where I knew they were specially honored, smoothed away all my difficulties and I found all things easy and agreeable. I was so much at home that it already seemed several years since my arrival. Then I understood by my own experience that there is vocation, not only for an order, but also vocation for a particular House of that order, as I had no attraction for any other convent; on the contrary, from the moment I entered that of Tours I felt that I was where God wished me to be."

Let us for a few brief moments interrupt these interesting details to make acquaintance with the house into which Perrine was led by Divine Providence.

The monastery of Tours is by no means the least considerable among the many which the daughters of St. Theresa have established in France. We behold in its foundation a visible proof of St. Martin's protection of his episcopal city.

Divine love had already formed a bond of union between the Carmelite Reformer and the Thaumaturgus of the Gauls, which her biographer has not neglected to mention. The virgin of Avila writes: "Today is the feast of St. Martin to whom I have a special devotion, for I have frequently received extraordinary graces from Our Lord during this octave."

It was, as we have seen, on the feast of this holy bishop that Perrine had received marked assistance in the pursuit of her vocation; it was also during the celebration of that same feast that she found, not far from the tomb of the glorious apostle, the asylum wherein her perfection was to be accomplished. Is it not an indication of the watchful care of Providence to have enriched the city of St. Martin with a community so thoroughly imbued with the Theresian spirit? It will be dur agreeable duty to trace, summarily, the origin of the monastery and its principal historical phases down to the time of the admission of sister St. Peter.

The monastery of Tours was established in 1608. Four years previous, that of Paris was founded by cardinal de Berulle, madame Acarie and Blessed Mary of the Incarnation. The latter was related to M. de Fontaines-Marans, seigneur de Rouziers, in the vicinity of Tours, whose favorite daughter had entered among the Carmelites of Paris, but because of ill-health she was obliged to return home. To indemnify this beloved child who still sighed for the peaceful solitudes of Carmel, M. de Rouziers proposed founding a monastery at Tours with the hope that she would be received as benefactress, thus enabling her to satisfy her pious desire, and at the same time remain near the paternal mansion. It was madame Acarie in person who negotiated for this foundation with the pious nobleman. Cardinal de Berulle appointed mother Ann of St. Bartholomew, prioress of the projected monastery, and nominated seven sisters to accompany her. This was the devoted friend of St. Theresa who expired in her arms. She had come from Spain with several other sisters, accompanied by cardinal de Berulle. The annals of the monastery have preserved the following account of the foundation: "We left Paris on the 5th of May and arrived here on the 9th. The journey was tedious and painful; but St. Theresa appeared and consoled her faithful friend. She seemed to walk by her side on a path strewn with thorns, exhorting her to continue her arduous undertaking in the following words: 'Courage! I shall assist you.' From the moment of their arrival, the sisters took possession of the house prepared for them, and the Blessed Sacrament was deposited in the chapel the Sunday within the octave of the Ascension, the 18th of May."

"On the same day, mother Ann of St. Bartholomew recommended the new monastery to Our Lord during her communion, supplicating him to bestow his graces on the little flock of missionaries present, and on all those who, in the future, would present themselves to serve Him. 'My adorable Master assured me,' said she, ' that he would grant my request; and from that moment to the present time I have witnessed the marvelous accomplishment of his promise.'"

At this period the population of Tours included a great number of heretics, descendants of the Huguenots who, in the preceding age, had been the cause of the most frightful civil wars. When they learned that a number of nuns were coming to reside in their city, and were even crossing the Loire, they exclaimed: "May they go to the bottom of the river before reaching the shore!" However, their impious desires were not realized. The grace of God soon triumphed and changed these hostile feelings. The nearest neighbor of the Carmelites cited them before the law because of a stray hen, but he was so filled with admiration at the sight of their exquisite charity, that he soon abjured heresy. This incident was much commented upon by the sectarians, who uttered all sorts of invectives against the Carmelites; one of them saying: "These Theresians are capable of making Catholics of us despite ourselves." . . . They would have had still greater reason to fear had they known how many prayers and penances were daily offered for their conversion in the interior of the cloister.

The new monastery had already attained such a reputation of sanctity that persons of the highest rank came from far and near to solicit the privilege of taking the holy habit. From the first year of the foundation, there were as many as twenty postulants at a time. Among those whom the venerable mother Ann of St. Bartholomew admitted to profession, we are pleased to find the name of one of the daughters of a Breton gentleman, Mlle. Querlingue, in religion Mary of St. Elias; another young lady from Rennes, Mlle, de la Riviere, in religion John of St. Joseph, who was afterwards sent to the monastery of Morlaix. These two being, as it were, the first among the most precious fruits of sanctity which catholic Brittany was one day to produce.

The holiness of the first professed was mirrored in the disciples formed by them. We have a proof of this in the fact that from among those who founded the monastery of Tours four were chosen to spread the Reform of St. Theresa; so capable were they deemed of implanting the true spirit. Many others were afterward taken from this monastery for the same purpose. But to return to our subject: Mother Ann of St. Bartholomew was specially favored by God. These are her words: "The Divine Majesty bestowed on me many graces, though I had no confessor with whom I could easily communicate, for our director understood no Spanish, nor I the French, yet I confessed as best I could, and our superiors came to visit us once a year. Our Lord supplied this deficiency by the consolations which he sent, for he now bestowed on me the graces of which I had been deprived at other times. These strengthened me in the practice of virtue and penance for many days together. It seemed that sufferings redoubled my strength and without reflecting on it, I felt myself closely united to God, and so to say, clothed with the spirit of St. Paul, which caused me to exclaim with him: 'What shall separate me from the love of Our Lord Jesus Christ!'I was, as it were, environed with the love of my Savior: if he had not sustained me by his almighty power and strengthened my nature against the many favors with which I was overwhelmed, I never could have been able to bear them. I repeated with the great Apostle: 'I wish to be an anathema and to die for my brethren and my Lord Jesus Christ.' And as it happens that on such occasions, the soul lovingly immolates herself without reserve, Our Lord once said to me: 'It is the glory of the Just-to do my will,' adding words so full of tenderness that I was as if beside myself with divine love."

In all the difficulties of this foundation, she applied for aid to St. Theresa, who appeared to her several times. Not to lose sight of her holy friend she wore a small picture of her. When quitting the monastery of Tours, mother Ann of St. Bartholomew left her mantle as did the prophet Elias to his disciple; doubtless her spirit likewise; for the religious of this monastery have ever been distinguished for the most sublime virtues, particularly for an inviolable fidelity to obedience, and for the vigilance with which they preserved in all its purity the true spirit of their holy mother, St. Theresa of Jesus. They were not unfrequently called upon to found or govern other houses of the order, upon which they drew down celestial benedictions. We refer to a sister from Quatrebarbes, in religion mother Elizabeth of the Holy Trinity, prioress of the monastery of Beaume, who died in the odor of sanctity. Others in 1617 founded the monastery of Riom, at Auvergne; again others, that of Nantes, in 1618, of Senz in 1625, and that of Angers in 1626.

The year 1616 was memorable for the erection of the church belonging to the monastery. The first stone was laid on Holy Tuesday March 29th by the Queen, Mary de Medicis, when returning from Midi after the marriage of her son Louis XIII with Ann of Austria. The edifice was blessed on Friday, the 3rd of May 1619, and dedicated to the Maternity of the most Blessed Virgin. The solemn consecration took place during the priority of Mother Margaret of the Blessed Sacrament, spiritual daughter of Blessed Mary of the Incarnation. The monastery then changed its primitive title of "Notre Dame des Anges" to that of "The Incarnation or, the Holy Mother of God," for it is mentioned in the ancient documents under these two appellations. At present it bears the latter title.

It is related that at the time of the canonization of St. Philip de Neri, M. Odoir, a good priest well known in the Order, came to Tours. The mother prioress requested him to offer the holy sacrifice of the mass, to obtain through the intercession of St. Philip, the restoration of two of the sisters who were ill. On retiring from the altar after having offered the Holy Sacrifice the saintly priest said to the prioress:

"Reverend mother, one of your sisters is restored to health," (which was really the case); he added: "The religious of your community are very pleasing to God, for whilst I was administering to them the holy communion, Our Lord seemed so desirous of reposing in their hearts that the Sacred Host departed from my fingers with great eagerness."

The Carmelites of Tours have always been remarkable for their great devotion to the Sacred Heart of Jesus. One day during prayer, the prioress beheld Our Lord, who showed her his adorable Heart wherein were lovingly enclosed all the sisters of the community. When Jansenism sought to devastate France by effacing the true spirit of Christianity from the hearts of the faithful, the Carmelites of Tours preserved intact the purity of the Lith, and accepted with entire submission all the decrees of the Holy See. On several occasions, the religious of this monastery were chosen by their superiors either to defend or to establish sound doctrine in other convents, in which the members had insensibly become imbued with the spirit of heresy. The strict adherence of the prioresses to the decisions of the Holy Church was even manifested in the writings of this period; every circular addressed to the different houses of the Order invariably terminated as follows: "We remain true daughters of the Church, submissive, by the grace of God, to all her decrees."

When the revolution of 1789 burst forth, the number of professed was nineteen, everyone proving herself worthy of her holy vocation. One day several of the municipal counsellors, under the title of commissioners, presented themselves at the parlor, forced open the door and entered the interior of the cloister to propose to the sisters what they termed, " The Oath of Liberty: "all peremptorily refused to take the oath, declaring that they had offered to God their vows, from which no human power could dispense them; that they knew of no liberty more glorious than the practice of their monastic duties.

In a few days the officers returned. Impressed with the idea that obedience to the superior was the cause of the previous failure of their efforts, they proposed a re-election, at which they themselves would preside, exacting that all the religious of the house, even the lay sisters and novices, should have a voice in the election. Imagine the astonishment of the officers when they found that the same superiors were unanimously chosen. "We have been fooled!" they exclaimed. Finding that these means proved ineffectual, they had resort to another expedient: that of speaking privately to each religious. They made every effort to spread disunion and trouble among the members of the community. But all their endeavors only served to cement more closely the bonds of faith and charity which existed among those good sisters.

It was not long before they were driven from their monastery and forced to seek shelter among their friends, who received them with fear and sorrow. Soon, however, they were arrested and thrown into prison. We cannot give an adequate idea of what they endured during their cruel imprisonment. One of the sisters, blind and aged eighty-seven, too feeble to walk, was left for four hours in an open courtyard where she was exposed to all the severity of the season; she contracted inflammation of the lungs and died eight days after, deprived of all assistance, but consoling herself with the thought that she gave her life for the love of her heavenly Spouse.

The other sisters were several times transferred to the different prisons of the city. One day, they received the announcement that they were to be taken out; the poor nuns thought they were to be brought to the place of execution; joy was manifested in their countenances for death had long been the object of their desire. On the way, they learned that they were only journeying to another prison. The populace had been bribed to utter all manner of abusive language against these holy sisters while they were traversing the public thorough fares. One of these saintly souls regretted that day to her last moment exclaiming: "Alas, must I die in bed after having lost such an occasion of martyrdom!" Language cannot depict the terrible sufferings they endured during these eighteen months of imprisonment. The bare boards were frequently their only bed, and their food was coarse and loathsome; the fidelity with which they kept their rules of abstinence, in the midst of their excessive sufferings, filled to overflowing their cup of bitterness; for notwithstanding all their privations, they constantly practiced their rule of abstinence. At length, the prison doors were thrown open and they were permitted to go forth. They dispersed among devoted friends and waited patiently the hour of re-union.

Nevertheless, they lived in all possible regularity, under the most exact obedience, religiously united to their Superior, who remained in office until after their re-establishment. Every Saturday she sent to each one whatever was necessary for the week; on Sundays they assembled for their religious exercises, held the chapter, and asked their permission, as if they had been in the convent. They possessed nothing in particular but guarded their vow of poverty as strictly as if in the cloister.

After the storm had subsided in the year 1798, they were enabled to resume their former manner of life. Then it was a source of consolation to them to reflect that during this long period of sufferings, their regular observances had never for one moment been interrupted, not even during the sad days of their imprisonment. Their first habitation was a miserable little house, where they were obliged to support themselves by the labor of their hands, but Providence soon came to their aid. A benefactress gave them the necessary money to purchase an old institution of which they took possession in 1805.

They then resumed anew the practice of their holy customs but were not able to observe the strict enclosure. It was only in 1822, after they had returned to their old convent, endeared to them by so many titles, that Almighty God accorded them this consolation. They found a part of the buildings destroyed, yet there still remained a portion of the old house which had been consecrated by the sojourn of the venerable Ann of St. Bartholomew and her first daughters. The church was in a dilapidated condition, in consequence of having been used as a ware-house during the six years of trouble; the main-altar, however, had not been disturbed, nor the large painting of the mystery of the Incarnation, under whose invocation the Carmelite Monastery of Tours had been placed. The Blessed Virgin seemed to have taken upon herself the duty of watching over and preserving the edifice consecrated to her, which the following fact, cited literally from the annals of the monastery, will prove.

"The proprietor of our house was earnestly solicited to sell the church for a theatre, for which, from its favorable position, it was well adapted. On the eve of the day on which the sale was to take place, one of the commissioners went to the church to conclude some business arrangements. What was his astonishment to see two little streams of water issuing from the painting! He approached and saw that these tiny rivulets came from the eyes of the Blessed Virgin. Astonished at the marvelous occurrence, he examined the picture very minutely, to ascertain if this proceeded from any natural cause, but could discover nothing. The painting was at an elevation of thirty feet from the door, and was suspended on a wall three feet thick, on which not the slightest appearance of moisture could be perceived. This man, who professed no religion, was so impressed by the event, that he ran in alarm to relate what he had seen to the proprietor, saying with great earnestness: 'If you sell that church for a theatre, you and your family will be lost forever, for I have just seen the Virgin Mary weeping there.' We know not if the proprietor attached any importance to this extraordinary fact: the church, however, from one cause or another, was not sold. The commissioner, in his fright, hastened to the abode of our Mothers to report what had taken place; several of whom went to the spot and bore testimony to the fact."

This miraculous picture is still to be seen over the main altar in the church of the monastery. The Carmelites also possess another very interesting historical picture worthy of veneration; a beautiful image of Our Lord, the original of which, it is said, is preserved at Grilles, and is regarded by pious tradition as the true portrait of our Lord Jesus Christ which he, himself, sent to king Abgare. A small number of copies of the picture have been taken, and are to be seen in Spain. M. Gauthier, a gentleman from Angers, brought one on his return from Spain with Cardinal de Berulle, where they had gone to solicit the Carmelites to establish a house of their Order in France. This picture, he kept in his possession for years, but finally gave it to a friend; at present, it is in the possession of the Carmelites of Tours. It is painted on wood; the countenance of Our Lord is life-size and exquisitely beautiful; the view of it inspires the beholder with admiration and love, so delicate are the delineations, and so vivid is the harmony of the coloring. Need we be surprised that from among all other religious houses, Our Lord should have chosen this particular monastery to rejoice in the possession of such an incomparable treasure! For it was here that he first manifested the mystery of his dolorous Face and chose this spot as the cradle of the devotion of Reparation.

The Carmelites of Tours preserve many other objects of inestimable value to them. Among others, a celebrated relic of St. Theresa, a large particle of the bone of her right wrist, with the authentic documents signed by the Archbishop of Grenada, by the Discalced Carmelite Monks, and by other dignitaries of the province of St. Ange, in Upper Andalusia. This precious relic was brought from the frontiers of Spain by a royal courier and sent to the Carmelites. Another treasure, with which they are enriched, is the mantle left them, as we have already mentioned, by the venerable Ann of St. Bartholomew. And still another equally treasured, the pall used at the profession of Mother Magdalen of St. Joseph, the daughter of the noble founder, of whom we have already spoken. It is under this same pall that, at present, the sisters prostrate themselves on the day of their profession. Lastly, they have the happiness of possessing a piece of the veil of the most Blessed Virgin, sent them in 1835 by the Carmelites of Chartres.

At the time of the admission of Sr. M. St. Peter, only seventeen years had elapsed since the return of the Carmelites to their monastery. They faithfully guarded these precious souvenirs of the great example of virtue which their ancient Mothers had left them. Some of these venerable religious are still living and sustain the primitive spirit of the monastery. The rules are observed in their full vigor.

Mother Mary of the Incarnation, a soul well-tried in every virtue and of whom we shall speak later, gave to the entire community an impulse as energetic as it was salutary. It was under the direction of this worthy Superioress, that our little Perrine was immediately placed. For such a school, the young postulant was already well prepared, by her worthy and able director, to mount by rapid strides to the highest summit of religious perfection. Let us hasten to return to her artless narrative, in which she herself will relate her first experiences in cloistered life.

5

HER NOVITIATE

"I looked upon myself as the little servant of the Holy Family."
(Words of the Sister.)

The life of a Carmelite, according to St. Theresa, should be one of special devotedness to the glory of God and the service of the Church by prayer and penance. The illustrious Reformer repeated continually to her spiritual children: "My daughters, we have not come to Carmel to repose or to enjoy ourselves, but to labor, to suffer and to save souls."

From the moment of her arrival, our little Breton postulant felt that she should be thoroughly imbued with this spirit. "The God of mercy," said she, "manifested the designs he had in view in calling me to the religious state; designs well suited to give me an exalted idea of the sublime vocation I had embraced. The object of all the previous communications with which Our Lord had hitherto favored me, was the sanctification of my own soul. I labored exclusively for myself, as I was only charged with the care of my own perfection. But when God called me to Carmel, where I was to devote myself solely to his glory, the necessities of the Church and the salvation of souls, hedeigned to teach me to nature of the devotedness, the spirit of sacrifice and the zeal for the salvation of others, sublime virtues of which, as yet, I knew nothing. On this subject I received the following communication, which I have always regarded as the foundation-stone of the *Work of Reparation*: for before speaking to me openly of this great work, Our Lord waited until I had obtained my superior's consent to make the act of perfect abandonment which he required of me. This communication remains engraved on my heart, but as I did not make a written account of it, I can only narrate from memory what transpired."

"One day, after I had received holy communion, Our Lord, accompanied by an angel, condescended to manifest himself to my soul. He showed me the multitudes that were daily falling into hell, and then expressed his wish that I should offer myself without reserve to his good pleasure; moreover, that I should abandon to him all the merits I might acquire in my new career, for the accomplishment of his designs. He promised me that he would take care of my interests, that he would cause me to participate in all his merits, and would himself be the director of my soul. The angel (elsewhere she states that it was the archangel Raphael), urged me to consent to this magnanimous proposal. It seemed to me that he envied my happiness, for being purely spiritual he could neither suffer nor merit. This celestial spirit assured me that if I consented to Our Lord's request, the angels would surround my deathbed and defend me against the assaults of the devil."

"How I longed to make this act then and there! I was almost on the point of offering the sacrifice to the Lord; but either because my Divine Master had advised me differently, or that I was afraid to stray from the path of obedience, I did not comply with his wish, thinking that I ought to have the permission of our reverend superioress. To obtain this, I briefly transcribed the communication and presented it to her, as I had been accustomed to do with my confessor. Our good Mother, not aware of the manner in which Our Lord conducted me, did not give much credit to what her little postulant related, but she wisely said: 'My child, this abandonment which you desire to make, is no ordinary act, therefore, as I have yet no authority over you I cannot counsel you, and for much greater reason, cannot permit you to make it.' As I had a very great love for obedience, I submitted respectfully to the opinion of our reverend mother; yet her decision grieved me. I returned to Our Lord and ' said, 'Behold, my sweet Savior, obedience prevents me from complying with thy demand;

but thou dost behold the inmost recesses of my heart, and therefore, know.that I have offered thee all that I can give.' Our Lord, for the moment, seemed satisfied with my good will; nevertheless, he inspired me several times to reiterate the same demand. It was only after I had obtained the permission of my superiors that he fully communicated to me the *Work of Reparation*. Our prudent mother, perceiving from this that I received extraordinary favors, took steps to ascertain the nature of the spirit which conducted me; she forbade me to pay any attention to these supernatural operations. Then I no longer heard any interior words, and Our Lord seemed to submit himself with me, in some manner, to holy obedience."

This superior, to whom Our Lord, for the moment, was thus *submissive,* was Mother Mary of the Incarnation; had he not appointed her his immediate representative to this vessel of election, to the chosen soul whom he proposed to make an instrument of mercy! It is important that we should make the acquaintance of this venerable mother immediately, as she plays a conspicuous part in the communications of Sister St. Peter.

The venerable mother Mary of the Incarnation was a Breton. She was born at Paimboeuf, under the "Directoire" on the 9th of January 1785. At that time, the law required children to be taken before the Municipal officers to have their names inscribed on the civil register.

This child was presented, bearing her mother's name, Marie Angelique. The municipal officers, all Revolutionists, were averse to such a *pious Christian name,* and gave her one of their own choices, directing that she should be called *Virtue.* Thus, it was that Divine Providence made use of the wicked to give a characteristic appellation to this child of benediction from the moment of her entrance into the world. All the innocence and strength of character comprised in the beautiful name, *Virtue,* was fully exemplified in her future life. At her birth she could only receive the sacrament of Baptism informally, because of the persecution; a few years later, all the attendant ceremonies were administered. She appreciated so well the grace of regeneration, that on hearing a person speak of infidel lands, she claimed: "Oh, how I pity the poor children of those countries who have not as I have had, the happiness of being baptized!"

Angelique early became inured to the sufferings of her parents having met with reverses of every description. Once her mother was congratulated for having a child of such promise, mature beyond her years, but she was heard to reply: "Alas, she has so often seen me weep."

This worthy lady, left a widow after the Revolution, removed to Tours. Her little daughter, though so young, gave early evidence that she understood the happiness of knowing and loving God. She had most celestial inspirations, and seemed naturally averse to all the pleasures of the world; God was not long in manifesting to her his designs. At the age of thirteen or fourteen, passing before the devastated church of the Carmelites, she felt inwardly moved to enter. Kneeling on the steps leading to the sanctuary, she gazed intently on the painting of our Blessed Lady which hung on the wall at considerable height, in front of the grating which separated the choir of the religious from the church. She then thought to herself: "How happy should I be, if one day I were admitted among those who have dwelt within these venerable walls!" Immediately she heard a voice reply:

"Persevere, and thou shalt taste this happiness." At this moment she was seized with a presentiment of sorrow; a crushing weight seemed to have fallen on her soul, and she fell prostrate on the pavement, shedding an abundance of tears: her sobs and sighs were re-echoed by the deserted building. Terrified, the poor child ran to a friend to relate what had happened; the latter said earnestly: "My child, I have long foreseen that you will one day be a religious."

The world was not long to retain this innocent dove, who at the age of seventeen flew to the bosom of Carmel. After the Revolutionary storm had swept by, the Carmelites found shelter in an old monastery purchased with the fruit of their toils and self-denials. Marie Angelique, renouncing the tender care of an affectionate mother, presented herself to share that poverty which was the portion of the daughters of St. Theresa, who soon discovered the treasure they had acquired and lost no time to enhance its value; they submitted her to the most rigorous trials of obedience in order to destroy her self-will completely. Their efforts were not fruitless, for when still a young professed, she was called upon as Mistress of Novices, to form others to religious perfection.

The many sacrifices and privations which the community had suffered during those years of distress had prematurely ruined her health and brought on a long and painful illness to which she finally succumbed. Nothing could induce her to deviate from her usual routine of labor, prayer, and penance. Appointed treasurer, she managed the modest finances of the house with such prudence and ability, that the monastery was soon relieved from the extreme indigence into which it had been plunged by spoliation.

Elected prioress in 1834, she made some important improvements in the old monastery, which had been restored to them in 1822. It was in this place that she had received the first call of grace. When obliged by threats of municipal expropriation to leave this venerable asylum, the task of constructing a new monastery devolved upon her. She succeeded marvelously in her enterprise, with the assistance of St. Theresa. Her charity was inexhaustible: from the depths of her solitude she extended both, spiritual and temporal aid to all the wants made known to her by Divine Providence. We find that she was instrumental in the re-establishment of the Carmelite friars in France, by the charity rendered two Spanish religious who had been brought prisoners to Tours. She procured their release, and provided for all their necessities until they were able to rejoin the reverend Father Dominic and other exiled priests who were to found a new monastery.

A person of superior mind, she elicited the admiration of all those with whom she had any intercourse; it was said, what a pity such a remarkable woman is shut up in a cloister!"

The venerable Mothers who had received her, considering her as the chain destined to link together ancient and modern times had, as she often remarked, bequeathed to her "the custody of the sacred traditions of the order *on the peril of her soul.*" She accepted it on those terms and under those conditions. To insure their preservation, she gathered together with pious respect from Tours and the other monasteries of France, the rules, religious regulations, and all the customs pertaining to monastic discipline. From these she compiled, "The Carmelite's Treasure" a most precious work, well adapted to preserve the traditions of the Order in France.

As superior, Mother Mary of the Incarnation knew admirably how to combine firmness with gentleness. Although it pained her to reprehend or chastise others, yet she never for an instant hesitated when the necessity of the occasion demanded, or the dictates of her conscience deemed it expedient. Her lively faith and experienced judgment were always guided by the rules of Christian prudence and by the most scrupulous discretion. One of her special gifts was the discernment of spirits. *Obedience* was the infallible mark by which she judged between the operations of grace and those of nature; this, in her opinion, was the touchstone of real virtue. When necessary, she administered humiliations in good doses, and manifested an apparent indifference for the communications confided in her.

Such was the course pursued by this prudent Mother in regard to the young Breton aspirant committed to her care. To discover the spirit by which she was influenced, the reverend mother adopted the method pursued by Perrine's former confessor and directed her to give a written account of all that concerned her celestial communications. Whenever her spiritual daughter presented herself with her paper, the Mother would take it quietly, lay it aside and continue her occupation, intimating thereby that she would attend to it When time permitted, after she had disposed of all other matters.

The special devotion of our young postulant was a tender love of the holy Infancy of Jesus. Let us not deprive her of the pleasure of describing the manner in which she was attracted by grace, previous to her reception of the holy habit.

"When but an infant in Carmelite life, Our Lord gave me a special attraction to the mystery of his holy Infancy and made known what he desired of me. The following exercise, consisting of a special devotion for every day of the month, was traced out in my mind; I practiced this exercise with great consolation and with much profit. I looked upon myself as the little servant of the Holy Family and offered to serve them. I longed to bear their livery in being clothed with the habit of the Carmelites, beseeching our reverend mother to grant me this inestimable favor, notwithstanding my great unworthiness. Accordingly, I received the holy habit on the 21st of May 1840, during the lovely month dedicated to her, through whose intercession I had obtained the grace of being called to the religious life. On that memorable day of benediction, I consecrated myself anew to the Holy Family in a most particular manner. The following is the formula which I wrote and placed on my heart during the ceremony: "Jesus, Mary, and Joseph! Most holy and admirable family, I beg of you to receive me today as your little servant; this is the most ardent desire of my heart. I beseech you to hear my prayer, for I am firmly resolved to be forever faithful; and though I cannot immolate myself by the vows of religion, nevertheless, I beg of you to receive my desire of fulfilling them, and to grant me the grace to accomplish them as perfectly as if contracted. O most Holy Infant Jesus! Grant that I may be as submissive to the Holy Ghost and to my superiors as you were to the most Holy Virgin and to St. Joseph. And thou, O Mary, conceived without sin, obtain for me that I may never tarnish the brilliancy of the angelic virtue of purity. O blessed patriarch St. Joseph, thou who hast practiced holy poverty in so eminent a degree of perfection, and who hast sacrificed thyself for the Holy Infant Jesus and the most Blessed Virgin, his mother, obtain by thy example and thy powerful influence with God, that I may love and practice holy poverty to my last breath, that I may make it a duty and a pleasure to sacrifice myself for my sisters. O most Holy Family! grant that I may glory in being your humble servant. Deign to receive me on this happy day, and give me in proof of your acceptance of my offering, the grace of acquitting myself worthily of the divine office, that I may recite it with respectful attention and loving fervor; grant that I may be as vigilant at matins as if I were in Heaven, enraptured by the grandeur of God and the splendor of his glory. Amen."

"After this consecration, I regarded myself as the little domestic of the Holy Family, and in all my occupations I had the intention of serving them at Nazareth. I had but one more ambition, that of being the little Ass of the Infant Jesus. If the royal prophet David looked upon himself as a beast of burden before the Lord, with how much more propriety could I not designate myself the Ass of the Infant Jesus? Reflecting that the Son of God reduced himself to such poverty for our love, that he was necessitated on his triumphant entry into Jerusalem, to send his disciples to borrow so humble an animal, saying on his part, that 'the Master had need of it,' I exclaimed: 'My good Savior, now that thou art in Heaven, I desire thou shouldst have an ass on earth, entirely at thy disposal, whom thou mayst lead about at pleasure, wherever thou wilt; accept me, I beg of thee. As well as I can remember, I was most desirous of knowing if Our Lord accepted my offering, and I believe I even prayed to the Holy Family with that intention. Afterward, I proceeded to my appointment in the following manner."

"Our reverend Mothers were then on their retreat; during this time, the postulants and novices took their recreation in the novitiate. One evening, as we were all assembled before a picture of the Holy Family at the hour of recreation, I proposed to my companions to make a sheepfold for the Holy Family in such a manner, that each would be consecrated to them according to the office, or title drawn by lot; the proposition was unanimously accepted. It was decided that one of us should be the ass of the Infant Jesus, another the ox, another the sheep, and so on. The convention was held, the billets drawn, and to my great joy, I was chosen by Providence to be the Ass *of the Infant Jesus.* 1 inquired into the characteristics of the ass, for I wanted to avoid its defects. A postulant, who possessed one in the world, gave me all the necessary information.—We could not have passed a more pleasant recreation.—My billet was couched in the following terms: 'The Ass of the Holy Infant is stubborn, he is idle; he will walk only in by-ways, but he has resolved to correct these defects. His office shall be, to keep the Infant Jesus warm, to carry him on his journeys; and in a word, to render to the Holy Family all the little services in its power.'"

"I was enchanted with my new title; but I thought there was still something more to obtain before I could validly assume the duties of my office. This was the approval of our reverend mother, whom I prayed to have the kindness to sign my billet; for said I, our dear Mother represents Our Lord; if I can obtain her signature, it will be a certain proof that the Divine Infant accepts me as his little ass. Our reverend mother was very much amused with our simplicity. 'I have no objection,' said she, 'to sign your little billets.' She became a child with her children, practicing the saying of St. Paul, making herself all to all, to gain all; and we thus obtained her signature. I was quite serious in thus offering myself to the Infant Jesus; I regarded it as a little contract by which I could comply with the request of Our Lord, made some days after my entrance into religion, that of giving myself entirely to Him together with all that I could do for the accomplishment of his designs; for I felt myself continually urged to make the act of abandonment. The permission of my superiors, only, was wanting. When our reverend mother signed my billet, I hoped that I could make my little sacrifice to the Holy Infant. However, to be more certain, I spoke to our reverend mother and asked her if she would be willing to give up her little Ass entirely to the Infant Jesus, that he might do with her as he wished. She replied: 'No, my child; tell Him that I only lend her, I cannot yet give her up entirely.'

"There were many other painful refusals in store for me; a perfect abandonment to God for the accomplishment of his designs might have entailed results which I could not then foresee, being so little initiated in the ways of the Lord. Our wise and prudent mother wished first to exercise this poor and 'miserable instrument in the virtue of obedience and in the renunciation of self-will. I offered myself to the Lord as a loaned Ass, through the hands of Mary and Joseph. This little act of simplicity was, I believe, very pleasing to the Divine Infant, for he began to direct me a- new in his ways; this was in fulfilment of a promise he had made after my entrance into Carmel. I regarded my soul as the poor stable of Bethlehem and considering the Holy Infant Jesus reposing in my heart, I adored him in union with the Blessed Virgin and St. Joseph, and I offered to be his little domestic. I was his little Ass in prayer, stimulating myself to keep him warm by the ardor of my love; his little domestic in action, by performing for the Holy Family all the duties imposed on me, imagining myself to be in the house of Nazareth. The Divine Infant inspired me to honor him each day of the month by a special devotion."

We give here an extract:

MONTH OF THE HOLY INFANT JESUS.

On the 15th of the month, she celebrated the Espousals of the Holy Virgin with St. Joseph, engaging herself to labor for them as their little servant.

The 16th was consecrated to the mystery of the Incarnation. On the nine following days, she honored the Holy Infant in the womb of his Virgin Mother; then she accompanied the Blessed Virgin and St. Joseph to Bethlehem.

On the 25th, she celebrated the birth of the Divine Infant.

On the 26th, she united her homage to that of the shepherds.

On the 27th, she adored him in his circumcision, when he was named Jesus.

On the 28th, she honored him in union with the Magi.

On the 29th, in his presentation in the Temple.

On the 30th, in his flight to Egypt.

The first seven days of the following month were consecrated to the Infant Jesus in his exile; then she honored his first steps, his first words, his first actions, his purity and his simplicity.

On the 8th, she celebrated the return of the Moly Family to Nazareth.

On the 9th, she contemplated Jesus commencing to work with St. Joseph.

On the 10th, she honored the obedience which the Divine Infant rendered his parents.

On the 11th, his affection for his Blessed Mother and for the faithful Guardian of his holy infancy.

The 12th, she consecrated to the Holy Child in his twelfth year, going to Jerusalem with the Blessed Virgin and St. Joseph to celebrate the Passover and to manifest his love.

On the 13th, she adored him in the midst of the Doctors of the Law, defending the rights of his Father.

On the 24th, she rendered her homage to the Holy Child, found in the Temple by Mary and Joseph, returning in their company to Nazareth, where he was subject to them. This completed the month of the Holy Infancy; the following day, the 15th, she recommenced. The thought of the Divine Infant, in union with whom she performed all her actions, rendered every occupation easy and agreeable, and thus the time passed imperceptibly.

"But," said she "Satan, pride itself, was jealous when he saw me honor the humiliation of the *Word Incarnate*. One day, when I had performed an action which undoubtedly, was very displeasing to him, he endeavored to be revenged as follows: That night, after retiring, and just as I was falling asleep, I felt on my head something like a great, ugly beast which seemed to be trying to smother me : immediately I had a presentiment that it was the devil, he was pressing my head. I cried out to the Blessed Virgin to come to my rescue. On hearing this sacred name he took to flight, I then offered a prayer of thanksgiving, after which, if I remember rightly, I began to sing these words, so terrible to the infernal spirits:

Et verbum caro factum est, et habitavit in nobis! This took place during the grand silence: though I did not really see the devil, yet from the extraordinary sensation experienced in my soul, I understood that it proceeded from more than an ordinary dream. Satan, undoubtedly, wanted to smother the Ass of the Divine Infant, but the Blessed Virgin came to her assistance."

This devotion of Sr. St. Peter to the Holy Infancy, was cherished by her to her last breath. Though by the call of divine grace, she was to accompany Our Lord in the most dolorous scenes of his Passion, yet she was incessantly drawn back to this first consoling mystery of his life, the sweet and innocent impress of which her virginal soul always retained.

To maintain herself always in contemplation of the Divine Infant, she ornamented two little statues, one of which she called her *little king,* and the other, her *poor king*; both being appropriately decorated to represent the character which her ingenious devotion gave to each one. She carried one or the other constantly with her: and on her deathbed we shall see how her pious and grateful charity easily found the means of gaining graces from her little Kings for the benefactors of her monastery.

6

HER PROFESSION

**"My child, it is not enough to sacrifice one
thing to God; *all* must be immolated to him."
*(The Mother Prioress.)***

S ister Mary St. Peter's novitiate was fast drawing to a close. The mere thought of the
happy day on which our fervent and generous novice would consecrate herself to
God by the sacred vows of religion, caused her to exult with impatient joy. She hastened
to manifest her eagerness to be admitted to her holy profession, and frequently entreated
her superior to grant her this favor.

"At last," said the sister, "she ceded to my pressing solicitations, notwithstanding my lack
of virtue and capacity, and decided to take the necessary steps toward my admission. Being
told that I would be obliged to present myself three times at the chapter before being
admitted, I had the inspiration to perform a little exercise of piety each time I presented
myself, to obtain for my celestial spouse, Jesus, the sole object of my desires. I addressed
myself to the three persons who have had special claims upon him: to the Eternal Father,
the Blessed Virgin and St. Joseph. In this way, I made my three demands for profession
with great devotion and gained him for whom I had longed unceasingly. Notwithstanding
my unworthiness, the community had the charity to admit me to my profession, and I
celebrated my spiritual nuptials with Jesus. L'Abbe Panager, cure of St. Etienne, who had
been my former director, came to preach at the ceremony. He took for his text: *Beatam
me dicent omnes generationes:* (All nations shall call me Blessed): He pictured the beauty
of the state I had embraced, repeating continually, 'Blessed art thou!' How true! Was

I not blessed' My vocation irrevocably decided, and all my desires accomplished! I was
supremely happy."

Our humble novice passes rather lightly over this important circumstance. We can
supply some interesting particulars of the period which elapsed between the time of
her admission by the community and the day of the solemn ceremony; these facts have
been taken from the annals of the monastery. The interval of several weeks was passed
by Sr. St. Peter in fervent and careful preparation for the all-important day. She made
a retreat of ten days with so much fervor and recollection, that she had not once raised
her eyes, so absorbed was she in God. The day on which she pronounced her vows, the
mother prioress, on leaving the room in which Sr. St. Peter had been congratulated by the
community, perceived a young novice very sad and pensive; turning towards the newly
professed the Mother said: 'Peter, go and console John!' Sr. St. Peter ran to embrace
her companion, promising her that her turn would soon come. In fact, the latter was
professed a few months later, notwithstanding the many forebodings to the contrary. She
never forgot the impression made on her on that occasion. In embracing Sr. St. Peter, it
seemed to her that she had approached an angel. Sister St. Peter's profession took place on
the 8th of June 1841, date worthy of record. On such an important occasion, the sister
was not without having given her Divine Spouse a new proof of her love. The following
is her act of CONSECRATION.

"O my God, deign to accept the sacrifice which I offer Thee in union with Jesus my
Savior, immolated for man. I offer thee through him and in union with him the entire
abandonment of myself, the sacrifice of my life. I remit my soul to thy all-merciful hands.
To thee O Jesus, my beloved Spouse, I offer my entire being on the altar of thy Divine
Heart, by the hands of the most Holy Virgin and of St. Joseph; through them I deposit
my vows, begging them to be the witnesses and the guardians thereof. Deign, O cherished
Family to accept the entire consecration which I make of myself to your service, I also offer
myself to thee on this day, in union with our holy Mother St. Theresa, and our Father St.
John of the Cross, for the accomplishment of thy designs over my soul. Look upon me
as thine. I pray thee to guard my holy vows; accomplish them in me by thy all-powerful
grace. O Jesus, my adorable Spouse, I am so poor, so miserable, so inconstant in virtue!"

"In union with the Hearts of Mary and Joseph, I make my profession and promise,
Poverty, Chastity and Obedience to God, to our Lord Jesus, and to the most blessed
Virgin Mary, under the authority of our lawful Superiors, according to the primitive Rule

of the Order of Mount Carmel of the 'Reform of St. Theresa' without mitigation, and this to the hour of my death. O Divine Infant, unite my sacrifice to thine."

"When presented in the Temple, thou didst sacrifice thyself for my redemption: today I offer myself to redeem sinners. O Mary, my tender Mother, and you my good Father St. Joseph, who presented two doves to the High Priest for the redemption of the Infant Jesus, deign, I beseech you, to offer to the Eternal Father, my body and my soul, to redeem this Divine Infant from the hands of sinners and to heal his wounds. Impress on me, I implore you, his divine resemblance; rather grant that it may not be I who live, but thou Jesus, who livest and reignest in me! O Jesus, Mary, and Joseph, with what ardor and joy would I not have gone to offer myself to serve you, if I had had the happiness of living when you were on this earth! With the same sentiments of love, I wish to serve this holy community as though it were you who dwelt in this house. I beseech you to accept all my labors, all that I have belongs entirely to you. Deign to regard me henceforth as your little servant and dispose of me as you will. Amen."

Sr. Mary St. Peter of the Holy Family.
(Unworthy Carmelite.)
June 8th, 1841.

The sister, on entering the monastery, had taken the name of Mary, patroness of all the Carmelites, and that of St. Peter, her baptismal name; thus, was she doubly placed under the protection of the Prince of the Apostles. On the day of her profession, she wished to become more particularly allied to the Holy Family; for this reason, she added to her other titles, as we have seen, that of the "Holy Family," which she lovingly cherished and by which she was known.

But to continue with her narrative: "Being thus entirely consecrated to Jesus as his little domestic, I was soon inspired by him to guard his flock in the pasture of his divine Infancy; and I arranged the plan of a little exercise in honor of the twelve mysteries of the first twelve years of his life; which I called the "Twelve Tribes of Israel", of which the following is an extract:"

"In honor of his first year, I offered him, through the Blessed Virgin and St. Joseph, our Holy Father the Pope, and all the hierarchy of the Church militant, under the protection of Sts. Peter and Paul.

The second year, I offered for the souls of all religious, under the protection of St. John and the holy Apostles.

The third year, for kings under the protection of holy king David and the Magi.

The fourth year, for the unfortunate freemasons, under the protection of the holy Martyrs.

The fifth year, for all comedians, under the protection of St. John the Baptist.

The sixth year, for infidel nations, under the protection of the nine choirs of angels.

The seventh year, for heretics and schismatics, under the protection of St. Ann.

The eighth year, for the Jews, under the protection of St. Ann and St. Joachim.

The ninth year, for unbelievers, under the protection of the holy Prophets.

The tenth year, for all obdurate sinners, under the protection of the holy Confessors.

The eleventh year, for tepid souls, under the protection of the holy Women.

Finally, the twelfth year, for the souls of the Just, under the protection of our holy Mother St. Teresa, and all the holy Virgins."

Such is what she termed the "Sheepfold of the Infant Jesus," most touching and admirable occupation of zeal and charity for the Church and the salvation of souls. Our Lord had inspired her with this devotion after her profession. According to her opinion, nothing could be better suited to the humble function chosen by her with so much love. — "My adorable Savior," said she, "soon assumed such power over me, notwithstanding my unworthiness, that I could truly say he had become the director and master of my soul."

In this divine school, the sister, docile and faithful disciple, made rapid progress in the contemplative life. The activity of her mind attracted her to the perpetual contemplation of the mysteries of the life of Our Lord. Taking for her starting point the Holy Infancy of Jesus, she passed successively over the scenes of his hidden life, his dolorous life and his glorious life, from his Incarnation to his triumphant Ascension. She distributed the hours of the day in such manner, that each recalled to her mind some circumstance in the life of Our Lord, to whom she united herself by faith and loving contemplation. She had such an attraction for this exercise that she performed without any apparent effort, what to others might seem tedious and complicated. We can form some conception of this from the concise report she drew up, in obedience to the mother prioress.

"At eight o'clock in the evening, I offer myself to the most holy Virgin and St. Joseph, as their little domestic, to guard their sheep in the pastures of the Infant Jesus, that is his mysteries and his sacred wounds; and I adore the mystery of the Incarnation until nine o'clock, when matins are sung; then I celebrate the birth of the Infant Jesus; I unite myself to the angels, to the shepherds, and the Magi who adored him in the manger. During the first nocturn, I adore his eternal birth in the bosom of his Father, and his divine life; during the second nocturn, I adore his birth in the stable of Bethlehem and his mortal life; at the third nocturn, I adore his sacramental birth in the Holy Eucharist, and his spiritual birth in our hearts."

"At each of the nine psalms, I unite myself to the nine choirs of angels."

"At the Te Deum, I adore the Infant Jesus manifesting himself to the Jewish people in the persons of the Shepherds."

During the psalms of lauds, I adore the Holy Infant circumcised and receiving the name, *Jesus;* afterward, I adore him with the Magi, as God, King, and Man.—This is my mental occupation during matins."

She thus, perhaps without being aware of it, adopted a method the most approved by liturgists and masters of the spiritual life, that of being united in spirit to Our Lord id the mysteries of his sacred life during the psalmody and recitation of the office.

Matins is the last choir-exercise of the day for the Carmelites, shortly after which the religious take the necessary repose. Sister M. St. Peter continued her homage to the Divine Infant. "Having retired to my cell," said she, "I am occupied until eleven, with the sheepfold and the sheep of the Holy Infant Jesus, beseeching that amiable Savior to pour his benedictions on them, and to apply to them his sacred merits. After this, I retire to rest in union with the Holy Infant reposing in the manger. In the morning, as soon as I hear the *reveil,* I arise and adore the Eternal Father saying to him, with the Infant Jesus: 'Behold me, my Father, I have come to do thy will.' Then I repair to the choir for prayer, in union with the Blessed Virgin and St. Joseph conducting the Infant Jesus to the Temple. During my prayer, I offer myself with him to his Heavenly Father; I renew the holy vows of my profession and give myself to this Divine Savior. Afterward, I offer him to his Eternal Father for the salvation of his sheep. Meditation being finished, we go with the Holy Family to Nazareth; soon the bell summons us to the 'Little Hours,' and we depart for Egypt. During the twelve psalms of these Hours, I adore the twelve years of the Holy Infancy; and honor his sojourn in Egypt, his return to Nazareth, and his stay in the Temple of Jerusalem, where he was found in the midst of the Doctors."

"After the holy sacrifice of the mass, the hour for work arrives, then I contemplate Our Lord during his hidden and laborious life. At eleven o'clock, I adore Jesus baptized by St. John: after noon till one o'clock, I remain with him in the desert; from one to two, I follow him in his public life. At two o'clock vespers commerce, then I adore his triumphant entry into the city of Jerusalem, and I go to the choir in union with our Divine Savior; during the office I keep myself in spirit at his feet, honoring the sentiments of his adorable Heart during the last week he passed with his disciples, and the excess of his love, which urged him to institute the sacrament of the Holy Eucharist."

"Afterward, we arrive at the Garden of Olives, and there I remain during the rest of the afternoon; I follow Our Lord through the different stages of his Passion in union with the Blessed Virgin. At five o'clock the bell calls us to meditation." According to the spirit of the Carmelite rules, the evening meditation is one of the most important exercises of the day; this will sufficiently explain the number and variety of interior acts performed by Sr. St. Peter during her meditation.

"At this moment," said she, "I adore Jesus crucified, and I remain either at the foot of the cross or in the Sacred Heart. I begin by an examination of conscience, and after humbling myself for my faults, I offer myself entirely to Our Lord, renewing my holy vows, in union with his sacrifice. After having thus given myself to him, it seems that he gives himself reciprocally to me with all his merits:he unites my soul to his, causing me to participate in the honor which he renders his Father as Victim. Then I lose sight of myself to be occupied with my heavenly Spouse, for the glory of God and the salvation of souls. I find in the Heart of Our Lord all the mysteries of his most holy life, his merits, and all his sheep. I offer each mystery to the Eternal Father for such and such a portion of the sheepfold of the Infant Jesus. After which, I present to this Divine Father the four quarters of the globe, which I have placed in the four wounds of the feet and the hands of my Savior: the twelve flocks of the Holy Family occupy the fold of the Sacred Heart. To these I also join the souls in purgatory, having placed them in the other wounds of this adorable body. Then

I offer this august Victim to the Eternal Father by the hands of the Blessed Virgin, as a sacrifice of expiation and of thanksgiving for all the perfections of the most Holy Trinity. Finally, I adore the last sigh of Jesus on the cross. Such is the method which Our Lord has given me to pursue during the evening meditation."

This method of prayer was particularly adapted to her disposition, and notwithstanding the seeming multiplicity of acts, we must concede that it is most simple, natural and practical. Habit, and the attraction of grace rendered it easy and delightful to her. She never lost sight of Our Lord; the meditation ended; she still continued her perfect union with him. "During the remainder of the day, I occupy myself till compline with Jesus reposing in the sepulcher; then I adore him rising from the tomb, and I contemplate him in his ascension to Heaven."

"This is, in general, the order of my daily exercises. But to facilitate the action of the Divine Master in my soul, I must practice a total renouncement of all that could flatter the senses: no reflections on self unless to humble myself. God alone, his will and his glory: such is my maxim. These words, *and he was subject to them,* and again, *I have not come to be served, but to serve,* are always in my mind. Our Lord gave me a thorough conviction of my utter incapacity to do anything good, and also of my abject misery. The Child Jesus led his little Ass by the bridle of his holy grace, I had but to renounce myself, and obey."

We need not be surprised at this interior self "renunciation" or at the "humility" with which the good sister seems to be penetrated; it was but the fruit of her continual application to the mysteries of the life of the Savior. The mother prioress, to whom these details were related in confidence, kept a constant watch over her, and became convinced that she was actuated by the impulse of divine grace. Nevertheless, to assure herself of the spirit which animated her, she spared her no humiliation but mortified her on all occasions, and at every instant opposed her wishes; in a word, she endeavored to make her pursue a more ordinary course.

"I made every effort to obey," said the pious religious, "but to no purpose; for I would soon find myself in the same path. Our mother permitted me to speak to a holy priest, well enlightened in the interior life. She said: 'My child, explain to him how you make your meditation and in what manner you are conducted by God.' I availed myself of this occasion with thankfulness and laid bare my interior to this good priest. Having thoroughly examined all, he said: 'My child continue your course without fear, let God conduct you as he wills, for you have established the foundation of your spiritual life on a solid basis,—mortification. Tell your reverend mother that I am satisfied; I will speak to her myself also.' After this, our prudent mother permitted me to abandon myself fully to the spirit of God; but she wisely counselled me to be faithful to grace, and not to remain inactive after the cessation of the divine operations in my soul. As I had no employment to distract my mind from the presence of God, the entire day was passed in an uninterrupted prayer, if I can thus express myself. My work was no hinderance to my continual union with Our Lord. Having thus no opportunity to practice virtue, I had not much merit; but our reverend mother, who continually watched over the spiritual advancement of my soul, soon gave me an office most fruitful in distractions, that of portress. My love of silence and prayer found no sympathy with my new office, but I regarded the command of our mother as an order from Heaven, and joyfully submitted, thinking that on that day, the feast of the Incarnation, the Infant Jesus had given me an evident proof that he had chosen me to be his little domestic, and that he would employ me in this office to perform all the errands of the house. I then renewed the consecration of myself to the Divine Infant."

It may be well to observe here, that the office of portress, according to the rule of the Carmelites, and as it was imposed on Sister St. Peter, is exercised exclusively within the interior of the cloister; she who is appointed thereto, receives all the commissions and messages from without, and transmits the same to those within the cloister. For this reason, it must not be confused with that of the Sister Tourieres who are in direct communication with the world, and whose obligations and duties are essentially different from the cloistered religious. The office of portress has its moments of fatigue. She who so willingly designated herself, the little "Ass of the Infant Jesus," was obliged more than once, to ask for relief from her Divine Master, through her superior. Besides the fatigue incidental to this employment, general business and preoccupation of mind, are the particular lot of those appointed portress. This was exactly what the mother prioress had in view in appointing Sister St. Peter, foreseeing that it would effectually cross the good sister in her habits of prayer and recollection; and indeed, it was a perpetual source of penance and self-renunciation: she practiced all the austerities prescribed by the rules, even adding others voluntarily; yet always maintaining herself within the limits of discretion. Her entire life, both interiorly and exteriorly, was one continued mortification, severing her completely from all the pleasures of the senses. She had asked for a statue of the Infant Jesus and in a short time received it. She relates the fact with her usual simplicity: "I often desired to have, a little statue of the Infant Jesus, to render my homage to him during the day; but I hesitated to ask our reverend mother for it. One day, it seemed that the Divine Infant urged me to insist on having one; I obeyed the inspiration, and my petition was granted. I now had the Holy Infant with me in the parlor, and I was supremely happy: I offered him all my little labors and demanded souls as a recompense. This Divine Infant gave me, in such profusion, all the graces I needed to fulfil my employment, that it was not injurious to my spiritual application, nor did it prevent my union with God when at prayer. All day long I labored for the salvation of the sheep of the Holy Infant.

Jesus, and at prayer, he repaid me a hundred-fold. By times during the day, he visited my soul with a powerful impulse of his grace. I would leave my work for a brief moment, when I felt his approach, that I might hearken to him the more attentively; but thinking that I should have permission I asked our reverend mother. As she never neglected any opportunity of exercising my virtue, she forbade me notice these interior operations. 'I only permit you, when your mind is disturbed, to pause an instant to recollect yourself.' With the grace of God, I followed minutely her wise counsels."

In 1843, Our Lord engaged her, in a special manner, to pray for Spain, which was then in a state of revolution. This Catholic country, the birthplace of St. Theresa and the cradle of the Reform of the Carmelites, would naturally have engrossed the attention of Sister St. Peter, and it was not surprising that she often remembered it before God at a period when the Spanish nuns and clergy were being persecuted and sent into exile.

"I have never," said she, "felt my soul so closely united to God as during that time. My Divine Master operated in me something which I can neither understand nor explain. It seemed that I heard him asking grace from his heavenly Father for that kingdom, and so urgently that I was astonished. He obliged me to beg mercy in his name;but I feel that I am unequal to the task of explaining this mystery of his love, therefore I abandon it."

God communicated himself freely to this generous professed. She felt more and more urged to make the act of entire abandonment with which she had been inspired after her admission to Carmel; but her Superiors always refused to grant the permission. However, this year, 1843, she unexpectedly had an occasion to renew her demand. The Carmelites were obliged to quit their old monastery and search for a site on which to build anew. The circumstances attendant on this change are intimately connected with the life of Mother

Mary of the Incarnation, and consequently with that of Sister St. Peter. The following facts, relative to this event, are taken from the annals of the monastery.

"For some time past, our house had been an obstacle to the various improvements planned by the city; moreover, our neighbor's new buildings overlooked our premises from which resulted serious inconveniences as to regularity, not to speak of the unhealthfulness brought about by such a state of things. Nevertheless, we would not have thought of making any change, for we could not bear the idea of abandoning the cradle of our religious life, hallowed by the virtues of our first Mothers, saintly ground which we had recovered at the cost of so much labor and sacrifice. But when least expected, unforeseen circumstances hastened the time of the dreaded change; several persons, desirous of purchasing the house, made some very advantageous offers; the inconveniences we experienced increased daily; the plans of the city officials were about to be put into execution, and we were compelled to decide on our departure. Before taking other measures, we had to procure the ground whereon to build. After much research, Divine Providence directed our Superiors to a place which seemed specially reserved for us. It was situated in a tranquil and solitary part of the city, near the archbishopric; there were no surrounding buildings, the air was pure, and in a word, the spot seemed specially chosen for our manner of life. We soon made the purchase depending on the treasury of our Heavenly Father, for we had not even half the capital necessary for such an undertaking."

"The first alms we received for this purpose merits a special mention. It came from a poor but virtuous old man, who touched with compassion at the sight of our destitution, gave all he had, as we afterward learned. His offering resembled the widow's mite, and was most pleasing to God, for it became a source of benediction. But to keep us perfectly detached from earthly things, Our Lord permitted that assistance should be rendered us only in accordance with our necessities, and at the very moment when all hope was lost, frequently by means unforeseen. Once in a moment of extreme distress, we appealed to St. Yves, the intercessor of the poor, and we received assistance truly extraordinary. He inspired a lady of noble birth, whose modesty forbids us reveal her name, to give us a special mark of her benevolence, though but little acquainted with our community, thus winning for herself our lasting gratitude, besides the title and privileges of a benefactress."

From the outset, this undertaking was a source of much anxiety to the reverend mother prioress, Mary of the Incarnation, as we can readily understand. Quite naturally she recommended the matter to Sister St. Peter and enjoined her to pray to the Infant Jesus to find a suitable spot for a habitation for his spouses. "With this intention, I prayed to the Divine Infant" said the sister, "and asked of him the land, but I believe I heard him reply: *Give me the land of your soul!* I understood perfectly what he meant. He, also, had a building to raise for the glory of his Father, and had long chosen the sandy ground of my soul for the accomplishment of his design;notwithstanding my unworthiness, he had ordained that so miserable a creature should be the means of adding greater *eclat* to his glory."

After prime, she went to the office of the mother prioress, who spoke of her anxiety in reference to the great enterprise with which she had been charged. "Our good mother," said the sister, "had need of a little relaxation of mind: I commenced to talk and soon made her laugh heartily: 'Reverend mother,' said I, when a man wants some money and has none, he sells his ass; if you will sell me to the Infant Jesus, I am sure He will give you some money to build the house.' Our reverend mother smiled at my singular proposition; but I persisted, saying: 'Mother, I am not worth much, but as the Holy Infant wants me and even asks for me, he will surely purchase me? Delighted with the thought of being sold for Our Lord, who permitted himself to be sold by Judas, for love of me, I then added: 'Mother, how much will you sell me for?' Our reverend mother perceived by my air of sincerity and by the great desire I manifested in making such a request, that Our Lord had perhaps some design in view; she seemed to condescend, and replied: 'Well, my child, you can say to the Infant Jesus that if I were rich, I would give you to him, but as I am very poor and in need of money to build his holy house, I am obliged to sell you; ask him then to purchase you.' This reply gave me great pleasure; I addressed myself to the Holy Infant and imparted to him the commission of our reverend mother: I besought him as a favor to purchase me, that I might then, be at his disposal."

"One night, while I was praying fervently, offering him the love of the shepherds, the Magi and the saints who had seen and adored him, I wove a little crown in honor of the twelve years of his most Holy Infancy. I thought this little homage was most pleasing to him, for I believe I saw him in the interior of my soul, and he gave me to understand these words: 'Tell your mother prioress that if she writes to such a person, she will assist to build the house.' Oh! What good news! Behold already a proof that the Holy Infant wished to purchase his little Ass. I went to our good mother to give her the message of Our Lord. The person in question lived 180 leagues from Tours; I was slightly acquainted with her, but our Rev. Mother had never heard of her. However, she wished to ascertain the truth of this communication, and wrote to the lady without giving any of these particulars. The reply was slow in coming and I began to fear a little; but the Divine Infant again assured me. At last, a letter came from the lady, in which was enclosed an order for five hundred francs. That was the first donation our mother prioress received; it was a guarantee of what our Divine Savior would do in the future. My heart was filled with joy at the arrival of the letter, and I said five hundred 'Laudates' to the Holy Infant in thanksgiving. I asked our Rev. Mother if that sum were not more that sufficient to buy an ass, and if she yet consented to deliver me to the Divine Infant who had sent her this amount. But she still wished to try my patience, and to discover the spirit which moved me; she explained that she required more money for the construction of the house of Our Lord before granting the desired consent."

The good sister then redoubled her fervor as much for the glory of Him who had claimed her, as for the assistance of her mother prioress, whom she saw in such pressing necessity. One of her practices was to say the beautiful invitatory for the feast of the Holy Name of Jesus; *Mirabile Nomen Jesus quod est super omne nomen; venite adoremus.* (The name of Jesus is admirable above all names; come let us adore). She repeated this thousands of times, engaging the other sisters to repeat it also, in order to form a series of invocations which she likened to banknotes on Divine Providence; her confidence never failed to have its reward.

One day, during her prayer, she found herself as if in the middle of a building. "Our Lord gave me to understand that it was a great and meritorious thing to erect a dwelling for him; He said that our Mother would have many difficulties to encounter in her undertaking, but that he would furnish the *stones*. He also directed me to tell her not to be troubled; that if the monastery were constructed according to the rule of St. Theresa, he would pay all, for she would receive assistance from divers sources. 'But,' added he, if the house be not built according to this rule, pay for it as best you can.'"

"I found my commission a little embarrassing, but I overcame my repugnance in order to accomplish the will of Our Lord. When I had communicated to our reverend mother what he had given me to understand, she told me that she had not been able to rest the night previous, in consequence of the uneasiness caused by the plan proposed by the architect, which was not at all in accordance with the usual mode of building. She procured another in perfect conformity with the customs of St. Theresa;—Our Lord was satisfied and was ready to fulfil his promise."

The *stones* which the sister had to furnish were, as she understood later, the prayers in reparation for the blasphemies and outrages committed against the glory of the Holy Name of God. These prayers drew down the greatest benedictions on the house. The work of Reparation would soon be made known to her. One day the pious virgin was speaking to her prioress of the abundant graces she had received before entering religion;the Rev. Mother replied that probably she had been unfaithful to God, since his favors were now withdrawn. "Offer an honorable *amende,*" said she, "in reparation for your faults and pray that he may restore your soul to the same condition hi which it was when he communicated himself to you so abundantly."

"I shall obey you, my mother," wrote the sister, "and I shall pray Our Lord, in your name to pardon me. My soul was at the time greatly agitated; prayer was a task, my imagination was like a furious courser, beyond control; but the Divine Master in his bounty heard the prayer offered him through obedience. The next day, on awakening, I heard an interior voice say: *Return to the house of thy Father, which is no other than my Heart.* These words produced a great calm in my soul. Having gone to prayer, I united myself to Our Lord in the most Blessed Sacrament, and I heard him say: 'Apply yourself to honor my Sacred Heart and that of my Mother, do not separate them; pray to them for yourself and for sinners, then I shall forget your past ingratitude, and I shall give you more graces than ever before, because you are now more united to me by your vows.'"

"A doubt presented itself, whether it was really Our Lord who spoke, but he gave me this assurance: 'It is I, Jesus, present in the most Blessed Sacrament, who speak. There are several ways in which I communicate myself to souls. Do you not perceive how tranquil and how united you are to me now; whilst for the past few days you were as agitated as the sea during a storm? My child, do as I have directed you, and you shall soon experience the salutary effects.'"

"Afterward," writes the sister, "he made me understand that I should not be attached to sensible devotion, and he gave me grace to see how we are often carried away by interior emotions, thinking we are most pleasing to him. Then, as he directed, I endeavored to honor these adorable Hearts, both interiorly and exteriorly, by embroidering scapulars of the Sacred Heart, and I prayed for the salvation of those who would wear them. Then I added: I do not seek sensible favors; provided thou art glorified and that souls are saved, this is all I ask."

The sister continued: "With this intention I offered my will to the Father, my memory to the Son, and my understanding to the Holy Ghost. I placed myself entirely in the hands of God, and I felt convinced that he would purify my soul by interior sufferings. Then I was plunged in an ocean of bitterness and desolation, I was lost in darkness and tormented by temptations: but that which caused me the most suffering, was my desire of loving and glorifying Our Lord. My soul was hungering for God, it seemed that all I did was of no avail, for I felt myself to be nothingness, sin and misery."

"I had a great longing for a book to solace me, and I asked one from our Rev. Mother. Notwithstanding her usual kindness, she refused, saying: 'My daughter, it is not sufficient to sacrifice one thing only to God, *all* must be immolated to him.' On another occasion, when suffering still more keenly, I desired to speak to her of my mental distress; but God inspired her to act in concert with him, to make me walk in the path of death to self; she, always so full of compassion, would not permit me this time to relieve my weary heart, but forbade me speak of my interior pains, even to my confessor, before a fortnight. With the grace of God, I submitted with a good will to this trial."

"The devil of blasphemy caused me no small amount of suffering, but I kept strongly attached to the cross during the temptation, not daring to say: 'O God, come to my assistance.' I offered my suffering to Our Lord for the salvation of souls and for the accomplishment of his designs. I said one day: 'O my God, I am now well aware of my nothingness and my misery!' Meaning thereby to say: It is enough, my God! I shall now know how to discern thy gifts and shall never attribute them to myself. I see that I am nothing but a poor and miserable sinner."

Finally, she felt urged to have recourse to her holy mother, St. Teresa, in whose honor she commenced a novena; the nine days had not passed ere her sufferings had altogether disappeared. The Lord now resumed with his servant the course of his extraordinary communications which had been totally interrupted for more than two years. But it was necessary that she should return to the *House of her Father*, that is to say, to the Heart of Jesus, whereas gold in the furnace, her soul would be purified by the fire of suffering and love. The Devotion of the Holy Face emanates from that of the Sacred Heart, one is the complement of the other. In the order of the designs of the Divine Master, his faithful disciple was to be conducted to the intimate recesses of his most amiable Heart, before being initiated in the mystery of Reparation by means of his dolorous Face." (*)

(*) — M. Dupont, establishing a comparison between the revelations of Blessed Margaret Mary and those of Sr. St. Peter said: "If the Heart of Jesus is the emblem of love, his adorable Face is that of the sufferings endured for our salvation." (Life of Mr. Dupont, vol. II,) On this subject a distinguished member of the Society of Jesus, Rev. L. P. Gros, has written the following, which furnishes matter for pious reflection: The heart is the symbol of love;—the face is the living mirror of the heart ; the face reveals what the heart contains, namely, love, sorrow with the other sentiments of the soul. For this reason the Church does not regard with a favorable eye the images of the Sacred Heart of Jesus, if the heart be isolated from the face; it is the face which authorizes us to say: behold such a one! When I have before me the face and the heart of Jesus, I have before me Jesus entire, his soul and its sentiments. Thus Jesus manifested himself to Blessed Margaret Mary, the face of Jesus in this vision, certainly was the light, the life, the word of the heart; that Face of Jesus, at Parray-le-Monial, was a dolorous face, a Holy Fac e, *Behold the heart which has so much loved mankind. . . . and they offer me nothing but ingratitude!* Surely it was not joy that was then expressed on the Face of Jesus !"

7

THE GOLDEN DAGGER

"The earth is steeped in crime! The Holy Name of the Lord
is blasphemed; the very Sunday itself is profaned: these fill
the measure of iniquity. In no age has crime been so malignant....
My Name is everywhere blasphemed; even by the little children!"
(Words of Our Lord to the Sister.)

F our years had scarcely elapsed since the little seamstress of Rennes had bid adieu to
the world, to enter among the Carmelites of Tours, whither she had been conducted
by her father. Clothed with the holy habit, and after two years professed, she generously
and unreservedly followed the interior attraction of grace, thus disposing herself to second
its every design, which till now had remained absolutely hidden from her view. Divine
grace suffers neither delay nor hesitation in the soul destined to taste the sweetness of its
consolations. Like the supreme wisdom of the Most High from whom it emanates, it
pursues its course with untiring vigor and prudence, performing all things with order,
weight and measure. Thus did divine grace act in the soul of Sister St. Peter. By alternate
hours of consolation and of desolation she was slowly prepared for its secret operations.
The hour is fast approaching, in which the object of these various movements of grace
will be made manifest to her; the communications which will have vouchsafed her, will
indicate, in a precise and circumstantial manner, the designs of the Most High over
this chosen soul. Her Divine Spouse, continuing his mysterious colloquies, will first
reveal that which is most offensive and most painful to his Divine Heart, and which in
consequence, provokes his just indignation. Then, after having made known the urgent
necessity of a reparation particularly adapted to the crime to be expiated, he suggests to her
a formula of prayer to console his Sacred Heart and to appease his anger. In short, the year

will not have passed until, to the great consternation of the sister, he, himself, will have designated by name the guilty nation which has drawn upon itself the vengeance of the Almighty. The communications which our Carmelite received on this subject refer to the first part of her mission, on which she has written a series of letters, to the original of which we shall adhere as nearly as possible. These are prefaced by the following declaration:

"Before commencing this narrative, I declare in all truth and simplicity, that the glory of God alone, and the accomplishment of his most holy will, have urged me to make known that which, I believe, Our Lord in his mercy has communicated to me in reference to the work of Reparation for blasphemy. I shall copy the letters which I have addressed to our very Rev. Mother Prioress, adding to them whatever may be necessary to make them more clearly understood; as also the remarks which I have since made, or anything else relative to the subject which I can now recall to mind. I declare, that the reason why I make these corrections is, that I usually write hurriedly, because of my duties as portress; I state as briefly as possible that which the Lord has operated in me. Our Rev. Mother, herself, has not always sufficient time to listen to a detailed account of these things at the moment of their occurrence. But as I suffer mentally until I have related to my Superior what has passed, I took the resolution to make note of all;after which my sufferings cease."

"After this little preamble, I shall write on in simplicity under the guidance of the star of obedience. I declare again that if the merest untruth could obtain the establishment of this work, I would never consent to it, for God is truth itself, and I am firmly convinced that he will defend his cause, for he has sworn it."

In the first letter, the sister gives several details which we have mentioned in the preceding chapter. We are now about to narrate the interesting communication which is the subject of her second.

It took place on the 26th of August 1843, the day after the celebration of the feast of St. Louis, who is specially honored as the protector of France, the defender of the Roman Church, and the avenger of the Divine Majesty outraged by blasphemy.

This date is not without its signification, which shall be noticed further on. A violent storm had suddenly burst forth from the fiery heavens and fell in torrents over the city of Tours, "Never," said the Carmelite virgin, "have I realized the justice of an irritated God as at that moment. Prostrate in an agony of fear before the Lord, I unceasingly offered

Jesus Christ to his heavenly Father for the necessities of our holy mother the Church: one of our sisters experienced the same emotions as I."—According to the doctrine of the Apostles, the phenomena of nature are the visible signs of things invisible and supernatural. The terrible rolling in the thunder and the gleaming of the lightning seemed to be the menacing threats of the Most High. The flashes of lightning were as arrows, ready to destroy the enemies of the Lord. At five o'clock, she commenced her evening prayer; placing herself in spirit at the foot of the cross, (according to her custom, as we have seen), she lovingly asked of Our Lord *the cause of his wrath.* Her Divine Master, wishing to try her, changed his usual manner, and said: "I have lent ear to your sighs, and have seen your desire to glorify me; yet, all this proceeds not from you, it is I who am the Author of all holy desires."

The sister continues: "Then he unfolded his Heart to me, concentrating therein the powers of my soul, and addressed me thus: 'My Name is everywhere blasphemed, even little children blaspheme it.' And he made me understand how that dreadful sin pierced and wounded his Heart, aye, more than all other crimes. By blasphemy, the sinner outrages him to his face, attacks him openly, and pronounces upon himself his own judgment and condemnation. Blasphemy is an empoisoned dagger, wounding his Divine Heart continually; he told me that he would give me a *golden dagger* with which to wound him delightfully, and heal the poisonous wounds caused by sin.".

"The following is the prayer which Our Lord dictated to me, notwithstanding my unworthiness, for the reparation of blasphemy against his Holy Name: he offered it to me as a golden dagger, assuring me that every time I said it, I would wound his Heart most lovingly."

THE GOLDEN DAGGER.

"May the most holy, the most sacred, the most adorable, the most unknown and the most inexpressible Name of God be adored, praised, blessed, loved, and glorified, in heaven, on earth and in hell, by all creatures formed by his sacred hand, and by the loving Heart of our Lord Jesus Christ in the most Blessed Sacrament of the altar. Amen."

The sister here suddenly interrupts her interesting narrative to explain an expression contained in this prayer.

"As I was not a little astonished when Our Lord said *and in hell,* he had the goodness to make me understand that his justice was there glorified. I beg to remark, that he did not only mean the place where the wicked are punished, but also purgatory, where he is loved and glorified by the suffering souls. The word *hell* is not merely applied to the place where the damned are confined, for our faith teaches us that the Savior descended into hell or Limbo, where the souls of the just were detained until his Coming; and does not our holy mother the Church pray her divine Spouse to deliver the souls of her children from the gates of hell? *A porta inferi erue, Domine, animas eorumy (Office of the Dead))*

To these explanations may be added, that St. Paul, in one of his epistles, made use of the same expression in an analogical sense, saying: "At the name of Jesus, every knee shall bend in heaven, on earth and in *hell.*"

She continues: "Our Lord, having given me this *golden dagger,* added: 'Beware how you appreciate this favor, for I shall demand an account of it.' At that moment, I seemed to behold flowing from the Sacred Heart of Jesus, wounded by this golden dagger, torrents of grace for the conversion of sinners, which sight gave me confidence to ask: 'My Lord, do you then hold me responsible for blasphemers?'"—This question shall have its answer later; for the present, the divine Master said nothing more. That which he had just communicated was sufficiently decisive, and deserving the most serious reflection. "Aware of my weakness," said she, "and fearing the demon, I prayed the Blessed Virgin to be pleased to guard that which her Divine Son had just confided to me."

She did not fail to take instant note of this important communication, and according to her custom, delivered it to the mother prioress as soon as written. The latter received it without appearing to attach much importance to its contents. But after the sister had retired, and the mother prioress had carefully perused it, a new avenue of thought was opened to her, and for the first time she began to suspect the gravity of the communications received by her spiritual daughter and foresaw the responsibility which would devolve both on her and on her community. For not only was the prayer in honor of the Holy Name of God to be repeated by the person to whom it had been revealed, but it was to be communicated and spread among the faithful.

As we can readily understand, this was a subject for reflection to a superior as prudent as Mother Mary of the Incarnation.

"This communication" said the sister, "has wrought a change in my soul, for I am constantly occupied in glorifying the most Holy Name of God. Our Lord inspired me to add to the *golden dagger,* some other prayer, to be repeated every hour of the day; he graciously accepted this exercise, desiring that it be promulgated. My Divine Savior made me participate in his desire of beholding the name of his Father glorified; he exhorted me to praise and bless that adorable Name, in imitation of the angels who are perpetually singing, *Sanctus, Sanctus, Sanctus*; that thus I would accomplish his desire, that of honoring his Sacred Heart and the holy Heart of his Mother. He likewise made me understand that this would not prevent me from honoring him in his sacred mysteries, that during his life, his Sacred Heart had suffered from blasphemy." At the end, she added: "I understand, moreover, that the more acceptable a thing is to God, the more odious does Satan try to render it, to disgust the soul; but if she be faithful, notwithstanding her repugnance, she will acquire great merit. Our Divine Savior gave me these instructions to help me resist the assaults which the devil was meditating against me, because of this work. His aim is its annihilation, as Our Lord made known to me, but his efforts will be fruitless."

The little exercise of reparation spoken of by the sister, and revealed to her on the feast of St. Michael, commenced with the *Magnificat,* followed by twenty-four verses, the first of which we subjoin:— "In union with the Sacred Heart of Jesus, come let us worship the adorable Name of God, which is above all names. ... In union with the holy Heart of Mary, come let us adore this Name... In union with the glorious St. Joseph come let us adore" . . . The last invitation is thus terminated: "Come let us adore the exalted Name of God which is above all names, and let us prostrate ourselves before him; let us weep in the presence of the Lord who has made us, for he is the Lord our God, we are his people and the sheep whom he conducts to his pastures."

Though these prayers contained nothing but what was in conformity with the spirit of the Church, yet the mother prioress would not at first allow Sr. Mary St. Peter to recite them but retained the formula which had been remitted her.

In the meantime, she took proper care to place bounds to the impetuosity of a zeal which astonished her, and which, in her opinion, might have been the effect of self-love. "But," said the good sister, "as I was persuaded that my superiors did nothing but by the special permission of God, I submitted to their orders, and did all in my power to obey. Our Lord, made a gap in the wall of obedience (if I can express myself thus) which I had opposed to him; through this he came into my heart to converse about his work, or rather he drew me to himself."

"One day, when speaking to our Rev. Mother, I told her that when at prayer I found myself entirely occupied in repairing the outrages committed against God by blasphemers. She reprimanded me severely and forbade me to continue; ordering me to apply my mind to meditate simply on my last end, or on any other similar subject. She reproached me for presuming to make reparation for others, whilst perhaps I, myself, had blasphemed God in my heart. 'Would you not do better,' said she, 'to meditate on these words which may be addressed to you some day: *Go, ye cursed into everlasting fire?*'"

With a grieved heart the poor sister retired from her superior. "Seeing that our reverend mother appeared to be so dissatisfied with me, I went to tell my sufferings to Our Lord, for it troubled me not a little to be obliged to change my method of prayer and to resist the attractions which he gave me. I was tormented with the fear of disobeying; but I did the best I could to follow the method of meditation indicated by our mother superior, and I then rendered an account to her. When she told me that I had fulfilled her desires, my soul became tranquil. One day, Our Lord made me understand that it was more necessary for me to obey my superiors than to credit what I believed to have heard from the Lord himself. With the assistance of grace, I have always been submissive to the least wish of my superiors."

Nevertheless, the humble virgin was prey to great mental sufferings. She obtained no consolation from anyone, neither from her confessors nor her superiors, "who, in their wisdom," said she, proposed to try me, to ascertain if it were really the work of God. It was then I felt the weight of that cross which, even before my coming to Carmel, Our Lord had promised to give me in religion." In fact, she now commenced really to carry the cross, and we shall see that she was never released from it until her last sigh. Let us now attend to her, as she reveals the manner in which she conducted herself towards her superiors: "When Our Lord communicated anything to me on the subject of his work, I dared not speak of it to our good mother, but I took note of it and left the writing in her office, very glad when she was not there. On one occasion, among others, I was all in a tremble before the Blessed Sacrament, holding in my hand a little letter which I presented to Our Lord before going to remit it. Sometimes the work of Reparation was a burning fire within me. I felt the necessity of speaking to someone who would take an interest in it, but I could not obtain the permission."

"At length, however, Our Lord sent me a great consolation: I was one day kneeling before our reverend mother, speaking to her of the sufferings occasioned by the work with which I was charged; our good mother said: What can I do for you, my child? Nothing, at all, you must bring forth this work by your own sufferings. As she was speaking, there fell from a book which she held in her hand, a little leaflet on which was printed an honorable amende to the most Holy Name of God, followed by an appeal to the French nation, *to appease the anger of God, irritated by blasphemy.* This had a striking resemblance to the communications which I had received, and which at that time appeared to be a mere chimera of my own. Our reverend mother was lost in astonishment. She had never before seen this paper, no one in the house knew anything about it; the book which contained it had not been taken from the library perhaps for twenty years; and it was in my presence that this incident occurred! I was in an ecstasy of joy, nor could I disabuse myself of the idea that Heaven commenced to speak in my favor."

The writing in question had been published in 1819, by l'Abbe Soyer, then vicar general of Poitiers, who became bishop of Lucan. To the first title of *Appeal to the People of France,* there was added a second, *Reparation, inspired to appease the Anger of God.* Therein it was staled openly that blasphemy drew down the anger of God on France; to avert which, prayers and supplications, similar to those proposed by Sr. Mary St Peter, were specified. "In her surprise," continues the latter, "our good mother said, smilingly, 'Well, sister, if I did not know you, I would think you were a sorceress.' I replied: 'Mother, I am confident that the holy Angels have brought this to light; for I remembered having invoked them before going to our Mother's office; undoubtedly it was they who caused this book to be taken from the library at the proper moment.'"

The mother prioress sought further information on the subject and wrote to l'Abbe Soyer for an explanation. The prelate replied that it was he who had published the "Appeal," at the solicitation of a Carmelite of Poitiers, named Sister Adelaide, a soul of predilection, with whom the Lord had held the most intimate communications. "That admirable Carmelite," said he, "was the most mortified, the most humble, and the most saintly soul I have ever met. It would greatly contribute to the edification of the members of your order if her life were written." Mother Adelaide died on 31st of July, of the same year, 1843; and just twenty-six days after her death, Sr. St. Peter, religious of the same order, was inspired to demand the work of Reparation for blasphemy as though God had awaited the death of one prophet before raising up another. *Uno deficiente haud deficit alter.*

"Another remarkable coincidence happened on the same day, the 26th of August. A pious gentleman had distributed among several of the communities of Tours, a prayer in honor of the Holy Name of God, to obtain through the intercession of St. Louis, king of France, the dispersion of the enemies of that divine Name. This prayer had been recited before the feast of St. Louis, and what was more admirable still in the dispensations of Divine Providence, was that the prayers had been circulated among all the religious houses of the city, as was afterward learned, the Carmelites alone being forgotten. On the very next day, the Lord communicated to the most unworthy of his servants, the fruit of the prayers of these holy souls."

The *very pious* gentlemen in question, is no other than M. Dupont, the *holy man of Tours.* He was on the friendliest terms with the Carmelites, and this occurrence, as may be supposed, only the more strongly cemented the bonds of friendship existing between them. For years he had burned with an ardent zeal for the reparation of blasphemy, and as a natural consequence, with a great devotion to St. Louis, king of France. This fervent Christian, as the sister relates, had received with great joy the formula of prayers called the *Quarantine of St. Louis,* which had come to Tours by post, no one knew from whence, in the early part of July 1843. Madam Deshayes, religious of the Sacred Heart, considered as one of the foundresses of the Institution, was the first to receive thirty copies; she gave one to M. Dupont who lost no time in having more printed. The prayer was in honor of the Holy Name of God, and in reparation for blasphemy. On the copy distributed among the faithful, there was the following:

"From the 16th of July to the 25th of August, inclusively, the faithful are called upon to unite in prayer for the necessities of the Church and State.... May thy Name, O Lord! be known and blessed, in all times, and in all places!" This prayer was recited during the forty days prescribed, in all the communities of the city. But what was most astonishing, was that notwithstanding the intimacy existing between M. Dupont and the Carmelites, (besides the circumstance that the Quarantine seems to have been put under the protection of our Lady of Mount Carmel), the mother prioress and her daughters, as the sister remarked, had not the slightest knowledge of the event. The day after the feast of St. Louis, 26th of August, immediately after the last day of the Quarantine, the pious sister received the divine communication, of which we have spoken. We cannot but be forcibly struck with the coincidence, as well as with the affinity existing between the words of the quarantine: *May thy Name be known, blessed,* and those of the "Golden Dagger" inspired to Sr. St. Peter, the same day: *May the holy Name of God be forever praised and blessed...*

M. Dupont, especially, attached so much the more importance to this, as he was then preoccupied with the idea of reparation for blasphemy. He naturally concluded that the prayers, offered in 1843 by a great number of holy souls, had been heard. "If faith does not oblige us," said he, "it at least allows us to believe that God has heard our prayers, according to his promise: *Where several are united in my Name, there am I in the midst.* It was only one year after the revelations made to the venerable sister, that we were informed of the very mysterious coincidence existing between the prayers of the quarantine and the invocation dictated her by Our Lord. It seemed as though Heaven had heard the supplication of earth, and planted the seeds of Reparation, which would ere long spring forth and blossom."

From the general aspect, it seems as if this year was predestined by Divine Providence for the work of Reparation. It was on the 8th of August 1843, that the Pope, Gregory XVI, promulgated a brief for the erection of a pious confraternity under the patronage of St. Louis, king of France, for the Reparation of blasphemy against the Holy Name of God. We find that at the same epoch, a Jesuit labored for some time in vain in a small country village of the diocese of Nantes, whose inhabitants were strangely addicted to blasphemy. But after his bishop had approved of an association in reparation for blasphemy, to which an indulgence of forty days was attached, he obtained the most salutary and abundant fruits. These events had the effect of causing the superiors of Sr. M. of St. Peter, to relax somewhat in their severity toward her.

"I was permitted to occupy myself with the work of Grod according to the inspirations given me. When our Rev. Mother returned to me the prayers of Reparation, I was carried away with joy, and every day I recited them with renewed devotion. My good Master gave me to understand that they were most agreeable to him. Soon after, he told me that I must request my superiors to have them printed; a new source of trouble for me, for our wise and prudent Mother, seeing that Our Lord continued to follow up his work, desiring as she did to see it established upon a solid foundation, continued to try me, in order to ascertain if it were truly Grod who guided me."

"One day she told me that I seemed like another Peter Michel. This man was a visionary, who had deceived multitudes by his false revelations; he had come to see our Rev. Mother, but she discovered the imposition at the first glance. Eventually, he was tried, convicted as an impostor and condemned to several years imprisonment. I knew not what to think of my communications on beholding myself placed on a par with this individual. Our Lord reassured me, however, by these words: 'As long as you continue humble and obedient, rest assured that you are under no illusion.'"

Shortly after these events had taken place, our Rev. Mother became very ill. Though she had often crossed me both for the good of my soul and to be convinced whether it was God who was guiding me, yet I loved her very tenderly and placed unbounded confidence in her. One day during my meditation (it was on the eve of the feast of St. Michael) Our Lord made me understand that I had pleased his Divine Heart with my little Reparation; that these prayers caused him to forget my past ingratitude; and that if the Community wished to obtain the restoration of our Rev. Mother, that she might be able to discharge her duties with less suffering, they should make a novena before the Blessed Sacrament, in reparation for blasphemy against the Holy Name of God, and also that they should say the prayers of the little exercise with which he had inspired me; that it was but just, children should aid their mother, and that if the sisters gave this satisfaction to his Sacred Heart, he would lavish graces upon the community."

"I could not refuse to impart this communication for Our Lord, who added, as if to induce me to comply with his request: 'Oh! if you could understand all I have done for you, and what graces I have lavished on your soul, you would be filled with astonishment on beholding the Creator thus abasing himself to his creature!' Then I said, 'My Lord, I will again do your bidding; for after all, I run no risk, I shall only be covered with humiliations.' I placed myself under the protection of the Blessed Virgin, and I communicated my mission to our Rev. Mother, whose sufferings were most violent. She consented to make the novena; but in order that the sisters should not know it was I who composed the prayers, our confessor had the kindness to copy them; they believed the new devotion came from him."

"For myself, I have never regretted my unlimited obedience to Our Lord, who is never outdone in generosity. On that same day, the feast of St. Michael, the Divine Master declared it his will that our mother should begin to promulgate these prayers of Reparation. As she was in a state of debility and suffering, Our Lord granted me as a token of my mission, the restoration of her health. He assured me there was nothing in this devotion contrary to the spirit of the Church, which has been established to glorify the

Holy Name of God. I promised him if he cured our mother, that she would not neglect his work. Then when she recovered I said: 'My Lord, I shall deliver your messages again, when and to whom you wish.' My Heavenly Spouse, faithful to his word, restored to health our beloved invalid, who was soon able to fulfil the important duties of her charge."

8

THE REPARATION

"You have offered yourself tome for the
accomplishment of my designs;
— this offering has won my heart."
(Words of Our Lord.)

T he mother prioress, who wished to test these first revelations, placed the young professed in direct communication with a man of God, well versed in spiritual matters, the Rev. Father Vieillecases, religious of Piepus, and Director of the grand seminary of Tours. Now that the communications were becoming of a more serious nature, that they tended to a practical end, and were destined to be made known to the world, her Superior felt the necessity of having a thorough understanding with the sister's confessor. Only those deemed indispensable in carrying out the designs of God, were told of these supernatural operations.

By the designs of Providence, two priests of the diocese became successively her directors, and thus were cognizant of the ever-varying phases of her life, with its interior illuminations.

These were Father Aileron, Dean of the parish of Our Lady la Riche, and the Abbe Salmon. The former had been the superior of the Carmelites for twenty-four years; it was he who received our little Breton on her arrival; and when the community were obliged to remove to another locality, he took a very active part in their temporal concerns; he chose the site, supervised the work, and in fine, seemed to be indispensable to these good sisters, who are so much indebted to his foresight and prudence.

He died in 1862, venerated and esteemed by all the clergy, who beheld in him a model priest. His parishioners admired and loved him as the true type of the Good Shepherd. Pious, charitable, and zealous, of remarkable self-abnegation and perfect disinterestedness, he displayed in the exercise of his holy ministry, as much delicacy of conscience as rigorous exactitude. He possessed a straightforward mind, solid judgment and good common sense; these admirable qualities combined to make him an able and discreet director. He was prudent in deliberation, giving no decision until after mature reflection. Simple, modest, and timid by nature, although firm in his resolutions once formed, he had but little relish for the extraordinary: both in his private conduct and for the guidance of others he preferred the ordinary way. With such dispositions, it will not be surprising that he paid very little attention to the spiritual communications received by Sr. Mary St. Peter; he would even laugh at them by times, when conversing with her and the mother superior. But by degrees, and after close observation, he recognized the divine origin of her revelations. He was, indeed, so fully convinced of this fact, that he was the first in the diocese who requested permission to establish in his parish the work of Reparation, demanded by the pious Carmelite, and was deeply grieved when the permission was refused.

This excellent priest professed a sincere admiration for M. Dupont, with whom he had frequent intercourse, as the latter was the prime mover in all the works of charity set on foot in the parish. When the Little Sisters of the Poor were established at Tours, it was in concert with Father Aileron that the pious founder made his negotiations and selected a site in the parish of Notre Dame la Riche. This good priest died on the 16th of August, the day after the feast of the Assumption. In his last testament he "willed and bequeathed to Notre Dame the fruits of his savings." His charity had rendered him so very popular that the municipality, wishing to show their high appreciation of his merits, gave his name to one of the streets in the parish de la Riche. He has, likewise, the honor of having achieved, almost at his own expense, the handsome architectural alterations which render the church of this parish one of the most interesting religious edifices of the city.

Rev. Father Aileron was an intimate friend of Father Salmon, his curate at his first parish St. Pierre des Corps, as likewise at Notre Dame la Riche. The latter was appointed confessor to the Carmelites in 1839, which office seemed in harmony with his austere and pious mode of life. He embraced this occupation with ardor and fulfilled its duties with the most rigorous punctuality for twelve years. He was the constant confessor of Sr. St.

Peter, and for six years (1844 to 1850) was resident chaplain of the community. He was endowed with qualities eminently sacerdotal. A man of prayer, a lover of the interior life, serious and reserved, yet, withal learned and laborious; he was an excellent and impressive preacher, though of a style rather antiquated. M. Dupont held him in the greatest esteem and consulted him freely on questions of theology and holy scripture. It was this reverend father who advised him to publish the pamphlet on the "Association against Blasphemy," approved by Mgr. Morlot.

Father Salmon possessed a taste for study, and practiced all the regularity of a religious, constantly employing every moment with the most scrupulous economy. He was the first among the priests of Tours to adopt the Roman Breviary, even before the archiepiscopal command, with the sole motive of being more useful to the Carmelites, who have always recited the Roman Breviary. He never dissimulated the joy which he savored at leisure in the recitation of his office, which drew forth the remark from Father Aileron: "His breviary and his Carmelites! with these, this good abbot so avaricious of his time, would willingly pass his days!" In fact, his love for Carmel and the Church was boundless. His zeal in the sacred tribunal was indefatigable, but unfortunately he was of a timorous conscience, sometimes amounting to scrupulosity, which caused him to suspect the influence of the devil in the simplest circumstances.

An incurable deafness rendered his ministry painful and fatiguing, increased his indecision and confirmed his doubts. He distrusted the communications made to Sr. Mary of St. Peter; they seemed to him to be the mere effect of imagination, and at times, his scrupulous mind caused him to fear a snare of the devil. But, by degrees, he recognized by unequivocal signs, the action of God in this pure and humble soul; and from the moment he became convinced, he rendered her every assistance in his power, defending her cause on every occasion. To his sincere regret he was obliged to resign his position as chaplain of the Carmelites, on account of an attack of apoplexy. He retired to the orphanage, of which he was a benefactor, (having donated their house); here he resided for some time with his intimate friend the Abbe Verdier. His days were peacefully ended at Langeais, in the midst of his virtuous and pious relatives.

These were the two grave and virtuous priests with whom the mother prioress held consultations from time to time, to be guided in her opinion concerning the manifestations made known to her by her spiritual daughter. Here was a question which involved not only opinion, but also action; and the responsibility became more evident now that she perceived the work was to become public.

The heavenly communications of the sister were frequent. Our Lord either concentrated all the powers of her soul in his Sacred Heart, as she herself expressed it, or seemed to come himself to reside in her heart, and there reveal his intentions. In both manners, a perfect union seems to have taken place; the will of the Lord, his sentiments, his desire to glorify his Father, to repair the outrages offered the Divine Majesty and to save sinners, all these became identical with the aspirations of the soul he penetrated so profoundly. The state of union to which the sister was elevated, without even the knowledge of it herself, was not very easily explained in the language of mortals. Poor little Breton seamstress, illiterate as we have seen, without any of the resources that study furnishes to mystical writers, when in compliance with obedience she took up the pen to expose her supernatural revelations, words failed her, or else were inadequate to depict what she beheld spiritually. This embarrassment became more palpable the day on which her celestial communications had, as their immediate object, not the sweet and winning mysteries of the Holy Childhood, but the austere and complicated work of the Reparation for Blasphemy. In a sort of preamble, the pious Carmelite plaintively bewails her incapacity, and the great difficulty she finds in giving utterance to the things she had seen, heard or understood. She implores indulgence, begging the reader to pay no attention to the style, but to penetrate the sense and the spirit of what she is writing, fully convinced that the Holy Ghost will enlighten her superiors to discern what has proceeded from him, light and truth itself, from that which may have originated with her, who is but ignorance and nothingness.

Moreover, as regards the interviews on this subject, which took place several times, she invariably declared that these "communications" were not "visions," neither were they "apparitions;" that the truths shown her, were not exhibited under an external form, nor did she physically hear what she was commissioned to relate. All this took place in the superior part of her soul. We must then suppose that she had been already raised to a high degree of union with God, who had favored her with communications the most sublime, and at the same time, the most independent of the senses. This observation is not without importance, later we shall have occasion to refer to it. For the present, far from being repulsed by the uncouth style of our humble Carmelite, let us in silent admiration, behold with what readiness and astonishing clearness she pronounces herself upon those matters over which the most learned theologian would hesitate before giving a decision. The following is further proof.

On the 3rd of November, the first Friday of the month, on which the Blessed Sacrament was exposed, and on which, in fulfilment of a vow made by the mother superior, two religious of the house should receive holy communion for the accomplishment of the designs of the Sacred Heart, the Divine Savior had desired that it be the "Community " who "should make him known," and who should spread the devotion of the Reparation. "Since," said he, "the Community *desires the accomplishment of the designs of my Heart, and prays for this intention, it is but just that it should have the honor of giving birth to this Devotion.'"

"Then," says the sister, "something extraordinary took place. My soul in the Heart of Jesus was as in a burning furnace; it seemed to me that it had quitted this miserable body of clay for a moment, to unite itself with God; my soul was delightfully lost, annihilated in Jesus, and I felt that he was its first beginning and its most happy end. I could no longer act, I could only say interiorly, 'My God, how admirable are thy operations! Thou art not so mysterious a God as is supposed.' I would have willingly added, 'Lord it is good to be here! Let us build three temples, to retain here the three powers of my soul in captivity.' This is what happened during mass: having had the happiness to receive holy communion, I took the liberty of saying to him: —'Behold, my Lord, now that I am so intimately united with thee, if thou wouldst be pleased to repeat what thou didst say to me at the beginning of the holy sacrifice of the mass!' But I felt that it was not his wish at that moment; then I gave myself up to what he was operating in me by this annihilation of which I have spoken. After the lapse of a few moments, he seemed to declare that he had remained silent to make me understand that it was not in my power to hear his interior voice when I would. After giving me this brief lesson, he continued: 'My daughter, you have offended me more, you have wounded my Heart more deeply than all the other sisters, because you have set an obstacle to my designs over your soul. Therefore, now you should try to surpass all the others by your love and zeal for the interests of my glory. It is not to afflict you that I tell you of your sins; have confidence for I will forget them all. There are two reasons why I choose you to make manifest my designs:—first, because you are the most unworthy; second, because you have offered yourself to me for the accomplishment of these designs: by this offering you have won my Heart. Be humble and simple; make known your imperfections and your defects; for this acknowledgment will redound to my glory.'"

Shortly after this communication, the mission of the Carmelite was clearly revealed. She writes as follows to her superior:

"My Divine Master told me to ask if you would wrench the sword from his hand, for a spouse possesses unlimited influence over her Spouse. It is his desire that the sisters of the community should make a novena in Reparation for blasphemy. If he chooses this spot to give free vent to his plaintive sighs, it is because he expects more consolation from us than from others. I seemed to read in his Heart that he had a burning desire for this work, that it might invoke his mercy on mankind." The manner in which the community was called upon to promulgate this work was to get the prayers, composed for this object, printed. The request of Our Lord was an urgent one. He commanded that the community should defray the expense of the printing, to bestow on it his choicest blessings, and return a hundred-fold. "I can no longer support this heavy burden. I deposit it with confidence into your hands, Rev. Mother, and I very humbly beg you to examine this affair before God; for I believe that he desires you to render him this service. For my part, now that I have performed my duty by delivering you this message of Our Lord, my soul is unladen of its burden." The fulfilment of this request implied many serious difficulties both as regards the public on one side, and the legitimate authority on the other. The necessity for a more thorough examination of the spirit which directed her daughter, prevented the mother prioress from taking any steps to obtain the necessary authorization.

"Our Rev. Mother," said the Sister, "having observed too much anxiety in me, and too great a desire to propagate the devotion of the reparation due to the Holy Name of God, showed me the enormity of my pride in asking to have these prayers printed and circulated, there being so many other beautiful prayers composed by the Holy Fathers of the Church. She forbade me to think on this subject; and even had the goodness to impose a penance on me. During this very charitable correction and during a second which I shortly after received at chapter, my stubborn nature had been so thoroughly broken in, that thanks be to God who had mercy on his unworthy servant, all the compliments in the world could not have produced the interior joy which I experienced after these humiliations. I endeavored to adopt the sentiments which our Rev. Mother proposed to me. I humbled myself before God and sacrificed to him my desire of asking for the establishment of this devotion, and promised to think no more of it, to become very obedient."

She observes, however, that she was not forbidden to practice interior acts of reparation; these she believed it her duty to perform.

"Our Lord," said she, "desired me to compassionate the sorrows of his Heart; for if this Divine Master were capable of sadness or of suffering, he would be saddened even unto death at the sight of the torpid state of man who, far from uniting himself to him, thereby to render glory and honor to his heavenly Father, is continually blaspheming his Holy Name, in union with Lucifer and his accomplices. How much it would please him if the faithful children of the Church would lovingly unite themselves with him in the Holy Sacrament of the altar, and with the holy angels to love and bless the Name of his heavenly Father! It is with these intentions that I offer my devotions in honor of the Holy Name of God, in union with the Heart of Jesus, the angels and saints, finding in such holy company, an adequate supplement for my unworthiness. I depose my prayers in the Sacred Heart, by the hands of Mary and Joseph, begging our adorable Savior to multiply them a million times, with the same power with which he multiplied the loaves in the desert."

Her cherished devotions once commenced, the good sister knew not where to stop. "With the same object in view," said she, "Our Lord inspired me to form a crown or chaplet composed of prayers in reparation. One day, during the holy sacrifice of the mass, my Divine Master gently drew me within the recesses of his Heart; and it seemed that he presented me this chaplet, which appeared to be of the purest gold, inlaid with precious stones. But thinking myself most unworthy of possessing such a great treasure and fearing to be assailed by robbers by the devil and his agents, I begged the Blessed Virgin to guard the beautiful chaplet in her most amiable Heart, and I asked Our Lord to grant some indulgences to it. I think this crown is very agreeable to him, but most odious to Satan. I am no believer in dreams, but since the time my mind has been so much occupied with the devotion to the Holy Name of God, and that I have prayed for the conversion of blasphemers, I have twice dreamed that I saw the demons under the form of wild beasts ready to devour me; but I saved myself from being torn to pieces by invoking the name of Our Lord, and the Blessed Virgin. Perhaps the novena of reparation made by the Community had robbed them of their prey. One day, during meditation, my good Master warned me of the rage of Satan because of this devotion, and at the same time gave me to understand these words: 'I give you my Name to be your light in darkness and your strength in battle. Satan will make use of every means in his power to annihilate this work from the very outset: but the most Holy Name of God will triumph and the angels will gain the victory.'"

There was, within the enclosure of the convent, a statue of our Lady of Perpetual Help, greatly venerated by the religious of the monastery. Our young Carmelite, anxious about the future of this work on which she had been forbidden to think, felt urged to confide her troubles to the Mother of Perpetual Help. "I wrote," said she, "a short letter, which I placed in the hands of the Blessed Virgin; my soul became tranquil, and I tried to be very obedient to our Rev. Mother."

What was the origin of this "Lady of Perpetual Help," invoked so efficaciously by Sr. Mary St. Peter? Perhaps our reader would be desirous to know something of its history. To satisfy his pious curiosity we shall quote textually from the annals of the Carmelites.

"In 1692, a statue of the Blessed Virgin was solemnly blessed. This statue may almost be considered miraculous and is invoked by the sisters under the title of 'Our Lady of Perpetual Help'. The following was the immediate cause of its dedication. From time immemorial, perhaps since the foundation of our monastery at Tours, there was consigned to the attic, a block of stone representing the Assumption of the Blessed Virgin, together with the clouds on which she was borne. This block was so heavy that several men could barely lift it; it was in such a dilapidated condition that the subject was almost entirely obliterated."

"A young lady, having an ardent desire to consecrate herself to God among the Carmelites, applied and obtained her admission. After some time she experienced such difficulty in reading the breviary, that it was decided to send her away as incapable of complying with one of the principal duties of a Carmelite, that of psalmody of the choir. The poor, disconsolate novice begged the mother superior to take into consideration her good will, assuring her that the Blessed Virgin who had obtained her admission would likewise teach her how to read the Office. On hearing this, the mother superior told her smilingly, (perhaps to put an end to her urgent entreaties to remain) that in proof of the sincerity of her desire, she should go and fetch the large stone from the garret. The novice set out immediately, full of faith and hope. What was the astonishment of the entire community beholding her return with the enormous statue! There was no longer room to doubt either the will of God, or the vocation of the young novice, who soon learned to read

the Latin perfectly, and as a mark of gratitude begged that the money intended to pay
for her habit on the day of her profession, be employed in repairing the statue of her
benefactress ; and as for herself, that she would willingly wear the habits already worn
by the other sisters; her wish was gratified. The statue was cut from the block of stone,
carefully repaired, blessed with great solemnity and installed in the ante-choir, Saturday,
the 13th of April 1692. It was saved from total destruction by one of the sisters during the
revolution, and on the return of our Mothers to the monastery, was placed in its present
sanctuary."

Allow us to add by way of comment, that "Our Lady of Perpetual Help" is now in the
recreation-room. It was here that Sr. Mary of St. Peter went, as we have remarked, to pray
so piously.

The mother prioress had not yet consented to the act of perfect abandonment, solicited
by her generous daughter, who in consequence, could only entertain; 'the desire of it.'
But this "desire" was most ardent because she believed it conformable to what Our Lord
demanded of her for the accomplishment of his designs. "He urged me to offer him the
donation of myself. The first time that he asked it of me, was a few days after I entered
religion. His designs at that time were unknown, but they were revealed to my soul
during the communications which he made on the subject of the work of Reparation for
Blasphemy; and I felt interiorly inspired to offer to God the sacrifice of my entire person,
and of all the merits I might be able to acquire in the holy house where I had the happiness
to dwell."

On the 21st of November, feast of the Presentation of the Blessed Virgin Mary, at
the renovation of vows, which is annually made on this day by the religious of the
community, she had written an act of donation which she had presented to her superior
for approbation, but without success. On the 24th of the same month, feast of St. John
of the Cross, all the time during mass, she was mentally occupied in considering the
guilt and wickedness of the world.—"I offered my holy communion in reparation for the
outrages committed against the majesty of God. This is my habitual practice since the
time that Our Lord urged me to repair the blasphemies uttered against the Holy Name
of God. I experience great consolation in thinking that Jesus, himself, comes into my soul
to offer their reparation, which can only be worthily made through his Divine Heart. For
this reason, when I receive him in the holy communion, I give myself entirely to him,
I annihilate myself in his Sacred Heart; then he performs in me the office of mediator

between God and man. But at this communion, on the feast of our father, St. John of the Cross, as soon as Jesus had entered my soul, he took possession of all its powers, and caused me to hear these words: —'I have as yet revealed but a part of the designs of my Heart; today, I desire to show them to you in their fullest extent. The earth is covered with crime! The sins against the three first commandments have provoked the wrath of my Father; *the Holy Name of God blasphemed, and the profanation of the Lord's Day fill to overflowing the measure of iniquity*; this sin has mounted even to the throne of the Most High, and has aroused his wrath, which will burst forth over mankind in an impetuous torrent, if his justice be not appeased; in no other time has iniquity reached such a degree. I most ardently desire the formation of a society well approved and properly organized, to honor the Name of my Father. Your superior is right in remaining inactive until this work can be established on a solid and permanent foundation, for otherwise, my designs would not be accomplished.'"

"This is, as near as possible, the commission which I have been told to deliver to my superiors. I experienced the greatest repugnance in accepting it, for I have never heard that an association had been established in the Church for the object which Our Lord mentioned to me. Then I said to him: 'O my God, If I were sure that it is thou who art speaking, I would have no difficulty in declaring these things to my superiors.' He answered: 'It is not your province to examine this matter but theirs. Have I not frequently communicated myself to your soul in the same manner as at present? Beware my child, for if from your want of simplicity, you would place an obstacle to my designs, you would render yourself responsible for the salvation of a multitude of souls. If, on the contrary, you are faithful, these very souls will be an ornament in your crown.' Our Lord gave me hereby to understand that he wished by this work of Reparation to show mercy to sinners. In conclusion he said: 'To whom should I address myself if not to a Carmelite, whose profession it is to glorify my Name unceasingly.'"

"This, Rev. Mother, although imperfectly detailed, is what I think I have heard from our Lord, for my soul was totally lost in God and I was seized with terror. I was inspired, at the same time with the words once repeated to Abraham, that if but ten just were found among the guilty, God would spare all; and it seemed to me that his justice would be appeased, and that he would show mercy to the guilty, if he could find devoted souls to say the prayers in reparation for blasphemy."

When terminating this narrative, our Carmelite added: "This is the substance of what Our Lord has given me to understand. I very humbly declare, Rev. Mother, that with the grace of God, I have spoken in all the simplicity of my soul. I have informed you of the commissions of my Divine Master as his little servant, and I leave all these things to your judgment, and to the wisdom of our ecclesiastical superior; as for me, my mission is fulfilled. The Holy Ghost, who directs superiors, will enlighten you to discern if it were he who has dictated to me all that I have just written. I shall submit my judgment to that of my superiors in this matter."

Thirteen days after this event, on the eve of the Immaculate Conception, the Lord, in his communications to his faithful spouse, reverted to the same subject, and this time the guilty nation is designated. "My soul is still trembling with fear at the thought of what Our Lord declared to me during this morning's meditation. He deputed me to relate it all to my superiors without fear of having been deceived, I shall do so in all simplicity. Our Lord having recollected the powers of my soul in his Divine Heart, manifested his anger against France saying, that he had sworn in his wrath to be revenged, if reparation were not made to his heavenly Father for all the blasphemy of which she is guilty. He declared to me that he could no longer dwell in this sinful France, which like a viper gnaws away at the bowels of his mercy. He suffers patiently all the affronts against himself, but the outrages committed against his Divine Father provoke his just indignation. 'France has suckled the breasts of mercy even unto blood, for this reason shall mercy cede to justice.'"

"At these words, I was so terrified that I cried out: 'My Lord and my God! permit me to ask you, if this reparation which you demand, be offered you, will you pardon France once more?' And he replied: 'I shall pardon her, but remember, only once more.' As this sin of blasphemy is publicly committed everywhere in the kingdom of France, the reparation must likewise be made throughout the nation in every village and in every hamlet; woe to those who do not make reparation!"

In conclusion, the sister observes, that her mind was not at all preoccupied with these thoughts after the revelation had passed; that she interiorly felt Jesus uniting her to his Heart, that it was there he made himself heard. "I submit all this to your wisdom, Rev. Mother, I am but a helpless child who has no other consolation than to refer all things to her Mother."

Sister Mary St. Peter left the choir in a condition difficult to be described: (this we know from the testimony of another sister). She was pale as death, covered with tears and bearing an expression of sorrow that was long discernible; these outward signs were always visible whenever she received any revelations of this nature; she appeared as if crushed under the weight of divine wrath.

We must explain this "terror" and this "sorrowful expression of countenance of the pious virgin of Carmel. Poor France, whom the Savior points out as the nation the guiltiest. Complaining of her blasphemy, he likens her unto a "viper" gnawing at the bowels of his mercy; he threatens to withdraw from amidst her children, if they do not hasten to repair by voluntary expiation the odious sin committed with so much impunity. She has suckled unto blood, the breasts of mercy; justice is ready to fall down upon her head. What French heart could listen to such menaces without emotion! Could hear such severe and solemn threats unmoved! The reproaches of the Savior were, alas! but too well merited, for her guilt is glaringly palpable. From every rank of society blasphemy issues forth with frightful impetuosity, attacking the Godhead openly, and wounding him as if with a poisoned arrow. To the vile blasphemy of the common people is added the doctrinal blasphemy of the freethinker. From the streets and thoroughfares of the city, it has succeeded in gaining entrance to the public-room, to the schools, even to the family fire-side; it enthrones itself in our theatres, in our club-rooms; it parades itself unblushingly before the public; it is to be heard in ordinary conversation; it forces its way into our books, our pamphlets, our newspapers, and in short, into the multitudinous collection of periodicals with which our literary market is daily inundated. It disguises itself under every possible form to suit every taste, but by preference adopting the tone of jest and pleasantry, so natural to the French character; it provokes the mocking laugh; by turns it can be philosophical or common-place, yet is always influential on the multitude. It attacks, first of all, the dignitaries of the Church, those most worthy of respect and the most elevated, then dogmatic teachings, aye, the very existence of Christianity itself; yet more, it hesitates not to attack God himself, to deny his nature, his rights, nay, his very existence.

This it is that "fills the measure of iniquity to overflowing," and cries to heaven for vengeance.

France, among all other nations, is named as the guiltiest, because she is the one most favored by heaven, the Beloved of Christ, and the Eldest Daughter of the Church. Blasphemy impedes her from fulfilling the providential role assigned to her; she places at the service of the impious of all other nations, the influence and ascendency which her wonderful resources and the natural genius of her people place at her disposal. Through the spirit of revolution of which she has become the center and the most active agent in Europe, and the practical atheism which she professes both in her government and in her laws, she plays the part of a universal proselytizer as baneful to the individual as to society at large. Need we be astonished that she in particular has been threatened with the wrath of God!

Fortunately, she has in heaven, among the angels and saints, many powerful intercessors; the glorious archangel, St. Micheal, for instance, but especially St. Louis, the greatest and wisest of her kings.

At the very time that Our Lord was communicating his mysteries to the virgin of Carmel, the influence of this saint was making itself felt. It was under the invocation of St. Louis, that the first cry for pardon for the blasphemer had been directed to the throne of the Most High; it was immediately after his feast, at the conclusion of the forty days prayer in his honor, that the corner-stone of the Work of Reparation had been laid. Rome herself, through the voice of her sovereign pontiff, seemed to have allotted her an adequate support, and an encouragement to foster the efforts already made for her salvation.

Let us be all attention while this little Sister, explains these coincidences.

"At this period, Our Lord desired to comfort my afflicted soul by a great consolation. I learned that there was established at Rome an association in reparation for blasphemy. What was my admiration and my gratitude when I beheld on a printed leaflet, a clause to the following effect—that by a brief dated August 8, 1843, the Sovereign Pontiff permitted the establishment of pious confraternities! What good tidings! I no longer doubted that the work with which I had been entrusted was the work of Grod. What filled me with the most admiration was this remarkable coincidence: on the 8th of August 1843. the Sovereign Pontiff issued a brief at Rome, and on the 26th of August, the same year, Our Lord manifested to a poor, miserable little Carmelite novice in France, this great work of Reparation for Blasphemy, which he wished my poor country to use as a shield against the fury of his just indignation."

She added: "Many pious souls then commenced to recite the reparatory prayers; pamphlets of the association were distributed, and there was even question of establishing this society in France." We shall soon see that the sister will receive promises of pardon and will perceive indications of hope. The guilty nation will not be chastised as it deserves, for it has been the kingdom of St. Louis and is still the kingdom of Mary! A special source of mercy is opened unto her.

9

THE ASSOCIATION

"He permitted me to behold the Association under the figure of an immense army of valiant soldiers, hastening to join him their Chief, to defend his Father's glory."
(Words of the Sister.)

Sr. Mary St. Peter felt strongly urged to make a perfect oblation of herself to Grod for the accomplishment of his designs. Prevented by her superiors from offering this act, the good sister, in all simplicity of soul, thought she could comply with the urgent demands of her Divine Master, by a little surreptitious means, which she herself, with her usual candor, reveals to us.

It was the feast of the Annunciation, on which the Church celebrates the Incarnation of the Son of God, patronal feast of Carmel at Tours.

"I felt an increased devotion to the holy Infant Jesus, and in union with one of the sisters, who also had the same attraction, we formed the design of consecrating ourselves in a special manner to the Divine Child on this, the day of his Incarnation, to render him more honor and glory. It was I who was to write the act of consecration; I composed it as conformable as possible to the act of perfect abandonment which Our Lord seemed to demand so imperiously. I could not do this without permission, but I was afraid to ask it because I dreaded a refusal. I did not seek the needed permission myself but induced the sister to ask our Rev. Mother for both, hoping thus to make in secret, the long-desired act of oblation to Jesus. Permission was granted. I was overjoyed, thinking that I had at last gained my object. But the holy Child is not a lover of fraud; he received my act as a simple consecration, as our Rev. Mother had intended in granting the permission. Therefore, he directed me to solicit the authorization of my superiors, that I might offer this act of abandonment with their full consent. I went to accuse myself of the fault I had committed and repeated to our reverend mother what our Divine Lord had given me to understand. She consulted our worthy ecclesiastical superior, and I obtained their mutual consent."

Let us add: this favor was not granted her immediately; an extreme delicacy of conscience had urged her to declare the trifling circumstance narrated above as a grievous fault, of which her superiors took advantage to try her the more; it being only after the expiration of nine months that she obtained what she desired.

Before giving the details of this event, the pious sister makes an observation. She says: "There is something singularly strange in this express desire of our Divine Lord, that I should offer him an entire abandonment of myself for the accomplishment of his designs. Is he not the Sovereign Master of all creatures? Is he not free to do with them as he pleases, to make use of their persons, their very lives in the manner he wills? Again, to think that he insisted upon having the full consent of my superiors before taking complete possession of my soul! But it was for this reason: that they, themselves, were to have a large share in the work which my Divine Master proposed to erect on such a questionable foundation. I was nothing in their hands but a useless instrument, which they were to employ in the work of God; and as they were to experience many contradictions on account of this work, he, in a manner, respected their free-will."

She continues: "I made this act on Christmas, 1843. On the eve, before matins, I placed it in the hands of the Blessed Virgin, beseeching her to offer it to Jesus, born at midnight in the stable of Bethlehem."

Act of perfect abandonment to the most Holy Child Jesus, according to the full extent of his desires, for the accomplishment of his designs, and for the glory of the Holy Name of God."

"O most holy and most amiable Infant Jesus, behold, the much desired day has come at last, on which, without fear of failing in the obedience due to my superiors, I can, with full liberty, offer myself entirely and unreservedly to thee, according to thy good pleasure and the boundless extent of thy power over my soul, for the accomplishment of thy designs."

"I am, indeed, most unworthy, but O Divine Infant, since thou hast desired it, deign, I beseech thee, to purify thy victim by the tears shed during thy holy childhood and by thy most precious blood. Prostrate at thy feet, before thy humble manger, on this night rendered forever memorable by thy most holy birth, I offer myself fully and entirely to thee, my divine Spouse, by the blessed hands of Mary and Joseph, upon the burning altar of thy Sacred Heart, under the protection of the angels and saints. I offer thee a perfect and entire oblation of myself for the accomplishment of thy designs, and for the glory of the Holy Name of God."

"O divine Child, thou who didst say to thy Holy Mother when she found thee in the temple of Jerusalem: 'Why hast thou sought me? Didst thou not know I must be about my Father's business?' I beseech thee to receive me on this day as one of thy disciples, grant that henceforth the one thought of my life may be to serve thy Eternal Father and to glorify his Holy Name."

"O most holy Child! I renounce today all that I have and all that I am, and I give myself to all that thou art. Do with me what thou pleasest, for the accomplishment of thy designs. I beseech thee, take sovereign possession of that which is thine. O divine Infant, for the love of thee, I divest myself of all things now and forever. Deign, I implore thee, in thy great mercy to clothe me with thy sacred merits perfumed with the precious odor of thy virtues, that on the day of judgment, I may receive a welcome from thy heavenly Father. Amen."

"I call upon our blessed father, Peter de Berulle, apostle of the Word Incarnate, and upon all the angels and saints of heaven, to witness this contract which I have just made with the Infant Jesus."

Sister Mary of St. Peter of the Holy Family.
(Unworthy Carmelite.)

"This contract having been made with Our Lord, I looked upon myself as belonging entirely to him; and notwithstanding my unworthiness, he continued to construct in my soul his edifice, to the glory of the Holy Name of God. At the same time, he urged me to solicit my superiors to have the prayers of Reparation printed and propagated. But when I presented my supplications to our Rev. Mother, she chided me severely for my presumption, saying that it would be much better to recite the beautiful formula of prayers written by the holy Fathers of the Church, that I was self-willed and obstinate to continue thinking of this work of Reparation. After she had said this to me, I had the idea of presenting all my disappointments as so much money to the Blessed Virgin wherewith to pay for the printing of the prayers which her Divine Son wished to have propagated over the whole world. In the meantime, God was granting numerous graces to the sisters of our community who recited the prayers either for themselves or for their parents. As they were entirely ignorant whence originated these prayers, they spoke freely to me about them. One sister said: 'Really, you can obtain from God all that you desire by making this novena of Reparation.' There was at the time, a sister very ill, who felt inspired to promise Our Lord that she would make this novena; on the third day she was perfectly restored and came to impart her joy to me. These were great consolations, for beholding that God has granted so many remarkable graces, I was confirmed in my opinion, that by the grace of God, the spiritual communications which I received, regarding this work, were not illusions. One day after communion, my Divine Master himself, wishing to console me, said these words, which have since been verified: 'My daughter, these prayers of Reparation shall be printed, and they shall be distributed.'"

"Our worthy and charitable superiors, who were seriously examining the action of God in my soul, commanded me to give them an account of my interior, in order to ascertain if it were truly God who led me. The following is what I wrote in obedience to their request."

"Reverend and very honored mother; with the assistance of the Infant Jesus and my good angel, I will now set about accomplishing your command, and state in writing the manner in which I make my mental prayer. It is a difficult task, but obedience and the grace of God, will render all things easy. By this time, very reverend mother, you are accustomed to my poor language; what you particularly desire is not well-turned phrases, but a simple statement of my interior dispositions at the present moment."

"Firstly, I have no merit in my mental prayer, for it is a second nature and a gift which, notwithstanding my unworthiness, I received from God from my childhood. As a remote preparation for this exercise, I try not to lose sight of the presence of God, and during the day I keep him company in the interior of my soul. Having left to my Divine Savior the care of my parents and of all that relates to myself personally, I think of him alone, considering myself as the little servant of the Holy Family. Consequently, in all that I do during the day, in my office as portress, I act as if I were in the holy house of Nazareth. I imagine that a servant has three duties to fulfil: to accompany his master whither he goeth, to execute his orders and to guard his flocks in their proper pastures; in a word, to work solely for the interests of his master and according to his will. This is what I try to do, with the grace of God. My interior occupation is to accompany Our Lord, through the mysteries of his life, to unite myself to him, and to offer him my homage. When I execute his orders, I think of these words of the Gospel: *And he was subject to them.* Every time the bell summons me to duty, I offer myself in sacrifice to the Eternal Father, on the altar of the Sacred Heart of Jesus, begging him to unite me to his Divine Son, that it might be Jesus alone that acts in me. When I have no preoccupying duty to perform, I entertain myself with him, I take his sheep to graze in his pastures, by this I mean in his sacred mysteries, the merits of which constitute the food and the nourishment of our souls. I pray for the pastors of the Church, for the conversion of sinners, and I try to keep my mind from all absorbing thoughts. I unite all my actions to those of my Divine Savior. Thus, exterior occupations very rarely disturb my soul, they only cause it to desire more ardently the repose and tranquility of mental prayer; and when the time appointed for this exercise draws near, oh! then Our Lord compensates me for all the little sacrifices of the day."

"I commence my meditation by an examination of conscience, after which I humble myself at the feet of Jesus for all my infidelities to him, beseeching him to pardon me and to purify my soul. Then I entertain myself quite naturally and simply with my amiable Savior, as would a child. Once, Our Lord gave me the following method of prayer, I do not know whether by words or by illumination:

Prepare your soul by recollection.

Purify it by contrition; Then fill it with God."

"As it is perfectly useless to continue pouring water into a vase once filled, so is it as useless to crowd the soul with reflections when one alone is sufficient to fill it."

"Sometimes I am interiorly urged to make my mental prayer in union with Our Lord offering himself to the Father for his glory and for the salvation of souls. Then I perceive myself entirely recollected in the Sacred Heart of Jesus, where I find ample food for reflection. Beholding that I am entirely divested of self and clothed with the Lord Jesus, I can approach his Divine Father with more facility, and being enriched with his sacred merits, I do not fear to demand extraordinary graces for our holy Mother the Church and for the salvation of souls. Frequently I follow this method of prayer, which is not wholly supernatural, all the powers of my soul being merely united in the Sacred Heart of Jesus; at these times our Lord acts in me and I in him; distractions are very rare because my imagination is transfixed, captive there. But when I am thus with him, and he wills to communicate something new concerning the Work of Reparation, a second operation takes place in my soul; I feel that I am incapable of longer acting, for it seems as if my mind were entirely annihilated to cede place to that of Jesus; it is then that my soul is capable of distinguishing his intimate conversation. The more perfect is this annihilation of all the faculties, so much happier is my soul, absorbed as it is in God."

"In this state the soul finds herself in him without knowing how she has entered therein; the attraction of grace predominates, seizing and possessing all her powers, elevating her above herself and absorbing her entirely in God! Oh, what delicious moments! Favor entirely gratuitous! I experience this perfect contemplation but rarely, for I am totally unworthy of such extraordinary graces. I make my customary mental prayer in the Sacred Heart of Jesus; there he teaches me his will, reveals his desires of laboring for the glory of his Father and for the salvation of souls; this is my most pleasing occupation. It is impossible for me to meditate for any length of time together, firstly, because I have not the strength, and again, because this attraction coming from the Heart of Jesus, draws my soul toward him, and I find myself captivated, confined in this divine sanctuary, like a little child in the womb of its mother. Then my will and all the affections of my heart perform all, and my poor mind finds itself relieved of all labor. It is Our Lord himself who has called me to this degree of mental prayer. At the beginning, I dared not follow this attraction for fear of not doing right by abandoning- the ordinary method; but Our Lord, wishing that I should follow his method, placed before my mind this comparison:—If a king invited me to his table, would it not be absurd to take my dinner with me, instead of partaking of the viands set before me on the prince's table to which I had been invited? Having consulted others in this point, I was told not to fear following the method inspired by the Holy Ghost, that this was the best way of meditating; of which I have made the happy experience, finding the viands of the Sacred Heart of Jesus much more exquisite than those which I could possibly prepare myself."

"The signal for the termination of this delicious repast is sometimes given before I have had the time to offer sufficient thanks to my benefactor. Then I briefly express my gratitude and take the resolution not to lose sight of him who has had the charity to treat me so magnificently, notwithstanding my unworthiness. Nevertheless, I am not without experiencing pain from time to time, for dryness and interior suffering are sometimes very necessary for my soul; in these times I accept whatever nourishment the Lord thinks proper to give me."

We have not been willing to retrench any of this interesting and confidential letter, written with such childish simplicity; we here behold, a humble, confiding soul, elevating herself by degrees to the most sublime heights of the contemplative life. At the school of the Sacred Heart and instructed by the Holy Ghost, the sister proves to be a faithful imitator of St. Gertrude, and a worthy daughter of St. Theresa. What admirable and astonishing progress she has made in the unitive life! Enraptured with her subject, her style becomes sublime;our illiterate little Carmelite, enriches her ordinary simplicity of expression with the most ingenious comparisons, and at times with conceptions, not unworthy the pen of our best ascetic writers. Her superiors had no longer room for doubt; it was plain that grace had taken entire possession of this holy soul, to mold it according to its designs, to make of it a privileged instrument in the great work so necessary to France and to the Church. The Divine Master was not slow in extending her spiritual vision, revealing in a more definite manner his intentions in her regard.

Not only was an ordinary association of Reparation necessary, but an arch-confraternity similar to that of Notre Dame des Victories, having a center toward which all the subconfraternities of the same work established in France, would converge as the rays of a disk to its center.

Let us attend to what Sr. Mary of St. Peter states concerning what was manifested to her on this subject, February 2nd, 1844. "For several weeks past, I have experienced nothing extraordinary as regards the work of Reparation; yet Our Lord keeps me in union with, him to glorify his Father, to repair the outrages offered him and to pray that his Name may be sanctified. But today, feast of the Presentation of Jesus in the Temple, it was my turn to receive the holy communion of vow."

The sister has already mentioned this "Vow." Mother Mary of the Incarnation had made a vow for the necessities of the monastery when a change of locality was in question. The terms of this vow were, that for the space of one year, two of the religious in turn according to rank, would pray every day for the accomplishment of the designs of the Sacred Heart, to draw down a special benediction on the community.

"It was my turn, to communicate," continues the sister, "and my good Master desired, notwithstanding my unworthiness, to manifest himself to my soul. Previous to the last occasion on which he addressed me, he was full of wrath against France, and I listened to his words with trembling and fear and wept bitterly. But today, I was inundated with joy, when he made known the pleasure experienced by his Divine Heart at the sight of the zeal and good-will manifested by his children toward the growing association. As his Holy Mother had adopted the arch-confraternity for the conversion of sinners, so had he taken under his protection that of the Reparation; these two associations were to act in concert, the latter, to repair the outrages committed against God, the former to obtain pardon for these outrages, the one through Jesus, the other through Mary. But Our Lord gave me to understand that the association which he wished to establish in France had two objects in view: first, the Reparation of blasphemy uttered against God; second, the sanctification of his Holy Name on the Lord's Day; consequently, the extirpation of blasphemy and the prohibition of manual labor on Sunday. Blasphemy and the violation of the Lord's Day are the principal sins which provoke the anger of God against France."

"To the rules and regulations prescribed by the association at Rome, there are others added to the one established in France; for instance, that the members should perform no manual labor, nor allow others to labor, and to contribute with all their might to the prevention of all kinds of manual labor on the days prohibited. Our Lord desires first, that this association be placed under the patronage of St. Martin, St. Louis and St. Michael; second, that each member recite daily a Pater, Ave, and Gloria Patri, followed by the act of praise which he gave me under the title of "The Golden Arrow," with an invocation to the holy patrons; but on Sundays and Holy days they should recite all the prayers of Reparation, in expiation for the outrages committed against God on these holy days and to obtain mercy for the guilty. I beheld this association under the figure of an army of valiant soldiers, hastening to join their Chief, to defend the glory of his Father. He wished that their name should correspond to the nobility of their undertaking, and for this reason, that they should bear the title of, 'Defenders of the Holy Name of God.' He also helped me understand that each member should wear a badge in the form of a cross, bearing on one side *Sit nomen Domini benedictum,* and on the other *Vade retro, Satana.* That he would give to this heavenly device a secret virtue to combat against the demon of blasphemy; that every time a member heard a blasphemy uttered, he should repeat the words written on this cross, and in this manner to wage war against Satan, thus glorifying God."

"Our Lord manifested to me, that the devil would make use of every means in his power to crush this work from the beginning. I felt as though I could shed even the last drop of my blood for so holy an association. Our Lord told me also that he had said nothing to me for a long time, because it was not necessary; that he did nothing undesignedly, but that it was expedient to give me this information today. He called my attention to the difference existing between the Association of France and that of Rome, on account of the violation of the Lord's Day. Oh, if we could know with what joy he looks upon this infant association, we would hasten to satisfy the long cherished desire of his Heart, by enrolling ourselves under the standard of this glorious militia, of which he is the commander-in-chief, to fight with the arms of his cross against the enemies of the Holy Name of God, and to submit them to his sway by rallying them under his standard."

The Roman association, to which the sister here alludes, was established by a decree of Gregory XVI on the 8th of August 1843. The headquarters of this association was at Rome, under the invocation of Peter Caravita, and was placed under the protection of St. Louis, king of France. Each member proposed to himself never to utter a blasphemy or an imprecation. Those invested with authority, should try to encourage their dependents to avoid his odious sin. If they cannot prevent its commission, they must, at least, offer an aspiration of praise, such as, *May God be praised! May his Holy Name be Blessed!* They should recite daily "Pater and Ave" for the conversion of blasphemers. His Holiness has granted many spiritual favors, notably a plenary indulgence once a month, on any day at option, provided the ordinary conditions be fulfilled; and at the hour of death, another plenary indulgence on the invocation of the Holy Name of Jesus; many other special indulgences are also attached thereto.

An association for the Reparation of blasphemy was not a new institution in the Church; thus we see that Sr. Mary St. Peter was greatly consoled on learning of the existence of a similar association at Pome, and she with good reason inferred from this fact, that the communications, made to her on the subject, were of divine origin. Yet, as it was a question of repairing and extirpating this evil, peculiar to our times, which was propagating itself with alarming rapidity, reparation for blasphemy, the only object proposed by the association of Rome, was not sufficient for that of France, where it was necessary to add reparation for the profanation of Sunday. It must be remarked that in the non-observance of the Lord's Day, the sister beheld an outrage committed against the sovereignty of God, and an injury done to the sanctification of his Holy Name, a crime in her eyes identical with that of blasphemy: in fact, when the day is no longer sanctified by the suspension of labor, the Holy Name of the Lord is not adored, blessed, known or glorified as it should be.

From the ignorance and contempt of which He is thus the object, results a social evil, so much the more pernicious and fatal to society at large and to individuals in particular, as it daily tends to become more general and more prevalent. On this point also, does France hold the first rank among culpable nations, for by her people, the precept of sanctifying the Sunday, is most daringly and unblushingly contemned. Protestant nations, Mohammedans, and even the Jews, officially recognize one day of public prayer; but in France, neither the state nor the laws ordain a day of prayer and repose from labor,—grave subject of astonishment and scandal to the great number of foreigners who throng her cities. These, therefore, are the reasons why the members of an association for reparation established in France, should pledge themselves not to labor on the days prohibited, and to be zealous in restricting others from performing servile work on these days. Moreover, it was just that the proposed association should be placed under the patronage of St. Michael, St. Martin, and St. Louis. Blasphemy and the violation of the Lord's Day are sins which attack God directly, in violation of the first three commandments, they confer no benefit on man, but are sadly prejudicial alike to his temporal and spiritual happiness. They are diabolical in character, the unhappy transgressor labors not for himself but for the devil, who not only degrades, but enslaves his victim.

It was therefore but just that the former enemy of Lucifer, St. Michael, the acknowledged champion of the "Eldest Daughter of the Church," as he was likewise of the ancient people of God, should be the first patron of a work whose watchword was *Vade retro, Satana*. We also know that St. Martin was one of the adversaries of the demon, driving him from Gaul with the remnants of idolatry, and from this has he become an apostle of charity and zeal, one of the glories of Christianity and the special protector of France.

The Association at Rome, being placed under the auspices of St. Louis, because of the just severity which he exercised toward blasphemers, it was but natural in France, where, unhappily, the traditions of his piety have been forgotten, that his protection should be invoked for an institution whose object is, to obtain by prayer and the rigorous observance of the divine commandments, that which this great king had already won by the solidity of his virtues and the wisdom of his laws.

Some weeks afterward, the sister refers to the same subject, February 26, 1844. "Our Lord," writes she to the Mother Superior, "desires most ardently that the work of Reparation be established, as he has given me to understand. I seemed to hear my Divine

Jesus from the recesses of the tabernacle address us these words: 'O ye, my friends and my faithful children! behold if there be any sorrow like unto my sorrow! My Divine Father and my cherished spouse, the Holy Church, are despised, outraged by my enemies. Will no one rise to revenge me by defending them against those enemies? I can no longer remain in the midst of an ungrateful people: behold the torrents of tears that flow from my eyes! Can I find no one to dry them, by making reparation of honor to the glory of my Father, begging of him the conversion of the guilty?' Such are the sentiments, reverend mother, with which God fills my soul, causing it to experience this interior pain which the Heart of Jesus glorified can no longer suffer. If a king or even an ambassador be despised or set at naught by a foreign nation, his countrymen fly to arms, the honor of the king must be avenged; troops are levied and the death of thousands is counted for naught. And yet, the most holy and terrible Name of the God of armies, of the King of kings is despised and blasphemed; his holy Day profaned by an infinite number of sinners, and no one is concerned, no one thinks of avenging him! But behold! Our Lord Jesus Christ, the ambassador from the kingdom of heaven, demands reparation of honor for his Divine Father, or proclaims war against us, for he has threatened France with his wrath. Shall we hesitate in our choice?"

After perusing these soul-stirring apostrophes, these burning ejaculations, we are overawed and we ask, what would have become of France, if the desire, communicated to the servant of God, had been publicly manifested and immediately fulfilled? Would the entire world have witnessed the misfortunes with which we have since been deluged? Would we have had to fear the evils which still menace us today?

The sister, in terminating, begs that the archbishop of Tours be informed of all that has taken place since the feast of St. Louis, concerning the work of Reparation.

"Would you please permit me," she writes to the mother prioress, "if our reverend ecclesiastical superior consent, to address the archbishop, for I have such an ardent desire to inform him of these things! I most humbly beg you to grant me this permission. Then I shall have performed all that lies in my power toward the accomplishment of the work which has been revealed to me, notwithstanding my unworthiness; but I shall write to his Grace, only when I feel my soul under the influence of the Holy Ghost, for I desire to make no use of my own convictions, being incapable of anything good; I shall beseech him to guide my pen."

In another statement she says: "Our Lord has given me such interior pain because of my desire to see his work established, that I have been unable to take any nourishment whatever. I can bear this burden no longer without falling under its weight, for this reason, I feel strongly urged to depose it at the feet of the archbishop."

10

THE ARCHBISHOP

**"Our Lord revealed to me that he charged
me with the care of France; that he would send me
as his ambassadress to make a treaty of peace."
*(Words of the Sister)***

Nothing of what we now know concerning Sister Mary of St. Peter, had yet passed beyond the walls of the cloister; as we have heretofore remarked, only the ecclesiastical superior, the sister's confessor and a few very intimate friends, had been informed by the mother prioress of all that had occurred; not even the archbishop had as yet received any information. The grave nature of the last revelation to the cloistered virgin, and her pressing solicitation to have the matter brought before the archbishop made it obligatory on the Rev. Mother to inform his Grace of all that had transpired.

The archbishop of Tours, Mgr. Morlot, had been transferred from Orleans to the archbishopric of St. Martin some two years previously. This prelate was a man of extreme delicacy of conscience and of exemplary regularity. The highest dignities were successively conferred on him, such for instance as the honor of the Roman purple with which he was clothed in 1854; and also with the title of Archbishop of Paris, to which dignity he was elevated in 1856; these honors served to increase rather than diminish his detachment from the transient honors and pleasures of this earth, and of which we have more than one admirable proof. His life, prematurely shortened by the incessant labors of his episcopal charge, was finally crowned by a most edifying death. At Tours as at Paris he has left numerous traces of his episcopal life of forty years.

His affable and courteous manner and. his cordial benevolence has rendered his name illustrious. He had a particular veneration for the Carmelites; it was with pleasure that in 1846 he assisted at the installation of these religious in their new monastery, and consecrated their chapel with the greatest solemnity. At the time of the disastrous inundation, which happened shortly afterward, he hastened to offer them the hospitality of his own palace, thus enabling them to continue in peace their religious exercises.

Prudence in a very remarkable degree was his characteristic virtue. Unhappily this natural propensity, fostered by his advancing years, his experimental knowledge of mankind, and by the critical circumstances through which he had passed, amounted at times to an almost excessive reserve occasioned by timidity, which, others, less circumspect, did not hesitate to attribute to apathy, or weakness of character. His caution and timidity were not unfrequently an obstacle to the progress of the affairs under his jurisdiction, yet he was right-minded and good-intentioned; but when a point of any difficulty arose, he allowed himself to be swayed by the opinion of his counsellors, who were often the cause of turning him from a decision prompted by his natural good sense. His administration had more than once suffered from this course of action of which we may judge from his conduct in regard to Sr. Mary St. Peter, and consequently toward Mr. Dupont, for whom, nevertheless, the pious prelate professed the highest esteem, of which we have given elsewhere some notable instances.

The holy man of Tours was the first to bewail in secret the excessive prudence of the archbishop; and although he, himself, suffered many a stern refusal, yet he never for an instant was wanting in the deference and perfect submission due his authority or to his person. Prayer was his weapon against the rigorous decisions of his Grace. One day a question arose touching the revelations of Sister St. Peter, when the pious layman received another refusal, very mortifying to his ardent zeal. On leaving the archbishopric he met an ecclesiastic, one of his friends, to whom he confided his disappointment. Both were walking on the solitary part of the Rue des Ursulines alongside the high fence which surrounded the episcopal domains. Drawing near the Carmelite convent, M. Dupont suddenly stood still, and taking a medal of St. Benedict from his pocket said: 'Come, we must have recourse to extraordinary means,' and after having devoutly made the sign of the cross on the medal, he threw it over the walls into the garden, saying: *Ascende superius,* (Let us seek aid from on high.) The answer was not long in coming. That same evening M. Dupont full of joy, went to his friend, the priest, and informed him that Mgr. Morlot himself had sent for him, and with the utmost urbanity had granted the object of his request.

Indeed, the worthy archbishop esteemed his virtuous parishioner. How many times had he not sent him pressing invitations to dine at his palace, but the humble "pilgrim of Rue St. Etienne," as he styled himself, always declined as politely as possible. One day, however, in deference to his aged mother, who urged the impropriety of so many refusals, he accepted the invitation; arrived with the other guests in the dining-room he observed that there was one place wanting at table in order to accommodate the number about to dine; one of the servants, in mistake, had just then removed the chair, which did not fail being observed by the attentive eye of our guest, who stooped down and whispered in the archbishop's ear: "You see Monseigneur, that I ought not dine with the great; there is no chair for me." Mgr. Morlot was quite disconcerted at the mishap, and while giving orders to his domestic to prepare a place, M. Dupont had already reached the bottom of the stairs and was out of sight before a messenger could overtake him.

A short time after the death of Sister St. Peter, when there was question of the nocturnal adoration, and still later, when the society of St. Martin for the clothing of the poor was established, the venerable archbishop manifested his eagerness to second M. Dupont in all his views. We have before us a sketch of the rules and regulations arranged by the very hand of the prelate, together with expressions of approbation for the zealous and charitable founder of these two holy works.

These details do not appear superfluous in order that our readers may understand the character of the prelate with whom Sr. Mary St. Peter will soon find herself in direct communication. It had already been decided upon by Father Aileron, ecclesiastical superior of the Carmelites, and Mother Mary of the Incarnation, that a minute account of all that had transpired from August 25th, should be presented to the archbishop. Mgr. Morlot, with his characteristic reserve, was not willing to give his opinion in a matter so grave and of such vital importance, without mature deliberation. He ordained that the various writings and statements which had been drawn up by the sister be brought him, and of these he, himself, took cognizance. He could not fail being impressed with the evidence of sincerity which pervaded every page and approved of the conduct of her superiors toward her, encouraging them to continue as heretofore. With regard to the communications themselves, he was so much impressed, that he did not hesitate to let it appear in his pastoral for the ensuing Lent of 1844, from which we extract the following, relative to the profanation of the Lord's Day: "Have the workshops been closed? Has manual labor been suspended on the Lord's Day? Show me the street or the throughfare of the city in which the noise of commerce has for one instant been interrupted! Everywhere the same clamor resounds, the same agitation, the same commotion sways the multitude as on weekdays. The children of men pursue their avocations with the same ardor as on the days assigned to labor. Here we behold them erecting stupendous edifices which the hand of God refuses to bless; there, exposing the produce of their industry, pursuing their speculations, their negotiations, their insatiable craving for wealth, for power, for honor."

"Look at our villages, pass on to our hamlets, what do we behold? The forgetfulness of Grod which necessarily follows in the train of profanation, and the countless other disorders, none the less deplorable. Yet the most diabolical of all these outrages committed against the majesty of God, is the shameful desecration of the Sundays and holydays: one part of the day is consecrated to business; the other, to pleasure; forbidden labor being always followed by disorderly pleasure. Servile occupation, is succeeded by intemperance and immorality."

Still enumerating the consequences of this profanation, the prelate continues: "On the one hand, we behold open revolts and scandalous outrages committed against the divinity of God; on the other, lukewarmness, nay more, total indifference in the fulfilment of duty. These provoke the wrath of the Most High, whose justice, though patient and long-suffering, is, nevertheless, inevitable; whose vengeance, though tardy, is certain; for Grod has no need to punish day by day; His power is eternal and not to be confounded with the justice of man, intimidated by the number of the guilty, and which, beholding the multitude to be punished, lets the sword fall powerless from its hand. It is not thus when God wishes to punish, it is not the number of the guilty which arrests his hand, he then counts but the just, and when these have disappeared from the face of the earth, his arm falls mercilessly."

The venerable archbishop was not satisfied with this appeal, addressed officially to his flock. On the 15th of March, he authorized in his diocese the association already founded at Notre-Dame de la Riche for the Reparation of Blasphemy. The pastor, Father Aileron, in establishing this society in his parish, had availed himself of the power conceded by the Pontifical brief of August 8th, 1843 (of which mention has already been made).

Permission had been granted to the sister, at her own request, to write to the archbishop.

"I had," said she, "the honor of writing to his Lordship; my worthy superiors had
already informed him of all that the Divine Master had made known to me regarding
the Work of Reparation. Then the pious prelate had the little circulars printed which
had been previously published at Nantes. He added his own approbation on the 15th of
March 1844, recommending the Association to the attention of the clergy of his diocese,
and expressing the desire that they would encourage the faithful to repair the outrages
committed against the sovereign majesty of God. A great number of these circulars were
distributed, but there was no association established according to the demand of Our
Lord; it seemed that the hour had not yet come. Let us adore in silence the hidden designs
of the Most High".

These last words indicate the disposition in which the sister had received the decision of
the archbishop; although grieved that the Association of Reparation was not officially
established in the diocese, yet she was consoled by the encouragement of the prelate, and
by the approbation which he had given to her communications. She hoped that the time
was not far distant, when he would place himself at the head of a movement, which she
believed so necessary for the salvation of France. Nevertheless, when she perceived that
he took such a neutral stand, she deplored it deeply, and attributed the cause to her own
sins; for she suffered "in seeing the Majesty of the Most High outraged with impunity, and
her countrymen, hastening to their own destruction." In her distress, the humble virgin
turned to her heavenly Spouse who had confided this noble mission to her, of which she
had so faithfully acquitted herself. Then the Savior gave her to understand that during
the interval, it was in her own soul he desired to make reparation; of this she thus gives an
account to the mother prioress:

"Permit me to relate in all simplicity, what has passed today within my soul, after holy
communion. Our Lord inspired me to present myself before him in the name of France,
to receive him in the kingdom of my heart, and to offer him my communion in a spirit
of reparation for the crimes of which our nation is guilty. After having received this
divine King, I prayed most earnestly for France; then he communicated himself to my
soul, telling me that he charged me with the salvation of France, and constituted me
his ambassadress to treat of peace with him; also that I should remain humbly prostrate
before him in the most Blessed Sacrament of the altar, praying for France and for the
establishment of the Work of the Reparation. Then he counselled me to reflect well on

the obligations of the office he imposed upon me; for when an ambassador withdraws from a kingdom, it is received as a sign of war. Our Lord gave me to understand that I must not voluntarily withdraw from his presence in the most Blessed Sacrament, but that I should remain there in spirit in the name of France. Then I answered: 'My Lord, I have given myself entirely to thee for the fulfilment of thy intentions, do with me what thou wilt.' And I prostrated myself, adoring the designs of God who makes use of what is most miserable and despised to perform his works: I accepted the charge which he imposed on me, praying him to render me fit to accomplish his designs over me, and to fulfil them himself in me."

"I have applied myself for several days to adore Jesus in the Blessed Sacrament. On quitting the choir to resume my occupations, I leave my heart at the feet of my good Savior, and in whatsoever part of the house I am engaged, I try to keep in his divine presence. This is the nature of the spiritual exercise which he demands of me at present; he wishes me to remain there at his feet, praying in the name of France."

The Divine Master lent a favorable ear to the humble prayers of his servant; he revealed to her the heinousness and enormity of the sin of blasphemy. "It seems as if Our Lord said to me: 'You cannot comprehend the abomination of this sin: if my justice were not restrained by my mercy, the guilty would be destroyed in an instant; even inanimate beings would feel my vengeance, but I have an eternity in which to punish the wicked."

"Then he made me understand the excellence of this Work of Reparation; how far it surpassed all others, and how pleasing it was to God, to the angels, the saints and to our holy mother the Church. Oh, would that we could understand the glory we could obtain by repeating these words: Mirabile Nomen Dei." (Admirable is the Name of God) in a spirit of reparation for blasphemy!" A short while after, she wrote the following : "You are aware that Our Lord, some time ago, directed me to pray for France, telling me to guard the sheep, of whom he was the Shepherd; that he chose me on this day to be his little shepherdess, giving me his mysteries and his most holy life for my domain; that I could draw forth grace from his divine wounds for his sheep. In fine, that he gave himself to me as a mine of gold wherewith to pay the debt which France owes to his divine justice, permitting me to draw on the treasury of his Sacred Heart. Then Our Lord gave me to understand, that I must be careful not to act as did the unfaithful servant of the Gospel, who made no use of his talent; that he would demand of me a rigorous account, and that I would find no difficulty in drawing from the mine of gold, which he himself had acquired by his labors and sufferings. I believe that he desired to find someone who would become a mediator between himself and France, in order that he might extend to it his mercy."

During this interval, the sister had had much to endure, for God did not spare her; interior sufferings were to prepare her to accomplish his work: her mind was at times overspread with darkness, and in the face of her arduous mission she was confronted with the experience of her own weakness and incapacity.

"This work," said she, (June 6, 1844) "is in me as a burning fire which causes me to suffer more or less, according to the good pleasure of God. During prayer I never cease begging of the Lord to spare France, to establish in all her cities the Work of Reparation, and to raise up apostolic laborers to preach this work. "Thou dost behold, my sweet Jesus, how poor and miserable I am; I implore thee to give all that I am now suffering to some soul more courageous than I who will render thee more adequate service.'"

Once, however, Our Lord caused her to feel his presence for nearly two hours. "During this delicious repose, I thought I heard his sweet voice say to me: 'Courage and confidence, my child! Courage and confidence! Engrave these words on your heart. Oh, if you only knew the advantage you derive in supporting these sufferings, you would thank me for sending them to you! I have come to visit you but not to remain with you in a sensible manner. You will partake of my chalice, but be consoled; although you behold me not, still I shall not be far from you, for I will hold the chalice while you drink therefrom. After this trial, I shall send you consolations; you have justly merited these sufferings by your infidelity; however, it is not in anger, but in mercy that I send you such trials.' I then took the liberty to ask him if the crown which I made in honor of his Name and of his holy mysteries was agreeable to him. He replied: 'All that is done to glorify me is most agreeable.' He counselled me to practice this exercise when I would be incapable of mental prayer."

A new aspect of things comes over the life of Sr. Mary St. Peter. The Carmelites had just quitted the venerable and cherished monastery which had been the cradle of their foundation. The following is the account we read in their annals in regard to this subject.

"Toward the end of the year 1843, our old monastery was sold, the purchasers having paid a reasonable price, with the express clause, that for the space of twenty years the chapel, (of which only the walls were left), should not be used for any other than its primitive purpose. After the conclusion of the negotiations, the moment came to put our hand to the work and commence anew. The plan of a monastery was made, which was as much as possible in conformity with the rules and customs of our order. Particular attention was paid to the arrangement of all the regular places of the house, in order to facilitate the practice of our holy observances. Our Rev. Mother Mary of the Incarnation, then superior, as well as our worthy ecclesiastical superior, toiled at this work with unremitting zeal and devotedness. God plainly showed that he had chosen them for this work, by the abundant benedictions he bestowed on their labors."

As we have said, a convenient site on the Rue des Ursulines, back of the archbishopric, had been bought. Mgr. Morlot solemnly blessed the cornerstone in the month of September, 1844. While awaiting the completion of the edifice, the Carmelites were obliged to remove to a small dwelling-house which had neither gratings nor cloisters.

Although beautiful in appearance and finely situated, it was small and inconvenient for religious, the absence of gratings being one of the greatest annoyances. In such cases, every Carmelite carried the grating with her, if we may be allowed the expression: a thick black veil enveloped her from head to foot, scarcely permitting her to breathe or to move. Such was the habitual condition of Sr. St. Peter during those two years, when as portress of the interior, she was obliged to communicate directly with persons from without, and to transmit the messages to those within. Let us listen to the naive complaints to which she gives vent.

"The time had come when Our Lord had prepared a great trial for me, for I was obliged to quit the dear convent where I pronounced my vows, and where I had been overwhelmed with graces by his merciful liberality. I found myself in a secular house having no grating, and I still held the office of portress which kept me in continual contact with seculars. Condemned to stay for nearly two years in this parlor, and observing that a great number of persons were always coming, some to solicit prayers for the sick, others for the conversion of those dear to them; some again to be consoled in their pains and sufferings, while others were drawn thither by mere curiosity;—this novel situation threw me into extreme affliction. Fearing to lose the spirit of retirement and recollection, for which I had such an attraction, I said to myself: 'Alas, can I ever hear the voice of my Lord here!' I went to our Mother and manifested to her this repugnance, which I experienced for my position. I would have been only too happy had she changed my office, or at least, if she had given me a companion to share my duties with me, yet, notwithstanding her great charity, she judged it better to leave me alone and unaided."

"To avoid the frequent visits of seculars, I said politely to all who presented themselves, that the mission of a Carmelite was to hold intercourse with God in silence and retreat and but little with man; that they might expose their sorrows to other religious, and seek consolation from those not living, as we, in seclusion; that we would pray for their intentions; all my reasoning was of no avail. I cannot help laughing even now, when I think of one good women who insisted on bringing her daughter to see me, in order, as she said, that I might give her some advice about her approaching marriage; as I declined to comply with her request, she was obliged to go and consult someone else, better posted than I on such matters."

"My good Master allowed me to suffer from this extreme repugnance for my new position for some time: but one day, he had the goodness to come and console me in the inmost recesses of my soul. He told me that I should not grieve thus at having an office which brought one in such constant communication with my neighbor; that I should receive these people with the same spirit of charity with which he welcomed all those who approached him when passing through the towns and cities of Judea; promising me that this office would not be injurious to my soul, and that he would draw much glory therefrom."

Six months passed, during which the communications, in reference to the Reparation, remained as if suspended, and the sister was conducted by a path of aridity, darkness and temptation. She seemed ready to fall under this weight when God favored her anew.

"He made me understand that the intelligence of man cannot conceive the heinousness of the affronts offered God by the sin of blasphemy. This crime pierces his Sacred Heart and covers him with wounds like another Lazarus. He pointed out the compassionate dogs who consoled poor Lazarus by licking his wounds, and invited me to render him a similar service, employing my tongue every day to glorify the Holy Name of God despised and blasphemed by sinners. I never stopped to consider whether this exercise would give me interior consolation or not; it was sufficient to think that I soothed his divine wounds and gave him some relief. It seemed that he also said: 'Do all in your power to have this Work established; I shall enrich you with my merits that you may obtain it from my Father. Ask in my Name and it shall be granted you.'"

Here terminates the first account of the sister, relative to the Reparation in general; she concludes with the following declaration:

"It is in the Sacred Heart of Jesus that I have found this Work; it is also in this Divine Heart, burning with zeal for the glory of his Father, that I remit it through the hands of the most Holy Virgin and of the glorious patriarch St. Joseph, under the protection of the angels and saints, in expiation to the divine mercy who has deigned to make use of so vile an instrument. I declare that it is I, Sr. M. of St. Peter of the Holy Family, unworthy Carmelite, who have received these revelations regarding the Reparation for Blasphemy, and who have written them, in obedience to the orders of my superiors, for the greater glory of God, and also for the tranquility of my conscience. I tremble at the sight of the mission imposed on me by the Lord.—A multitude of souls will be saved if his designs be accomplished. I also declare that I have spoken with all truth and sincerity."

"At this time a circumstance took place which the sister herself relates. A priest who had heard something of this Work, came one day to beg me to pray for two graces: one for himself, the other for one of his confreres. The question at stake was the salvation of a soul, and also the shielding of the reputation of two persons in whom they were greatly interested. This priest said to the saintly religious: 'I believe in the Work with which the Lord has charged you; but in proof of your mission, beg for these two graces. If you obtain them, I promise that my confrere in the ministry and myself will devote ourselves to propagate this Work.' I accepted his proposal, telling him that I would undertake the mission confided to me in the name of obedience; for when I ask any special grace, from God in the *name of obedience,* I obtain it more readily. He consented and took his leave. I went immediately before the Blessed Sacrament to pray my good Savior to defend his cause for the glory of his Name, and to grant the two priests the favors which they desired assuring him that they would become, as they had promised, zealous defenders of his Name; after which I made use of all the little eloquence, I possessed to touch his Divine Heart, commencing with a novena. Our Lord gave the proof required to make known the truth of his Work: the priest who had spoken to me, received the grace he so much desired, on the evening of that same day; the second also received his request a little later. He told me that the Lord had heard his prayers beyond his most sanguine expectations, and that the unfortunate affair in question, had eventually turned to the glory of God and to the happiness of those who had, at first, been so much grieved."

11

THE LITTLE GOSPEL

"When Jesus received his Name, Satan was vanquished and disarmed."

After the negative decision of Mgr. Morlot, there was a short respite in the revelations made to Sr. Mary of St. Peter, regarding the Work of Reparation. Our Lord, during this interval, was pleased to console his servant by holy meditations on the mysteries of his Passion and of his Holy Name; or by animating her zeal for the deliverance of certain souls detained in purgatory. One of these seemed io have awakened her sympathy in a special manner. We shall quote the sister's account of what passed on this subject; it will enable us to judge of the holy ardor which prompted her to assist those among the departed who seemed to be most in need of help.

A most frightful and unprovided death had recently terrified the people of France. The Duke of Orleans, eldest son and heir presumptive of Louis Philip, was one day driving through Paris, when his horse took fright and became unmanageable, the Duke imprudently precipitated himself from the carriage, and was almost instantaneously killed by the violence of the fall. The news spread through the country like a flash, and even reached the Carmelites of Tours. Everywhere it had produced the greatest commotion, the more so, as the Duke, a few years previous and to the great scandal of the catholic world, had married a protestant princess, notwithstanding the admonitions of the Archbishop of Paris. His sudden death was regarded as a well-merited chastisement from God.

"One Sunday morning," writes the Sister, "when I was making my ordinary meditation, the thought of the Duke of Orleans crossed my mind; I had been vaguely apprised of his death, but had forgotten to pray for the poor prince after his decease. During the office of the Little Hours, I suddenly became conscious that his soul was suffering in purgatory, and in great need of assistance. It seemed to me that the nearer I approached the Divine Heart of Jesus, the more my emotion increased; tears so choked my utterance, that I could with difficulty recite the office. I felt great sympathy for this suffering soul, whom the Lord desired to rescue from the flames, and I offered the holy communion for him; the Lord Jesus also inspired me to offer his infinite merits to his heavenly Father. During my thanksgiving after holy communion, it seemed that our souls met in the Lord. I then said to him: 'Poor prince, what remains to you now of the grandeur and riches of this world! How pleased you are today to have the benefit of the communion of a poor Carmelite! Remember me when you enter the kingdom of Heaven!'"

"Our Lord engaged me to pray for him with more than ordinary charity, and with greater ardor than that which I felt in praying for my relatives. He suggested to me to offer, with this intention, all that he had suffered when crowned with thorns and derided as a mock king, during his Passion. I spent the rest of the morning in prayer for the prince before a picture of our Savior crowned with thorns."

"Three times a day I recited, at the foot of the altar, six Pater and Aves, and Gloria Patris, in order to gain the numerous indulgences attached to these prayers for the souls in purgatory."

"The next day, Monday, I was again urged to receive holy communion with the same intention. The suffering soul seemed, as it were, chained to my soul; I carried it everywhere with me, all the mortifications which I performed were offered for its relief."

On the 20th of March, the sister writes as follows to the mother prioress:

"The fortnight is now terminating, during which you have permitted me to offer myself to God for the soul in whom I am so deeply interested, and to abandon myself to the divine pleasure, to suffer all he would judge proper in order to obtain its deliverance. Permit me, Rev. Mother, to give you an account of all that has passed in my soul from the 26th of February until the 19th of March."

"I shall simply say that I have been to this poor prince, like the mother of a sick child, whose tenderness and anxiety keep her constantly on the alert in search of some new remedy to restore him to health. Night and day have I sought to relieve him; at length, I begged my guardian angel to allow me no rest until the dear soul would be happy in heaven. I believe that he has charitably heard my prayer, for I felt continually urged on to offer all I did for him. All my communions, except one which I was obliged to offer for one of our departed sisters, *all* that I have done, has been performed for the release of this soul. The holy sacrifice of the mass, the stations of the cross, and all the mortifications which I have been permitted to perform:—I have had the consolation of offering all to God for him. I have suffered but little physically, you have beheld my face swollen, it is true, but this was comparatively nothing; my greatest pain was to have had no more to suffer; the sweet union and interior peace I had been enjoying, has been followed by dryness and temptation; for he has hidden himself from my sight, and permitted that I should feel my unworthiness. Yet, if the Divine Master has afflicted me with one hand, he has sustained me with the other, and has given me the courage to say to him: 'My God, that this poor soul may possess and glorify thee the more speedily, I accept all these sufferings; provided I offend thee not, my Lord; this all I desire.'"

"The feast of our father St. Joseph, was approaching; I prepared myself by a novena, supplicating him to obtain of God, the speedy deliverance of this poor soul, promising at the same time, to continue the penances which were permitted me. On the eve of the feast, my ardor was inflamed anew. I was suffering very keenly from the intensity of my desires. In the refectory, I felt more inclined to weep than to take my meals. My soul was in great affliction, but from supernatural motives, for I had never known this prince. If I ever felt the privation which my vow of poverty imposed on me. Oh, it was at this moment! Were I still possessed of any means; I would most certainly have had requiem masses said for this poor soul; but a consoling thought came to my mind. I said to myself: I have renounced all things for my heavenly Spouse, consequently he has given himself entirely to me; therefore, what is his, is mine. Then, full of confidence, I offered to the Eternal Father all the treasures of his Divine Son, as a supplement for my poverty, and I formed the intention of offering for the soul of this poor prince all the masses celebrated throughout the world."

"Then Our Blessed Lord gave me to understand that there was yet one more act of charity I could perform for him,—to offer the holy communion I was about to receive, thereby gaining the indulgence applicable to the souls in purgatory. I consented, but not without a little reluctance, for I had counted on this great feast to think a little of my own private necessities, and to apply to my soul the fruit of this indulgence; but since the Lord had ordained it otherwise, I submitted to his holy will. I have still continued to intercede for the prince with all the powers of my soul, and all the affections of my heart."

"Since this day, reverend mother, I have no longer experienced any anxiety, I feel entirely free from responsibility, and say nothing for him now except the *Laudate.*"

"I believe that my little services, united to the fervent prayers of our sisters, have procured his relief. It was undoubtly through the intercession of the most Blessed Virgin that he obtained his salvation, and through the powerful aid of our father St. Joseph that he gained his entrance into Heaven; for I think, and am even convinced, that he must have been delivered from purgatory on the feast of this great saint. However, of this my Divine Lord has given me no certainty; I adore his designs without any wish to penetrate them, for I am most unworthy."

"The prince, as is well known, came to an untimely end by a very terrible accident; he may have made a sincere act of contrition which saved him from eternal death. The mercy of God surpasseth all his works!"

Three years later, the sister received the assurance that this soul, the object of so many fervent prayers, had indeed obtained its deliverance.

On the 26th of April, 1846, she writes: "After holy communion, our Lord Jesus said to me: 'Allow yourself to be guided by the impulse of grace.' I obeyed, and my Divine Savior commenced his operation. But how shall I speak of what I beheld! O infinite goodness of my God! assist me, that thou mayst be more loved, more known and blessed on earth! 'Look!' said he suddenly to me, 'Behold him for whom you have prayed! I bring him to you to thank you for what you have done. Behold the excess of my mercy in his regard! Had I allowed him to dwell longer on the earth, he would, in his ambition, have encircled his brow with a temporal crown; and now, in Heaven, I bestow on him a crown of glory.'"

"By an intellectual view, I beheld this soul standing by the side of Jesus. 'Ah!' said I to him, 'It is Jesus, not I, whom you must thank; as for me, I am mere nothingness: it is his merits that I have offered to God for you.' The soul then said to me: 'It is to the Blessed Virgin I owe my salvation, for when I was brought before the tribunal of God, I was covered with the infinite merits of Jesus Christ; and it is through the intercession of St. Joseph that I have been delivered from purgatory.' 'Oh, most fortunate soul!' I exclaimed, 'Pray for France and pray for me; and in a transport of gratitude to the infinite mercy of

God, I repeated: Fortunate soul, pray for me; let us prostrate ourselves in prayer at the feet of our Lord Jesus Christ; pray that I may obtain the grace to fulfil my obligations to him.' Our Lord said: 'Now, he will pray for you: and I kept repeating, pray for me! But interrupting myself, I asked: 'How shall I invoke you henceforth?' He answered: 'I am called *Ferdinand*, call me *Ferdinand; Ferdinand* is my name.' It seemed to me that he thus repeated his name several times as a proof of the truth of what I beheld, for I was not aware that this was his name. He added: 'I now reign with Jesus Christ; I am crowned in Heaven.' I said to him: 'I know the mercy of God is unbounded, still I dared not hope that you had already entered into glory.' But I understood that this was only permitted by an extraordinary grace from God."

"All that I saw, heard, and understood of the excess of the divine charity toward this soul, threw me into an ecstasy of joy; my emotion vented itself in tears and sobs. But at this delicious moment, the parlor-bell rang, and as it was obedience that called me, I left our Lord Jesus to go and fulfil the duties of my office. Wishing to test the truth of what I had just experienced, I asked a sister whom I met the name of the prince in question. She answered: 'His name was Ferdinand.' Her answer impressed me deeply, for I saw in it a proof of the truth. This operation of God in my soul was the strongest I have ever experienced." An account of the extraordinary event was placed in the hands of Mgr. Morlot, who beheld therein a communication so manifestly supernatural, that he thought it his duty to write to the pious mother of the deceased, Queen Amelia, who was very uneasy over the eternal fate of her son. As can be readily conceived, the letter was a consoling balm to the heart of the distressed lady.

This extraordinary fact, so minutely made known to our Carmelite of Tours, is not without precedent, or analogy in history. A similar instance is related of the deliverance of a soul from purgatory, by the prayers and sufferings of one of the first daughters of the Visitation, Sister M. Denise de Martignat. The circumstances are detailed in the life of this religious, by Mother de Chaugy. "Our Lord one day lead the sister to the borders of purgatory, and pointed out to her the soul of a great prince whose death had occasioned much regret, and the shedding of many tears; he was a most powerful prince when on this earth, and now, more destitute than could be imagined, for during his life he had not amassed many good works, which alone constitute the wealth of eternity."

Our Lord said to her: "My daughter, you have already offered many prayers for the salvation of this soul: now behold him, and continue to pray."

This prince was killed in a duel. "But," explained the sister, "by a master-stroke of divine mercy, he received the grace to make a sincere act of contrition for his sins at the last moment, and instead of being cast into hell, which he had but too justly merited, he was condemned for a great number of years to the purifying flames of purgatory." Sr. Denise de St. Martignat offered herself as a victim to expiate the sins of this poor soul, and to relieve him of a portion of his debt. From that moment, she was afflicted by the most peculiar maladies and excruciating sufferings. Several times, the soul of the deceased appeared to her, thanking her and encouraging her to continue and suffer still more for him. Shortly before her death, the servant of God received the announcement that the soul of the prince was greatly relieved; but less happy than Mary of St. Peter, she did not know the precise moment of his final deliverance.

Another saintly practice served as a stimulus to the zeal, ever active and ingenious, which animated Sister St. Peter for the salvation of souls. The Carmelites were still living in the house on Le Place St. Gregoire, (of which we had already spoken), while awaiting the completion of their monastery. Sr. Mary of St. Peter, portress for the interior, was perpetually besieged by visitors who were desirous of receiving consolation or advice. She would fain have excused herself from these pious importunities, in order to preserve the spirit of recollection.

"These good people," said she, "felt that the little Breton nun, simple as they themselves, understood and sympathized with them in all their troubles and afflictions, seeking to encourage them to resignation by the solacing words of religion; they returned to their homes happy and contented, but soon came back to the convent with their neighbors. Notwithstanding the charity I felt for them, I nevertheless excused myself as much as possible from receiving them, in order not to fail in the spirit of silence, so necessary for a Carmelite. Our Lord, beholding my desire, gave me the means of gratifying these people and also of comforting them in their maladies, by inspiring me with the pious practice of wearing the 'Gospel of the Circumcision.' Behold in what manner I arranged this practice in conformity with what had been communicated to me on the subject."

"The devil uses every means in his power to snatch from Our Lord the inheritance won by his holy cross; and he is incessantly seeking to rob this Good Shepherd of the sheep purchased at so great a price. To prevent this ravenous wolf from approaching the sheepfold, Jesus desired, as he made me understand, that I should proclaim to all, that his sheep were marked with his Holy Name, and carried about them the Gospel announcing to all nations that the Word Incarnate was named *Jesus*. My amiable Savior made me understand the depth of virtue contained in that sacred name, the very mention of which puts the devil to flight.—Those who will have recourse to this act of piety will receive great graces.—He told me, also, to place below this Gospel, the words recalling the victory which he had gained over Satan in assuming, through love for us, the name of Jesus. This little devotion was, first of all, approved of by my superiors; their charity permitting *the Gospel of the Circumcision* to be printed, and a picture of the Infant Jesus to be engraved on the same leaf, with the initials of his adorable name. The leaf was then folded and enclosed in a small covering of woolen material on which was embroidered a cross with the Sacred Heart; it was to be worn as a medal around the neck. It also received the approbation of the Vicar General, as being in conformity with the spirit of the Church; for we see from history that the first Christians had the habit of wearing the holy Gospels."

"Our Lord told me that these pious little objects of devotion should not be sold, but that they should be distributed in his name, in order that everyone might be able to procure one easily. That he asked this alms from the community for his glory, for which he would richly compensate us, and that he, himself, would transact the business of the house. Our worthy superiors gave me permission to comply with the desire of the Divine Infant; soon a countless multitude were enrolled. They wore the gospel with great devotion, and the Infant Jesus was not slow in granting them many special graces."

"I was continually occupied in distributing these little gospels, but although I was very assiduous in the work, I could not meet the demand of all who desired them. Our good sisters then kindly offered to help me. I was charmed with this new commerce which redounded to the glory of the Holy Infant. I made a very pretty little gospel for him, which I placed round the neck of his little statue. As I have said, he told me that these little objects of devotion were not to be sold, but as many wealthy persons wished to purchase them, I placed a small purse in the hand of my little king with the following inscription thereon:

If you wish, give to Jesus; it will enable us to purchase infantile clothing for him.

"The Divine Child rewarded the good people a hundredfold for their alms, with the graces which he granted them. Quite a considerable amount was thus amassed in his little purse, with which our reverend mother purchased clothing for Jesus. By this I wish it to be understood, corporals which are linens used in the service of the holy sacrifice of the mass. The sisters of the community, by the direction of our reverend mother, prepared these corporals, which were presented to the Holy Infant with grand ceremony on the feast of Corpus Christi, and afterward distributed among the poor parishes of the diocese. We also made a trousseau for a poor infant, in whom we pictured the poverty of the Infant Jesus at his birth."

The good sister informs us, furthermore, that Our Lord asked as alms that these prayers be distributed as soon as possible; at the end of the prayers, he desired should be written: "When Jesus received his name, Satan was vanquished and disarmed. He permitted me to behold the amount of glory which accrued to him by celebrating his victory in these words, which make the demons gnash their teeth with rage. He promised that he would bless all who would wear this gospel and would defend them against the attacks of the devil."

The Lord afterward informed her, that as this grace had been drawn from his heart, that the engraving of the Sacred Heart, together with the instruments of his Passion, should be stamped on the little covering containing this gospel, which would answer the same purpose as a seal on a reliquary, which guarantees the authenticity of the relic. In honor of the five letters which form the name of Jesus, and in virtue of his five wounds, he promised to grant five special graces to all who would practice this devotion.

1st.—To preserve them from death by lightning.

2nd.—To protect them against the snares and the malice of the devil.

3rd.—To deliver them from a sudden and unprovided death.

4th.—To assist them to advance with faculty in the path of virtue.

5th.—That he would give them the grace of final perseverance."

As this last favor appeared excessive to the pious Carmelite, the following words of holy scripture occurred to her mind and reassured her: "Whoever will invoke the name of the Lord shall be saved." (Rom. X. 13.)

These little gospels required no other blessing than that given to the palms used on Palm Sunday, in commemoration of the triumphant entry of Our Lord into the city of Jerusalem.

"Whilst I was seeking," she writes, "the means of covering these little expenses,—(here she is referring to the first gospels which she had made) my Divine Master directed me to address myself to his servant, M. Dupont, and to say to him, that the Infant Jesus requested of him this work of charity as the tithe of all the benefits he had bestowed upon him; for this work was most agreeable to him. I then said to my Divine Savior: 'If you would only promise me some recompense for him, or at least some grace for his family!' To which Our Lord replied: 'His love for me is so pure that he will perform this service without offering him any inducement. For his disinterested love and devotion, I will recompense him magnificently in Heaven; as for you, you must do this little commission for me, because you are my little servant. Do not fear to ask in my Name; and you will have the same merit as if you performed the entire work yourself.'"

We can imagine with what eagerness M. Dupont responded to this request. In this, as well as in the works of piety and charity which gave him a certain eclat in the city of Tours, he proved worthy of the eulogy which the Lord was pleased to bestow on his generous love, and was well deserving the interest which the good sister manifested toward him and his family. We read in his life, that this fervent layman, with all the candor and simplicity of his ardent faith, aided the virgin of Carmel to pursue her cherished devotions, especially those in reference to the Infant Jesus. Before the little gospels had been printed, he, himself, copied them, and assisted to distribute them among the faithful; esteeming himself well repaid by the prayers which the sister promised for his daughter Henrietta, who at the time was preparing to receive her first communion.

On the feast of the most Holy Trinity, the Lord encouraged his servant anew to propagate this pious practice.

"Behold, as near as possible," said she, "that which our Lord Jesus made me understand. 'My child, be not afflicted because the work of your little gospels allows you no time to enjoy my presence, it is much better to sacrifice these consolations, that I may not be offended, for already has it been the means of preventing the commission of enormous crimes.'"

Addressing herself to the mother prioress, the sister adds: "Our Lord again informed me that with the money received for these little gospels, you might have fifty masses celebrated for his greater glory, and for the salvation of souls: and that afterward, if sufficient would be received, to pay the expenses of a new edition of the prayers of Reparation; that I should thereby recognize that there is no illusion on my part, but that it is my Divine Savior himself who has communicated with my soul."

"You are aware," continues she, "that I thought no more of asking for the reprinting of these prayers, because the archbishop thinks they cannot be easily understood; and today, Our Lord desires them for religious, that they may invoke his mercy on France, and appease his justice, so that the wicked may be confounded. I abandon these things to your better judgment, reverend mother, all that I seek is, that the holy will of God be accomplished."

The most wonderful graces were not wanting to sanction this devotion so simple, and at the same time, so ancient in the Church. The following are some of the wonderful facts which Sister Mary St. Peter herself had taken care to note down. "We shall narrate them in her own words:

"At the time of the enlistment of soldiers, several of the young men of the city, urged on by the solicitude of their mothers who feared to lose in them their stay and the support of their old age, came to me in their sorrow to seek my prayers. I advised them to wear the little gospel, and they were not, in consequence, called upon to enlist in the army. These scapulars also wrought conversions, Among others, that of a young person who was a continual source of sorrow to her parents, owing to her violent bursts of passion; but she was induced to wear a little gospel; this alone was sufficient to vanquish the demon, to whose influence she had so long yielded; she soon asked pardon of her parents and went to confession. A hardened sinner, reduced to the last extremities, obstinately refused to receive the sacraments: his venerable pastor, saddened on beholding this sheep of his flock about to become the prey of the infernal wolf, had recourse to the little gospel, one of which he placed at the foot of the sick man's bed, the latter was immediately touched, asked for the priest and died a good Christian."

"Another, who for many years had abandoned the practice of his religious duties, was inspired to wear the little gospel, and to recite the prayer attached thereto: from that moment, he felt urged by a powerful impulse of grace, soliciting him unceasingly to return to God. For several months he resisted the call, but finally, yielding to the power of the Holy Name of Jesus, he threw himself at the feet of a confessor; his perfect conversion filled with joy those who had for so many years grieved over his past conduct."

"Many persons have experienced the marvelous effects of this salutary devotion during their maladies or corporal infirmities. A little girl had been suffering from a terrible fever, which had reduced her to the last extremity; all were expecting the angel of death, when her uncle tied around her neck the little gospel; they recited the prayers during nine days and the child was perfectly restored. For seven years, a lady had suffered from an ulcer in her throat which, at times, prevented her from taking her proper nourishment, she had difficulty even in swallowing the holy communion; many different remedies had been given her, but all to no purpose.—Having put on the little gospel, she was cured so promptly, that those who took care of her were greatly astonished, until she made known to them the holy remedy to which she owed her restoration."

"Agreat number of women in childbirth have been miraculously delivered by this little gospel; upon these especially it has operated the most extraordinary effects."

"A little girl, to whom we gave a gospel of the Holy Name of Jesus, fell and was seriously injured. When she was picked up, she was unable to make any movement; her disconsolate parents feared that her limbs were broken, and wished to send for the doctor immediately, but the child cried out: "No, no, don't go for the doctor, but give me my little relic, the good Jesus can heal me!" The little gospel was put round her neck, and she immediatelv ceased crying and fell into a profound sleep. On awaking, she was so completely cured that she did not feel the slightest effect of her fall. Thus was the faith of this child recompensed; all who believe like her shall not hope in vain.".

"Many missionaries carried this gospel of the Holy Name of Jesus to foreign lands; I shall give, in conclusion an account of the conversion of a great sinner."

"On the 26th of December 1845, a person weeping bitterly, came to recommend to our prayers a man reduced to the last extremity. 'There is no use speaking to him of the sacraments,' said she, 'for he is furious.' We gave her a little gospel to be placed round the neck of the sick man, with the prayers to be recited in honor of the Holy Name of Jesus. This lady full of faith and zeal, having learned that some men were going to sit up all night with him, begged them to try and put the little gospel round his neck, and to recite the prayers attached thereto. They acquiesced and were so successful in their mission that the obstinate invalid was suddenly changed, and appearing calmer, they proposed sending for the priest. He assented, much to their surprise, and after his confession, received the Holy Viaticum, and died in the best disposition. Satan, furious on beholding the escape of his prey, in revenge turned all his rage against me. God alone knows what I endured at the moment of the death of this man; for two hours, I was surrounded by a legion of demons, I was as if possessed. I seemed to hear their horrible voices soliciting me by their most seductive language; never have I had a similar combat to sustain, but the Divine Spouse of my soul fortified me by his power; and his grace rendered me victorious. I ran and threw myself at the feet of our reverend mother who was terrified at the pallor of my countenance. I discovered to her the agony of my poor heart and she had the charity to console me; when she gave me her benediction, I was immediately relieved and passed the rest of the night in peace."

These prodigies have continued even in our days. We shall only cite one more example, which happened at Tours quite recently. A foreigner had long neglected his religious duties and had even shown very little respect for our holy religion during his public career. He was finally attacked by a mortal malady, and those interested in his salvation beheld him with sorrow, refusing to listen to all the advances made on this subject. Finally, a lady, who had for a considerable time conversed with him without making any impression, adroitly slipped under his chin a little gospel, and prepared to depart. She had not gone from the door of the sick-room before the invalid called her back saying: "However, I do not wish to appear before God without having set in order my accounts with him; send for a priest, if you please." From that moment he was entirely changed, and thought only of his salvation, and of the best means of repairing lost time by a sincere and public repentance.

It was in this manner that our Divine Lord sustained his servant, by giving her the occasion of making a trial, and so to say, a preparatory test of that which was to be more largely accomplished by means of the great Work of Reparation. By the Little Gospel, he glorified his name, the blessed Name of Jesus; he healed the sick, he brought back sinners to the true fold. By the Work of Reparation, he will glorify the Name of his Father, this Holy Name of the Eternal God, outraged by blasphemers. He will cure the sick, save the sinner, and convert France, that nation formerly the glory of Christian Europe, now gangrened even to the heart with godlessness and impiety. But mercy shall be extended to her, a child of the cloister shall point out the path of salvation, and France shall once more be reinstated in all her glorious privileges. Such is the object of the noble mission confided to the humble daughter of Carmel.

12

THE HOLY FACE

**"I seek another Veronica to soothe and adore my
Holy Face, which has so few worshippers!"**
(Words of Our Lord)

The spiritual delight which Mary of St. Peter received from the meditation on the Holy Name of Jesus, consoled her somewhat for the delay made in the propagation of the Work of Reparation. Our Lord had made no allusion to the subject from the 19th of November 1844.

But on the 17th of June 1845, the Divine Master once more referred to this theme so dear to his Sacred Heart and encouraged his servant to have an interview with the archbishop. Nothing less than a command from such a source, could have compelled this humble and timid maiden to place herself in direct communication with a Prince of the Church; for she was now to entreat him most earnestly in the name of God, to establish this Work; a serious undertaking in his eyes from which he always seemed to recoil.

She writes: "I then suffered an interior martyrdom which God alone knows; I could take no nourishment; existence was a burden. My heavenly Spouse told me not to fear speaking to Monseigneur; that he himself, would accompany me and suggest what I should say. My divine Savior kept his promise; for I spoke to this worthy prelate with the simplicity of a child, conversing with the respect due to his dignity without being over-awed."

The archbishop consented to pay a visit to the sister, whom he already held in great esteem, because of her rare virtue. When she came into his presence, she fell on her knees and kissed his feet; she then implored him to finish the Work which he had so happily begun for the glory of the Holy Name of God, explaining to him the manner in which the Lord urged her to further his designs. The prelate replied: "My child, I desire with all my heart, to establish this Work, and to give it all the publicity it merits; but this is an undertaking of some difficulty; you cannot see all the obstacles. If at present there is so much difficulty in obliging the people to perform their obligations of precept, what would be said of me if I were to propose practices of piety hitherto unheard of? Would not the wicked be excited to blaspheme God more than ever? Commend our present embarrassment to God, and pray fervently for me; ask for new lights; if the Lord deign to enlighten you further, you must make it known to me." He added, as if to tranquillize her with regard to her interior dispositions:"My child, that which you experience bears not the impress of an illusion; no, sister, quite the contrary; I recognize therein the hidden workings of God. We have made inquiries and have ascertained that many persons have had the same inspiration as you on the subject of this Work of Reparation, which now exists in Italy, and there is a movement in its favor in many dioceses of France. It is my desire that pious souls embrace this devotion, but that you, should offer yourself to God as a *Victim*. Offer your penances and all your works as a sacrifice of Reparation for the Church and for France; unite yourself to our Lord Jesus Christ in the most Blessed Sacrament of the altar, to render through him honor, praise, and glory to the three divine persons of the adorable Trinity; endeavor to stay the arm of the Almighty, that it may not fall heavily upon us. Address yourself to the Sacred Heart of Mary, and offer to the Eternal Father, through the hands of this august Mother, the most Precious Blood of her Divine Son, his sufferings and all his merits; and I hope we shall thus appease the anger of the Almighty."

The archbishop continued his conversation with the sister, exhorting her particularly to glorify Jesus in the most Blessed Sacrament of the altar. "Every Thursday," said he, "make an honorable amend to God: Friday, recite the Litany of the Passion, and on Saturday, that of the Blessed Virgin. When Our Lord inspires you, my child, you may recite the prayers of Reparation: but I prefer you to recite more ordinary prayers." The pious sister then told him, that sometimes she feared her own imagination interfered with the operation of God;but the prelate reassured her again, saying: "Since you do not tenaciously cling to your own opinion, and that you remain within the limits prescribed by obedience, abandoning these things to the judgment of your superiors, you should remain perfectly at ease." In conclusion, he said: "I find all that you have related to me very excellent; beg the Lord to send me the light of the Holy Ghost; and do all things for the glory of God."

"These counsels were as a healing balm poured over my soul; they filled me with consolation, for my confessor had declined giving an opinion on what had transpired in my soul regarding the Work of Reparation, saying that the archbishop had received from the Holy Ghost the power of pronouncing judgment, and that I should submit to his decision. Then I was more than ever convinced of the divine will, and although Monseigneur had not given me much hope that he would establish this work, as he foresaw many grave difficulties, yet this did not prevent me from hoping that all obstacles would be removed when the time appointed by the decrees of Divine Providence would arrive. The following are my reasons for this conclusion:If the communications, which I have received from God in regard to the Reparation, are not illusions, as he who has received the grace from on High to judge, has declared, then this work will most assuredly be established, for the word of God is all-powerful; if, on the contrary, Monseigneur had declared that they were illusions, I would have abandoned the Work entirely, for by the grace of God, I have always had more confidence in the decisions of my superiors, than in the interior communications which I believed to have received from God; in the latter, I might be deceived, but faith can never be deceived, for our Divine Master has said of superiors: 'He who heareth you, heareth me;' therefore, we cannot err in obeying our superiors. These words of the Gospel have always struck me forcibly; they are engraved on my heart; and in the practice of them, I have received wonderful graces with the assistance of those who have had the direction of my soul." These solid reflections give us a wonderful insight of the soul of our humble and obedient Carmelite and will corroborate the opinion of the venerable archbishop concerning her revelations. No one is ignorant of the fact that in matters of revelation or heavenly communications, the touchstone is humility and a perfect submission of judgment to the decisions of those appointed by the Church as her immediate representatives.

Sometime after, Mgr. Morlot consented to give his approbation to the prayers of Reparation, and after having indicated the corrections which he deemed necessary, granted the permission to have them printed. "But," continued she, "this was not immediately done. Our Lord gave me to understand that if the prayers alone were printed without a notice on the object of the work to be established, it would not be sufficient, because the faithful should be informed of the designs of his will, in order to awaken their interest in the Work, and to induce them to recite the prayers; and then we shall see them adopted by a multitude of pious souls who will recite the prayers of Reparation with the same avidity as the bees seek the flowers of the field. He made me also understand that these prayers would obtain great graces for the conversion of sinners."

She then speaks of the work on blasphemy, entitled the "Association of Prayers," composed by l'Abbe Salmon. The author adds a few reflections on the profanation of the days consecrated to God; then followed the prayers of Reparation. There was also subjoined the "Little Office of the Holy Name of God," which had been compiled with the aid of two venerable canons, friends of the Carmelites. The expenses of publication were defrayed mostly by the contributions of M. Dupont.

"Monseignor," continued the sister, "approved of this little work which soon met with great success; and in a short time, more than 25,000 copies of the prayers of Reparation had been distributed. From the different cities of France application came to Tours, for authority to propagate this devotion for the glory of the Holy Name of God, and the prayers were recited everywhere with great devotion. In reference to this subject, Our Lord told me that this new harmony appeased his anger; but that he wished an Association established *according to the manner indicated.*"

In conformity with the exhortations of the archbishop, she began to importune the Lord to deign to grant her new light on the establishment of his Work. But it pleased the Divine Master to lead her once more in the path of trial. She could no longer think of anything but her sins; she believed herself to be but the phantom of a Carmelite, far removed from what she should be in reality, and that her sins were the cause of this Work remaining incomplete. With a heart laden with sorrow, she besought Our Lord to choose another instrument more worthy than she for the accomplishment of his designs. Then, regarding herself as very culpable before Grod, she made a review of conscience with her confessor, and took the resolution to lead, in the future, a life more in conformity with the knowledge she had received of her own misery and nothingness. This was only the beginning of a new series of struggles and interior combats. She was assailed by a thousand temptations, to which was added the privation of all sensible consolation; it seemed that her soul was not even in the state of sanctifying grace; she was reduced to a state of agony, experiencing disgust and bitterness in the very devotions which formerly had been so cherished. She scarcely dared receive holy communion.

One day, when she was hesitating to receive holy communion without having previously exposed her sad condition to her superior, the following happy thought presented itself to her mind: that this Bread of the strong would give her courage. While awaiting the mass to begin, with new faith she took her crucifix, and recollecting that Our Lord had told her that the praise contained in the "Golden Arrow" would wound his Heart in a most delicious manner, she pronounced the formula ten times in succession, then resolved to present herself at the holy Table and receive the Blessed Eucharist in reparation for the blasphemies uttered against the Divine Majesty of God. Nothing more was needed to touch the heart of the Divine Spouse. He tenderly drew to himself this soul who, in spite of her desolation, had come to unite herself to him, in order to indemnify his heavenly Father for the outrages offered him.

"Oh, how good is God," exclaimed the sister. "How great is his mercy! After having received this God of love in holy communion, I said to him with faith: 'O heavenly Physician! I remit my soul into thy hands; and immediately my adorable Savior made me experience the effect of my prayer, drawing me to himself alone that I might forget all my sorrows. He told me it was his express will that I should persevere in the exercises of Reparation in spite of all the efforts of the devil who was trying to fill me with disgust and repugnance, because he wished to annihilate this work, were it in his power."

The Masters of the spiritual life have remarked that the Word Made Flesh, in his intimate relations with souls of election, has unexpected and sudden times of visitation, causing them in one moment to pass from tears to joy, from temptation to peace, from the most obscure darkness to the most brilliant light. Mary of St. Peter experienced this in the present case; as if to compensate her for the painful state which she has just described, Our Lord favored her with one of his most consoling and most fruitful communications. The Work of Reparation through the Holy Face was suddenly revealed to her. She was transported in spirit to the road leading to Calvary. "There," said she, "Our Lord gave me to behold in a most vivid manner, the pious Veronica, who, with her veil, wiped his adorable Face covered with spittle, dust, sweat, and blood. My divine Savior gave me to understand that the wicked by their blasphemy renew all the outrages once offered to his divine Face; these blasphemies, poured forth against the Divinity, like the vile spittle of the Jews, disfigure the Face of Our Lord, who offered himself as a victim for sinners.

Then he told me that I must imitate the zeal of the pious Veronica who so courageously passed through the crowd of rough soldiers to offer him some relief, and whom he gave me for my protectress and model. By endeavoring to offer reparation for blasphemy, we render Christ the same service as this heroic woman, and he looks upon those who act thus, with the same complacency as if they had performed this act during his Passion. I observed that Our Lord had much love for this holy woman. For this reason, he said that he desired to see her particularly honored in our monastery, and he invited me to ask any grace that we wished, in the name of the service rendered him by Veronica."

It was the first time Our Lord spoke to his faithful servant of his Holy Face, and that he proposed the example of this noble Jewess, of whom tradition preserves an immortal souvenir. The statement is clear and succinct. The marvelous economy of the Reparation for Blasphemy is here presented entirely in its germ. We shall behold it bud forth and blossom in the succeeding revelations.

After relating the preceding facts, our Carmelite adds:

"The effects of this communication in my soul were so marvelous, that I could not but admire the power and condescension of Our Lord. Before receiving this communication, I was in an abyss of sorrow; and after having partaken of this Bread of Life, I was as if resuscitated from death, and my soul was dilated with joy; I went to seek our reverend mother to inform her of what the Divine Master had just communicated to me concerning his Holy Face, in regard to the Work of Reparation. I said to her: 'Reverend Mother, Our Lord promised to grant any grace asked for through the intercession of the pious Veronica. What shall I ask for you?' I felt interiorly urged to propose this question to our reverend mother, for Our Lord assured me that I would be heard; and I thought that if he granted the favor proposed, it would be a proof of the truth of the last communication I believed to have received. Our mother replied: 'If God desire that we should soothe his Divine Face, and if he be disposed to grant us a grace in consideration of the services of the pious Veronica, the favor which I desire you to ask is, that he would have the goodness to veil the faces of his spouses, who will be exposed to the eyes of seculars, if the ground adjoining our garden be sold to strangers; therefore, intercede with him to obtain it for us; if he grant you this grace, your superiors will have a visible proof of the spirit which conducts you.'"

The mother superior, Mary of the Incarnation, was at that time occupied with the construction of the new monastery on the Rue des Ursulines. On one side of the enclosure, there was a piece of ground which commanded a view of the Carmelites' garden, a great inconvenience, as can easily be understood for cloistered religious, who by their rule, should be sheltered from the curiosity of the world. With the gayety and apparent indifference with which she generally spoke to her spiritual daughter, the reverend mother held the above conversation to which we have just listened. The sister obeyed the order of the prioress and began a novena in honor of the Holy Face; but said she naively: "Thou knowest well, my Divine Lord, that I only desire this ground for thy sake and for the glory of thy Holy Name."

Before obtaining possession of the ground, there seemed to be insurmountable obstacles to be overcome; for this reason, the sister became importunate in her entreaties to the Lord, knowing that its acquisition would be a visible sign of her mission; we shall notice in what manner this grace was granted.

For the present, let us listen to her describing the manner in which she rendered homage to the Holy Face, from the time she received the first communication. "I experience a special protection from the pious Veronica, and I am continually occupied in the adoration of the august and most Holy Face of Our Savior. I feel that my soul is in the hands of God, like an instrument of which he makes use at his own good pleasure. I felt urged during those days, to expose to Jesus that which our worthy archbishop had suggested to me concerning the work of Reparation for Blasphemy when I had the privilege of speaking to him. Yesterday, after holy communion, I conjured Our Lord to deign to give me more light on this subject, saying to him: 'Thou knowest, my Lord and Savior, that it is for Monseigneur I make this request, and in virtue of holy obedience.' But my Divine Savior did not judge it necessary to answer me. He only concentrated the powers of my soul most profoundly in the contemplation of his adorable Face."

On the 27th of October, from the moment she entered the choir for the morning meditation, the Lord communicated himself to her anew, according to his ordinary custom, and as if in answer to the prayer addressed to him in the name of the archbishop, he exposed his designs on the Work of Reparation.

"It is at the present moment, reverend mother," said she, "that I stand in need of the light of the Holy Ghost to direct my pen, for I know not how to write that which I have seen and heard. I shall relate it as carefully as possible."

"Our Lord, having concentrated the powers of my soul in his Divine Heart, applied me to the contemplation of his adorable Face; he made me understand by internal rays of light, that this holy and august Face, offered to us for our adoration, is the mirror of the ineffable perfections comprised in the most Holy Name of God."

It is impossible for me to express this intellectual view, unless in the words of the Apostle St. Paul, 'God is the head of his Christ.'* (Cor. XI 3.) Which words I have since read; they struck me most forcibly, for I recognized in this thought what had been communicated to me supernaturally."

"I understood that as the Sacred Heart of Jesus is the visible object offered to our admiration to represent his immense love in the most Blessed Sacrament of the altar, likewise, in the Work of Reparation, the Face of Our Lord is the sensible object offered for the adoration of the associates, to repair the outrages of blasphemers who attack the Divinity, of which it is the figure, the mirror and the image. In virtue of this adorable Face, offered to the Eternal Father, we can appease his anger and obtain the conversion of blasphemers." The co-relation existing between the devotion to the Sacred Heart and that of the Holy Face could not have been better expressed. The Holy Face is a picture of the Divinity outraged by the opprobrium of blasphemers, as the Sacred Heart is a picture of the immense love of Jesus in the Holy Eucharist.

The sister was also favored with another light. "Our Lord" said she, "showed me that the Church, his Spouse, is his mystical body, and that religion is the face of this body; then he showed me this face as the butt of all the scoffs coming from the enemies of his Holy Name; and I saw that blasphemers and sectarians renew in this holy face, all the opprobrium of the Passion. I beheld, also, by this divine light, that the wicked, in uttering profane words and in blaspheming the Holy Name of God, spat in the Divine Face of Our Lord and covered it with filth; that all the blows aimed at the Church and at Religion by sectarians, were the renewal of the numberless buffets which our Divine Lord received in his Holy Face, and that these unfortunate wretches drew forth perspiration in drops of blood from his Divine Face, by thus maliciously destroying his works."

The word *religion,* employed here to signify the face of the mystic body of Jesus Christ, is easily explained. We may understand it to mean the doctrine of Jesus Christ, which teaches us what we are obliged to believe and practice, and the worship which we must render to Clod. Religion, in this sense of the word, is the face of the Church, because her doctrine renders visible the features by which we recognize her even as we distinguish and recognize a person by the features of his countenance. This face of the Church is, at the same time, the Face of Jesus Christ; for the Church can have but one head, which is Jesus Christ, and consequently but one face which is likewise that of Jesus. Finally, in a mystic sense, it can be said that the doctrine of Jesus Christ, that is the Christian religion, is as much his face as that of the Church, because it is by this doctrine that we recognize him as he is himself. Therefore, the expression inspired to the sister, justifies itself, and we can but admire the nicety and depth of the word.

Nothing, therefore, could be more conformable to the spirit of Reparation which Our Lord proposes to himself. In our days, more than ever before, the face of his mystic body, the Church, is the butt of all the outrages of his enemies. Sectarians vomit forth their blasphemies into his face, as so much ignoble filth ; they launch at her a thousand injurious invectives, even falsehoods which recall to mind the buffets received by the Savior during his Passion; thus do they seek to destroy his labors; and after the lapse of centuries since the time he passed in the world, 'doing good,' they exult in their endeavors to overthrow what he has established, and to counteract the fruits of the salvation brought to man. This face of the Church, also, stands in need of being consoled and comforted, and we are not surprised that Christ has repeated to his servant, the request already made in favor of his Spouse, placed like him on the road to Calvary.

"Then, at this sight," she continued, "our Lord Jesus Christ said to me: 'I seek for more Veronicas to console and adore my Divine Face, which has but few worshippers.' He made me understand anew that all those who devoted themselves to this work of Reparation, would perform the same office as Veronica. After which he addressed to me the following consoling words: 'I give you my Holy Face as a recompense for all the services you have rendered me for the past two years; you have done but little, it is true, but your heart has conceived great designs; therefore, I give you this Face in presence of my Eternal Father, in virtue of the Holy Ghost, and in sight of

the angels and saints; I present you this gift by the hands of my Holy Mother, and of St. Veronica, who will teach you how to honor it.' Our Lord continued: 'By this Face, you will perform prodigies.'"

She understood that this precious gift was not for herself alone, but that it was to become the distinctive symbol of the projected work. "For," said she, "my Divine Master manifested his desire to see his Holy Face offered as the appropriate object of devotion to his children, the members of the Association of Reparation for Blasphemy, and he seemed to invite me to reveal his adorable Face under this aspect." She undoubtly felt, at the same time, the excellence of the grace accorded her by Our Lord. "It was, he told me, the greatest grace he could have given me after that of the sacraments, and for which he had prepared and cultivated the soil of my soul by the interior trials which I had suffered a short time previously. I also learned that he deputed St. Louis, king of France, protector of this Work of Reparation, because of his zeal for the glory of the Name of God; and tor protectress, he designated the pious Veronica, in gratitude for the services rendered him on the Toad to Calvary."

"After having favored me with these remarkable revelations regarding the Reparation for blasphemy, he added: 'Those who do not now recognize in this, my work, close their eyes, and will not see.'"

"Toward the conclusion, I felt a little uneasiness with regard to the veracity of this revelation, because of its length; but Our Lord assured me, saying that he had many means at his disposal by which to manifest himself to souls, that he accommodated himself to my feebleness, and that I had already experienced that he had communicated himself to me before in this sweet and peaceful manner. He was as a tender Father giving me his orders and informing me of his desires; but for this purpose, it was necessary that my soul should not be disturbed by passion of any kind, neither of joy or pain, which might cause agitation and impede his communications. When by his pure bounty, he condescended to make himself understood, all passed so sweetly and impressed me in such a manner, that I could only apply myself to that which my Divine Master, in the excess of his bounty, was pleased to communicate."

"He had promised after my admission into religion, that if I would make him a perfect act of self-abandonment, with all my merits, for the accomplishment of his designs, that he himself would conduct my soul in his ways. I can here testify, to the glory of this amiable Shepherd, that he conducts me step by step as one of his sheep, notwithstanding my unworthiness; he leads me at will, to graze now in one pasture, then in another; sometimes in delicious valleys, again in sandy deserts, according to the necessity of the spiritual health of his poor little sheep. — I have thought it might not be useless to make known in a few words this conduct of our Lord in my regard, that the communications, which I believe I have received from my Divine Master, may the more easily be credited. May his Holy Name be blessed for having taken so much care of a miserable sinner!"

(*May there not be, in effect, a mysterious sense applicable to the devotion of the Holy Face in these words of the Apostle: *Caput Christi Deus?* (God is the head of his Christ.) May we not infer that the word, Caput, (head), signifies not only the authority God possesses over Jesus Christ considered as man, but that the *head* of the Savior, taken in its literal signification, expresses in a particular manner the figure of the Divine Majesty?

What favors this interpretation is the unity of idea contained in the passages in which these words are found, and the conclusion drawn by the Apostle. Jesus Christ is the head of mankind, as man is the head of woman, and as God is the head of Jesus Christ. If it were here only a question of the power which God possesses over the humanity of Jesus Christ, Jesus Christ overman, and man over woman, it would suffice to conclude, that woman ought to be submissive to man, man to Jesus Christ, even as Our Lord himself is submissive to his Father.

But St. Paul goes still further. He desires that man should respect Jesus Christ, his chief, his head, by uncovering his head when- at prayer. That woman should veil her head when praying, for man is her chief. We observe here an idea of dignity attached to the word chief, or head, taken in its literal or physical sense: dignity of man as head of woman; dignity of Jesus Christ, the chief of mankind, dignity and majesty of God in the august head of Jesus Christ.

Still better, we may infer the dignity of the adorable head of our Lord from one of the following passages in which St. Paul says: "Man should not cover his head, being the image and glory of God." True, the sacred text simply says, that man is the *image* and the *glory* of God, without particularly mentioning the head; but according to this, why forbid him to cover his head, if not because this *image* and *glory* reside principally in the head? Now, if the head of man be worthy of so much dignity, with how much more reason should we not consider the august head of Jesus Christ as the picture and the emblem of the Divine Majesty, and his Holy Face as the image and the glory of God?)

The above is found at the end of Sr. St. Peter's writings. It reveals to us an extended horizon of information and light on the devotion to the most Holy Face of Our Lord Jesus Christ, and is its own commendation

13

VERONICA AND THE GOOD THIEF

**"Two persons have rendered invaluable service to
our Divine Lord during his Passion: Veronica on
the road to Calvary, in offering her veil to wipe and
soothe his Adorable Face; the Good Thief on the cross,
acknowledging and defending his Divinity."
(Words of the Sister)**

Two days after the feast of the apostles, Simon and Jude, the heavenly Master
continued, during the evening meditation, to instruct Sr. Mary St. Peter on the
new subject which had been presented to her contemplation.

"Our Lord," said she, "deigned to abase himself, and hold converse with my ungrateful
and sinful soul. That which he revealed to me will, I think, reverend mother, give you
much pleasure to learn. It was with difficulty I could persuade myself that he had granted
me such a great favor as that of presenting me with the gift of his Holy Face. Therefore, I
besought him to give me a visible proof of the invisible grace which I believe I had received
from his divine mercy; it was perhaps in proof of its reality that he communicated to me
what I am now about to relate." "Having taken for the subject of my meditation, the
treason of Judas, I reflected with sorrow on the enormity of the outrage offered to the
Sacred Face of Our Lord by a kiss so perfidious; and it seemed to me that the Divine Master
invited me to kiss the likeness of his Holy Face with love, in a spirit of reparation. After
having offered several acts of praise, I felt that Our Lord was attracting me to himself;
I obeyed this secret action of grace, and my amiable Savior deigned to give me some

instructions on the excellence of the gift he had bestowed on me, in presenting me his adorable Face; and he again had the goodness to accommodate himself graciously to the weakness of my intellect by a simple comparison, saying: 'As in an earthly kingdom we can procure all that we desire by having coin stamped with the image of the king, so also with the precious gift of my humanity, which is my adorable Face, you will obtain in the kingdom of heaven, all that your heart can desire.'"

"These divine lights or heavenly illuminations, which, for want of capacity, I am forced to express by means of such feeble terms in trying to have them thoroughly understood threw me into an ecstasy of joy, and I experienced something interiorly which it is impossible to describe. I besought my Divine Master to instruct me and to render what I beheld a little more intelligible to my poor comprehension, for the powers of my soul were as if paralyzed."

The idea of the "piece of coin" filled the sister with joy and confidence. Naturally enough her thoughts reverted to the ground contiguous to the monastery garden which commanded a view of the interior of the house; the same lot of land which the mother prioress had told her to ask of Our Lord. "It seemed to me," said she, "that I was to purchase it by offering this Holy Face, and our Lord Jesus informed me that before the expiration of another year, we would be in possession of the ground desired; of this he assured me and added, that I must not be anxious how it would come about."

"In reality, the affair which seemed to be despaired of, was quite suddenly brought before our notice. The proprietor, who hitherto could not be induced to sell, came voluntarily to offer his land on the most favorable conditions; the contract was concluded, and strange to relate, a few days after having affixed his signature thereto, he died very unexpectedly."

Though afflicted at the sudden death of this good baron, the sister, nevertheless, offered thanks to God for the benefit obtained. "This favor filled me with consternation, for I regarded it as a tangible proof of the gift I had received, that of the Holy Face; and I tremble at the thought of the account which God will demand of me, if I know not how to improve this divine talent for his glory and the salvation of souls."

At the termination of these communications which unveil to Christian piety so vast and so luminous a horizon, Sister St. Peter had an interior vision on the same subject, October 30th, which sublime conceptions she expressed in the following terms: "Remember, O

my soul, the instruction which thy celestial Spouse has given thee to-day on his adorable
Face! Remember that this divine Chief represents the Father who is from all eternity, that
the mouth of this Holy Face is a figure of the Divine Word, engendered by the Father, and
that the eyes of this mysterious Face represent the reciprocal love of the Father and the Son;
for these eyes have but one and the same light, the same knowledge, producing the same
love, which is the Holy Ghost. In his beautiful silken hair contemplate the infinitude of
the adorable perfections of the most Holy Trinity; in this majestic head, the most precious
portion of the sacred humanity of thy Savior, contemplate the image of the unity of God.
This, then, is the adorable and mysterious Face of the Savior, which blasphemers have
the temerity to cover with opprobrium: thus they renew the sufferings of his Passion, by
attacking the divinity of which it is the image."

A number of special communications, rapidly succeeding each other, will develop and
explain these consoling truths. Our Lord, to manifest the propriety of the choice he made
of his Holy Face, as the principal object of these reparatory adorations, declared to Mary
of St. Peter that he gave her this Sacred Face that she might comfort and soothe him by
her homage and the odor of her praises, then he adds: "According to the diligence you will
manifest in repairing my image disfigured by blasphemers, so will I have the same care in
repairing your soul which has been disfigured by sin. I will imprint thereon my image,
and I will render it as beautiful as when it came forth from the baptismal font. Abandon
yourself, then, to my good pleasure, and be disposed to suffer everything necessary to
restore this image to its pristine beauty. Be not troubled if you experience sadness and
darkness, for these have the same effect as the somber hues in a picture which only throw
out the more brilliant. There are those who possess the art of restoring health to the body,
but the Creator alone has the power of restoring the beauty of the soul. I have given you
the knowledge of this Work of Reparation, I have shown you its excellence, and now I
promise you the recompense. Oh, could you but behold the beauty of my face! But your
eyes are yet too weak."

"On the 6th of November, she received a new communication on the subject of the Holy
Face in regard to the Work of the Reparation. The Savior makes use of the soul of his
servant as a channel through which to reach the souls of men redeemed by his Precious
Blood. He declared to her that he wished to make her understand the virtue of his adorable
Face, to restore the image of God in the souls who have effaced it by sin. "He made me
observe the power which this Holy Face exercised over his unfaithful apostle, St. Peter,

rendering him penitent by one glance. Jesus cast upon him one look, and Peter wept bitterly. By an illumination from on High, I perceived that this adorable Face is, as it were, the seal of the Divinity, having the power to impress itself on the souls of those who apply to themselves this image of God; it is this sight which causes me to salute the Holy Face, in these words:"

"I salute thee, I adore and I love thee, O most amiable Face of my Jesus, my well-beloved, most adorable seal of the Divinity! I give myself to thee with all the strength and power of my soul, and I very humbly beseech thee to renew in us the image of God."

"Very reverend mother, if these communications have come from heaven, this work is verily the Work of the Reparation; for man is invited to repair the outrages committed against God, and by a return of love, God promises to repair his image in man's soul in virtue of his adorable Face. What a mystery of love! Let us then relieve and soothe this august Face of our Lord, disfigured by numberless blasphemies, and our Divine Master will efface from our souls the filth and hideousness of sin. This is what Our Lord has imparted to me; it seems that in thus discovering to us the virtue and power of his Holy Face, he has grand designs of mercy over the souls of mankind."

"We have in this precious gift an infallible means of appeasing the wrath of God the Father, irritated against blasphemers; we shall beg him to cast a glance at the Face of his Divine Son, and the thunderbolts of justice will fall harmlessly from his hands. O God, our protector, look upon us and cast thine eyes on the Face of thy Christ!"

Our humble Carmelite sets a just appreciation on the means offered man to stay the arrows of divine justice. From the beginning of the year following, the Lord gave her new lights, and confirmed her in the mission of mercy which he had already confided to her.

On the 5th of January 1846, she wrote: "Our Lord gave me to understand that the ground which we have bought from his heavenly Father by the offering of his Holy Face, is a figure of the patrimony for the living we are to purchase for a multitude of souls, with the mystic document of this adorable Face. Then the divine Pastor presented me a flock of sheep, telling me that he appointed me their shepherdess: he made me understand that these poor sheep had been bitten by the serpent, and were poisoned with the venom of blasphemy; that I must lead them to graze on the pastures in the realms of his divine mysteries, that there they might be healed, and that I should place them in the adorable

wounds of his sacred body, marking them with the sacred effigy of his Holy Face. He
foretold that I would undergo much suffering, because this flock of blasphemers was
in a special manner under the guidance of the Prince of Darkness. The Lord gives me
to understand that Lucifer willingly abandoned to his subordinates the charge of the
other troops of sinners, as for instance, the lewd, the intemperate, the avaricious, but the
blasphemers, he kept as his favorite flock. It is he, continued the Savior, who has caused
you to have so much repugnance for this Work of Reparation, but fear not! St. Michael
and the holy angels will protect you; with my cross which I give you for your shepherd's
crook, you will become a terror to Hell. He made me understand that he had withdrawn
me from the world and called me to inhabit his holy house, to accomplish this mission.
And as I expressed a certain anxiety, regarding the truth of the communication I had just
received, being always afraid of an illusion, he said to me: 'Be tranquil. Satan has too great
a horror of the cross to make use of it in his operations.'"

"In one of my meditations, the date of which I have forgotten, our Divine Lord chided
me for my negligence in not praying for blasphemers, and showed me how I had given
occasion to the evil spirit to tempt me to doubt of his mercy; it seemed that he said: 'Did I
not give you an example to pray for blasphemers when I was suspended on the cross?' He
likewise declared to me that he had wonderful designs of mercy on this class of sinners,
that he wished to make use of me as an instrument for the accomplishment of his work.
He made me understand that this reparatory work embraced not only reparation for
blasphemy properly so called, but for all manner of invectives uttered against the Church;
however, it is specially applied to blasphemy against the Name of God."

Thus, is verified what we have previously stated of that kind of blasphemy professing to
be doctrinal, which attacks religion and the Church. This is the real, the direct object
of the Work of Reparation; for all the invectives hurled against the Church or religious
worship, are at the same time an outrage offered the Name of God thrice holy. The year
1846 had set in, and nothing in the exterior course of events gave any indication whatever
that the desires of the sister were soon to be put into execution. On the 23rd of January,
she received a communication which she relates in these words: "I can no longer restrain
my tears at the thought of what Jesus has just told me after communion; behold the
terrible words of this meek Savior: 'The aspect of France has become hideous in the eyes
of my Father, provoking his justice; offer him therefore the Face of his Son, in whom he
has placed all his complaisance, in order to draw down upon France his forgiveness, else

she will be severely punished.' There lies her salvation, that is, in the Face of the Savior. 'Behold,' added he, 'the wonderful proof of my goodness towards France! Yet she repays me with ingratitude!'"

Affrighted, the pious sister added: "Is it really thou, my Lord, who communicates this to me?" Our Lord replied: "Would you have been able to procure it yourself in your last communion? I have purposely left you in profound darkness for eight days, to make you discern that now it is my operation which you experience." Docile and convinced, she immediately began to say this prayer which she repeated continually: "Eternal Father, we offer thee the adorable Face of this thy well-beloved Son, for the honor and glory of thy Holy Name and for the salvation of France."

"My poor heart," said she, "is wounded by a sword of sorrow. Our Lord directed my attention anew to the contemplation of his sacred head crowned with thorns, and to his adorable Face outraged by the enemies of God and of the Church. Once more I heard his sorrowful plaints, and my aimable Savior told me, that in our community he sought for souls to repair the outrages inflicted on him, and to heal his wounds by applying to them the wine of compassion and the oil of charity. He informed me that if the members of the community devoted themselves to this exercise of reparation, he would bestow upon them a kiss of love which would be a pledge of the eternal union; new and consoling promise, most worthy of this gracious and merciful Savior. Such a favor responds most admirably to the desire of every Christian soul and to the aspirations of mankind in general, expressed by the Spouse in the Canticle when she asks of the divine Word to 'come forth' by the Incarnation from the bosom of his Father, in order that she might listen to his voice, behold his countenance and be admitted to the kiss of peace from his sacred lips. (Cant. L., I.; IV. I.), while awaiting to contemplate him face to face in the splendors of his glory."

After this touching elucidation, she continues: "It seems to me, reverend mother, that Our Lord bids me thank you for what you have already done for him in this Work of Reparation for Blasphemy, and if possible, to prevail upon you to continue. I had some difficulty in resolving, to speak of these things, for I feared an illusion; and I told him, that notwithstanding my desire to see him glorified, I never would have uttered a single word which was simply an effect of my own imagination: but he urged me to plead his cause that he might be relieved from his cruel sufferings. For nearly two hours I was conscious of the presence of this divine Savior in my soul. 'My Lord,' said I to him, 'deign to choose a more worthy instrument, a Teresa or another Gertrude!' My sighs and tears afforded some relief to my poor, sad heart! This day was a one of bitter, but happy suffering, for it seemed that Jesus made me understand that the willingness with which I shared all his pains, was a source of much consolation to him."

"Oh, my good Mother, I beg of you in mercy for the love and consolation of Our Lord, send to our houses these prayers of reparation which are so agreeable to him. I have said them twice during the course of the day, begging our Divine Lord to receive them as the precious perfume which Mary Magdalen poured over his sacred head on the eve of his Passion."

"Behold, as near as possible, reverend mother, what has passed in my soul; for five weeks my divine Master has operated nothing extraordinary. I have been continually occupied in offering reparation for blasphemy, and in sighing for the birth of this Work, but always in great peace of mind. I have been also occupied in guiding and caring for the flock which has been committed to my care; every day I take them to graze in the divine pastures of the mysteries of the life and Passion of the Good Shepherd, who has given his life for his sheep that not one might perish."

We here understand what she means by these "divine pastures" where she leads the flock committed to her care; they are the mysteries of the life and Passion of Our Lord, as enumerated by St. Dominic in the devotion of the holy rosary: the joyful, the sorrowful, and the glorious mysteries. By them our Savior has merited for us the graces which nourish and give life to our souls; the fruits of which are found in the sacraments of the Church, especially those of penance and the Holy Eucharist, two fruitful sources, wherein the sinner can find the means of purifying and nourishing himself according to his necessities.

The pious Carmelite had been chosen to be the "Shepherdess" of these heavenly pastures; certainly not that she was to preach these "mysteries" or administer the "sacraments," which are functions appertaining exclusively to the priesthood. But the mission assigned to her was, as her seraphic Mother St. Theresa teaches in her rule, to aid apostolic laborers by prayer, contemplation and by the exercises of the interior life, thus to obtain the light and unction necessary for the ministers of the Church to bring sinners back to Jesus, and to clothe them with his merits, that they might find in these mysteries the grace necessary to sanctify, nourish and save their souls. This mission of charity was, four days after, more fully explained by Christ himself. He informed her that two persons had rendered him special service during his Passion, the first of whom he had already spoken, — the pious Veronica, who served his sacred humanity by offering him wherewith to soothe his adorable countenance on his way to Calvary; the second, the Good Thief, who from his cross as from a pulpit, undertook to defend his cause and proclaim his divinity, even at the very moment he was being blasphemed by the other thief and by the Jews.

"Our Lord gave me to understand that both the one and the other are the two models given to the Work of Reparation, Veronica, the model for those of her sex who are not ap¬pointed to defend his cause by their eloquence, but to soothe his Holy Face in reparation for the blasphemy of sinners, by prayer, praise and adoration; the Good Thief, as the model for his ministers, who in the Work of Reparation should defend him publicly. "

"My amiable Master caused me to notice the magnificent recompense which he bestowed on these two persons, the one in leaving her his divine portrait, the other in assigning him a place in his heavenly kingdom, as a testimony of the esteem he had for the services they rendered him. Then he promised me that those who, in reparation for blasphemy, would defend his cause by prayers, words, or writings, would be defended by him before his Heavenly Father and that he would make them partakers of his kingdom. It seemed to me that he told me to promise in his Name, to those of his ministers who would preach this work, to his spouses who would endeavor to soothe and honor his Holy Face in reparation for the blasphemy of sinners, that at the hour of death, he would purify their souls by effacing the stains of sin, and would restore to them their primitive beauty."

"Methought also that he said: 'Write down these promises, they will make more impres¬sion on the minds of men than all I have hitherto said to you concerning this Work, because of the promise of eternal life, which although not the purest motive, is at least, not unworthy of consideration, since I have given my life that sinners may obtain the kingdom of heaven. He added, if you keep these things secret, through fear, you will be guilty of injustice to mankind.' My Divine Master spoke to me thus because I hesitated to believe this communication, for I am always afraid of being deceived."

"This is, reverend mother, a precise account of what has passed in my soul. The communications which I have just received have greatly disturbed me, I am filled with interior sorrow, and I suffer from a devouring fire; I tremble and humble myself before God, adoring his divine operations in a miserable atom."

If the reader be astonished at the important position assigned the Good Thief in the
Work of Reparation, let him recall what is written in the Gospel, that "whilst the Good
Thief was hanging on the cross, there came from all parts those who blasphemed: And
the people stood, beholding, and the rulers with them deriding him saying: He saved
others, let him save himself, if he be Christ, the elect of God. And one of these robbers
blasphemed him saying: 'If thou be Christ, save thyself and us.' These words of the wicked
thief contain a positive blasphemy, for they are equivalent to saying: If thou dost not
descend from thy gibbet, and take us with thee, thou art not the Christ as thou dost
profess; thou dost prove thyself an impostor by thy very powerlessness. What more cruel
injury could be offered to the Son of God! But the other answering, rebuked him, saying:
"Neither dost thou fear God, seeing thou art under the same condemnation, and we
indeed justly, for we receive the due reward of our deeds, but this man hath done no evil."

Behold a true type of zeal and of courageous charity! This fervent convert could not suffer
that his companion in disgrace, at the very moment of appearing before his Sovereign
Judge, should be so far lost to the fear of God, as to join with those who blasphemed
the Messiah, as if the kingdom of Christ was to be extinct at his death; he reproached
him for his perversity and audacity; and full of faith, humility and contrition, confessed
his sins and accepted with resignation the chastisement due their enormity. From his
gallows, he renders public testimony to the innocence and holiness of Jesus. He endeavors
to silence his blasphemers, and he proclaims his greatness at the very moment that all
wore anathematizing him. The cross of the Lord was in his eyes neither a scandal nor a
folly, but the wisdom and virtue of God; in this patient, meek One crowned with thorns,
he adores the Sovereign Lord and the King of kings. Casting a respectful and suppliant
glance toward this dolorous Face bruised and bleeding, he says, "Lord remember me when
thou shalt come into thy kingdom." So heartfelt a prayer deserved an immediate response.
The divine Face of Jesus directed toward him a glance, full of compassion, and in these
ineffable words assured this model reparator of the immediate vision of his Face glorified.
"Verily, I say unto thee, this day, thou shalt be with me in Paradise." The eulogy given
to the Good Thief by the holy Fathers and Doctors of the Church is inexhaustible. St.
John Chrysostom, considering his faith, extols it above that of Abraham, of Moses and
of Isaiah. "These," said he, "have beheld Christ seated on the throne of his magnificence,
surrounded with glory, and they believed; whereas the Good Thief beholds him in agony
on an infamous gibbet, yet he adores him as if he beheld him in the realms of his glory;
he beholds him upon the cross, and he prays him as if he beheld him seated on the clouds

of heaven; he beholds him as a criminal condemned to death and yet he invokes him as a God."

According to the same Doctor, he became on the spot an evangelist and a prophet. He preaches Christ crucified, and he proclaims the eternity of his reign.

Tradition recognizes him under the name of Dysmas. The Roman martyrology places him among the ranks of the holy martyrs on the 25th of March, and the Breviary, in the feasts proper to particular places, indicating his feast as of double rite on the 24th of April. The prayer of his office contains a significant passage; the Church asks of God, who is ever powerful and full of mercy, and who justifies the wicked, to move us to repentance by the merciful regards of his only Son who converted the Good Thief, and to grant us the same eternal glory. A more worthy model could not have been offered to the zealous worshippers and propagators of the reparation.

As for Veronica, her life, although not written in the Gospel, is sufficiently well-known and authenticated by tradition. The heroic deed to which Sr. St. Peter makes allusion, is the sixth station in the Way of the Holy Cross. Her veil is at Rome in the basilica of St. Peter, of the Vatican; from time immemorial it has always been considered as one of the most precious relics of the Passion of Our Lord and has been the object of the greatest veneration. Since the time of the communications made to the Carmelite of Tours, and thanks to the zeal of M. Dupont, the authentic copy of this venerable image in France and in the Catholic world, is the object of special devotion, and is the exterior symbol of reparation for blasphemy.

The pious Veronica, herself, is the patroness and protectress of the work. Her heroic example would, most naturally, be offered as a model to all generous souls who devote themselves to reparation.

14

LA SALETTE

"My Blessed Mother has warned mankind of
my wrath in her desire to appease it."
(Words of Our Lord)

T he revelations received by Sister Mary St. Peter on the worship of the Holy Face, as have already been detailed, seem to announce a Second phase in the history of her communications. These taken together, have a.characteristic unity, and their object will now become more definite. Henceforth it will be easy to follow up the regular course pursued by Our Lord, and to comprehend the nature of the communications made to his humble servant.

She was early imbued with his divine spirit, and by degrees the necessity of reparation became more apparent to her. In order to be more fully convinced of its absolute necessity, he leaves her for some time to her own reflections; then he gives her special instructions and indicates the worship of the Holy Face as the means of accomplishing this reparation, developing the appropriateness of this devotion with as much clearness as depth.

The sister had not as yet fathomed the secret dispensations of the Most High and could not imagine by what means the Work of Reparation was to be accomplished; but divine Providence was preparing the way. There was one to whom we have already referred several times, who was to become the principal auxiliary of the virgin of the cloister. This most worthy instrument in the hands of God, was M. Dupont, a resident of Tours for over ten years; his reputation for sanctity was such, that he was everywhere spoken of in the city. He had gradually contracted a pious and intimate friendship with the daughters of St. Theresa, more particularly with Sister St. Peter. During the year that Henrietta, his favorite child, was preparing to make her first communion, her virtuous father took every care to prepare her worthily for so holy an action. He commended her to the prayers of the pious Carmelite, who wrote him a letter on this subject, June 4th, 1844, which merits a record here, at least in part.

"I accept with pleasure," said she "the proposition of daily offering the touching prayer to the Holy Infant Jesus which you have sent us, that he may prepare this young heart to receive him with the most perfect dispositions. I am not worthy of communicating directly with the Infant Jesus, but I will beseech. Mary and Joseph to offer my prayer, and to present your dear little daughter to the Holy Child, that the day of her first communion may be the day of her espousals with him."

"Permit me, dear sir, to beg a favor of you, in the name of the child Jesus: that you would please offer him three wax tapers, to be burned in honor of the Holy Family that you may to obtain the accomplishment of your desires; for the Child Jesus takes a special pleasure in illuminations; he has granted a great grace to Sr. Margaret of the Blessed Sacrament, after having performed this simple and innocent practice of devotion. Our good and reverend mother has often given us the means of offering him this pleasure, but at present I am very poor, and have no candles to offer him."

Henrietta's father was not slow in fulfilling this pious request of the sister, which was perfectly conformable to his own ideas. We shall cite another letter, dated July 26th, 1845, when the Carmelite virgin wrote to this holy man requesting him to lend her a pious book treating on the Holy Eucharist:

"Our reverend mother begs you to procure me a book entitled, *Triumph of Jesus in the Most Blessed Sacrament.* She does not know where the one belonging to us has been put, for we have not seen it since our removal, and as have no fervor I want to procure this book whatever it may cost, for I hope to find wherewith to enkindle in my soul the love of Jesus in the most Blessed Sacrament."

Mgr. Morlot was not ignorant of the relations existing between the pious layman and the Carmelites; when in the month of March 1844, he had authorized the publication of the prayers of Reparation, M. Dupont, with his consent, became the zealous propagator. In the month of October following, Monseigneur wrote to him, enclosing a letter which he had just received on this subject; "I take the liberty of addressing this letter to M. Dupont, begging him to answer it for me. I also enclose two copies lately received from Rome, which makes me desirous of a new edition of the prayers for the association, under the patronage of St. Louis, to which should be added a notice on indulgences more to the purpose than the present one."

> "Yours most humbly and devotedly in Our Lord,
> F. N. A. B. of Tours."

This intimate and confidential friendship with the Carmelites on the one hand and with the venerable archbishop on the other, at once revealed the important part assigned M. Dupont in this work; Providence was planning the delicate mission which he was soon to fulfil.

But we have come to the year 1846; after what we have related in the preceding chapter, a long silence of six months ensued, that is from March 23rd to October 4th; nothing more was revealed concerning the work of Reparation and devotion to the Holy Face. Divine Providence seemed to be leaving time for reflection to these holy souls, to prepare them for the efficacious grace which France was about to receive. In fact, nothing less than a miracle was about to be performed, to enlighten and move all Catholic hearts to repentance.

We here refer to the apparition of the Blessed Virgin at La Salette, on the 19th of September, 1846.—Between this ever memorable event and the communications of Sr. St. Peter there exists a marvelous affinity, which we must not fail to observe. The authority of Mr. Dupont in such a matter, is of the greatest importance; the account in detail which we have in his own words will serve to guide us. Before opening the subject, the pious narrator certified to the "truth" of his narrative, "in which" states he, "according to my poor conception, we may behold a prophetic announcement of the glorious event which took place at La Salette."

"In 1846, toward the beginning of the month of September, on the eve of departure for St. Servan, in Brittany, I went to receive the commissions of the reverend mother, who had some relatives at St. Malo."

"I was obliged to write a long list, so numerous were the commissions given me, and in the meantime, we entertained ourselves on the divine mission of Sister St. Peter."

"'I shall relate to you what she has just told me,' said the reverend mother, arid as I had a pencil in hand I wrote as follows: "Our Lord addressing himself to the sister said: My Mother has spoken to men of my displeasure; she desires to disarm my justice and she has shown me her maternal heart, saying: 'O my Divine Son, behold this heart which has so loved thee! Let me shower benedictions on my other children! After which she descended to the earth. Have confidence in her.' I placed these lines in my prayerbook and thought no more about them. Was I not in the presence of a mysterious language, in which the past was confounded with the present and the future!"

"Reflecting on these things, I came to the conclusion that I was not mistaken in my conviction that the sister was the favored confident of Jesus Christ. This conviction was confirmed when on the 22nd of October, of the same year, I received a copy of the first letter of M. le Cure de Corps, respecting the apparition of the Blessed Virgin at La Salette, which took place on the 19th of September. This was the fulfilment of the prediction made in the first part of September to Sister M. St. Peter. I made a copy of the note I had taken at the Carmelite monastery and hastened to remit it to the Cure de Corps, who replied without delay. From the outset, I believed in the heavenly mission of the sister; today, if I can so express myself, I believe double-fold."

M. Dupont concludes with an observation explaining why this communication is not to be found among the sister's letters, which at the same time throws more light on the method of direction pursued by the mother prioress with regard to her spiritual daughter.

"I made it a rule," said he, "never to commit to paper anything related to me concerning the communications of this sister. But it is evident in the case just related, that I acted on a happy inspiration, as the fact of which I had taken note, was not to be found among the collection of her revelations. Regarding this omission the mother prioress said to me: 'I always require the sister to write what she has to relate to me, but it is probable that in the circumstance referred to, I listened to her account, and through forgetfulness, I may have departed from my ordinary custom to which I adhered merely to keep the sister humble, I generally say: My child, in obedience, go and write what you wish to tell me, I have no time to listen to you now. It may be that in the course of five years, I have several times forgotten to tell her to write what she desired to say, especially when the communication was short and repeated with her usual volubility, in which case she would have been very careful not to have had resort to her pen.'"

This explanation, so natural, is very simple and seemingly quite sufficient. M. Dupont concludes that the servant of God had, some weeks previously, announced the apparition of La Salette, and the merciful intervention of Mary in favor of France.

He adds: "Is it not most astonishing to behold our august Mother, confiding to two poor little children the sorrows of her maternal heart! Was it not sufficient that she had been sprinkled with the blood of her Divine Son on Calvary! Is it possible that an impious generation shall recall to her mind the frightful scenes perpetrated in the streets of Jerusalem by their blasphemous language! What would have become of us, if Mary had no longer power to arrest the arm of Jesus!"

Nevertheless, M. Dupont "rejoices, and is full of hope in consideration of this mark of the love of our heavenly Mother. The beautiful crown which she took in her hands before speaking to her people, announces that the succeeding revelations will be truly glorious. The most holy and Immaculate Mother of Jesus would surely not have accepted this mission if her poor children of earth would have received it to plunge themselves more and more into crime, and to draw upon themselves more terrible scourges of divine justice. For this reason I have much hope for the future of France."

The account of this miraculous apparition, communicated by M. Dupont to the Carmelites of Tours, created a sensation among them, as can be easily imagined. The mother prioress looked upon this event as a wonderful and striking proof of the celebrity which was one day to be given to the Work of Reparation claimed by Sister St. Peter in the Name of God. The mission confided to the little shepherds of the mountain was evidently identical with that of the cloistered virgin of Carmel.

Another circumstance made known afterward to M. Dupont, and not unworthy our notice, is that long before these events took place, the pious sister had herself ardently solicited the intervention of the Blessed Virgin. Let her relate the fact herself: "Monseigneur would not take any decided step to forward this work; his prudence preventing him taking the initiative. I saw quite plainly that there was neither hope nor consolation for me but in prayer, and the intercession of Mary, our most powerful advocate; and I recited the rosary every day to obtain grace for France, and also the establishment of the Reparation in all the cities of the kingdom. All my prayers, all my communions, all my aspirations and all my thoughts were offered for the establishment of this work, so dear to my heart. I desired, if it were possible, to proclaim it all over France, by making known to my countrymen the misfortunes which menaced them. Oh, how I suffer in being the only confident in a matter of such importance, and which I am obliged to keep secret within the walls of the cloister! Oh, most Holy Virgin, I implore you to come to some pious soul in the world, and make her a partaker of that which has been communicated to me in reference to France!"

We all know in what a striking manner the Blessed Virgin heard this prayer. Mary again showed that she is the "Refuge of Sinners;" she interposed herself as an afflicted and loving mother, between the wrath of God and guilty France. She presented herself to her Divine Son whom she had nurtured in his hours of infancy, and begged him to extend his mercy to these, her other children; and that mankind might not be in ignorance of her intervention, she descended to the earth. With her own feet has she tread our soil, and has chosen the humblest messengers, who have since become so celebrated, Maximin and Melanie, two poor peasants of that part of the Alps, called "La Salette." Through their infantine mouths, the Blessed Virgin has rebuked *her people,* as she lovingly styles France, her cherished kingdom, reproaching them for their impiety, so openly manifested by their contempt of the commandments of God, notably by blasphemy and the profanation of the Sunday.

"If my people will not submit," said she, "I shall be forced to let fall the avenging arm of my Son; He is so justly irritated that I can with difficulty restrain his anger. Oh, if you knew how much I suffer for you!"And the tears streamed from her eyes; the image of the crucifix was on her heart; the instruments of the Passion, the hammer and the nails on either side, lay on her breast. [*]

The two shepherds related what they had heard and seen; they underwent cross-questioning and contradiction, but their message become known, and gave to the Christian world an impulse which has not since ceased. In vain have the powers of earth endeavored to place obstacles in the way of the apparition becoming known, they but confirmed the testimony of the children; Catholic France recognized her crime and feared the chastisement; she has entered the path of reparation.

Our seraphic little Sr. St. Peter intones & hymn of gratitude and joy on this occasion: "I render thee thanks, O divine Mother ! for having given me these two little shepherds as sounding trumpets, to cause the mountains to re-echo in the ears of France, that which was made known to me in solitude. The voices of my two little associates were soon heard all over the earth, and their announcements produced a great impression on mankind. The striking relationship between their communication and those which I have received, leads my superiors to think that it might be useful to give information of the fact for the glory of God and the advancement of his work. Our Lord in the Gospel has said: 'Blessed be thou, O Father, because thou hast concealed these things from the great and wise of this world and hast revealed them to little ones.'"

"It seems to me that these words can be applied to the poor little instruments of which God has made use for the establishment of the Reparation in the Church. O my God, how incomprehensible are thy ways! Who would not be astonished on beholding the instruments which our Lord Jesus and his most Holy Mother have made use of in bringing forth this work! They have chosen from earth a helpless trio most ignorant and despicable, in whose souls He has worked wonders of grace, to render them capable of acting in concert for the accomplishment of the designs of the most adorable Trinity and for the glory of his Holy Name. The first is a little shepherdess, who consecrated herself to the Child Jesus to watch over his sheep from the mountain heights of Carmel; the others are two little shepherds who tended their flocks on the mountains of La Salette. These three little beings are commissioned to announce pardon and mercy if the people return to God by penance."

The three messengers labored together at the same work, each one performing his part according to his profession; the little shepherdess of Carmel is charged to pray, to write and to maintain silence in her solitude; the little shepherds of La Salette, on the contrary, to proclaim their mission from the summit of their mountains, to appear in public before the multitude who would come to listen to their predictions. Soon the entire nation was aware of the crimes, for which Heaven reproached the land, which enkindled the divine wrath against them: they are in consternation and demand what is to be done to disarm the vengeance of an offended God.

Be consoled, O France! the shepherdess of Carmel knows the secret! Go and visit her. Like the shepherds of La Salette, she will say to you: God is provoked against his people because of blasphemy and the violation of the Sunday. Over four years she has heard the growling storm in the distance, threatening to descend in torrents over France: but your fate is in your own hands. Offer reparation for your crimes and you will obtain mercy; you will then behold "the milk and honey," flowing forth from the "Mountain of God." Mary is this mysterious Mountain, who by the excellence of her virtues is raised above the angels and saints.

However, let not our confidence be presumptuous. Let us pray earnestly, and weep over our sins; for a time will come, not far off in the future, when France will be shaken even to her very foundations. Then shall she tremble, but she shall not be overwhelmed if the Work of Reparation appear before the eyes of the Lord in every city of the kingdom; those now marked out to be reduced to ashes will be but slightly injured."

[*] **A strange fact, relative to La Salette, and bearing every evidence of truth, dated November 25th, 1846, only five weeks after the apparition of the Blessed Virgin, has just been made known to us. In this manuscript we read of a curious incident, which we do not find mentioned in any of the writings of the period, and which is interesting to us, as binding together the two devotions of La Salette and the Holy Face. A lieutenant, leading the recruits to Corse, passed through the village of Corps. He desired to see this child Maximin, who was brought to the hotel where he was stopping. After having heard the child's story of the apparition, the officer asked him to sell a piece of the stone upon which the Blessed Virgin had rested. "Oh! no, sir," said the little child, "I will give you a piece of it, but I could never sell it." So saying, the child give the officer a fragment of the stone which he broke in halves. What was his astonishment on beholding on the stone a representation of the Face of our Lord Jesus Christ crowned with thorns. He traced a copy of this miraculous head and gave the sketch to the mother of the child, after having affixed his signature, as did als o another officer, who had witnessed the occurrence. The precious stone itself, he kept in his possession and would never consent to part with it. The narrator has drawn on his letter, a picture of this head; it is a simple sketch in outlines, with no shading, and a very good likeness of the Sacred head of Our Lord, crowned with thorns. Without attaching to this event more importance than necessary, we may, however, remark that at this time**

there was nowhere question of the devotion to the Holy Face, except in the writings and communications of Sister Mary St. Peter.

15

THE SINS OF FRANCE

"If you but knew how agreeable the
sight of my Face is to my Father!"
(Words of Our Lord)

A fortnight after the Virgin of the apparition at La Salette had threatened France with the divine wrath, Sister Mary St. Peter, who in the solitude of Carmel was still ignorant of this important occurrence, wrote (October, 1846) to the mother prioress:

"Permit me to give you an account of the sad presentiments I experienced this morning after a communication which I received during the holy communion. You are aware, reverend mother, that for several months I have experienced nothing extraordinary. Our Lord, during this time of trial, has deigned to purify my soul by great interior sufferings, he has withdrawn his presence from me. But today, as soon as I received holy communion, my Divine Master gave me to understand that he desired me to remain at his feet. I obeyed, and then he caused me to hear these sad and dreadful words: 'My justice is aroused because of the profanation of the holy day of the Lord. I seek a victim!' To which I answered: 'Lord, thou know that my superiors have given me the permission to abandon myself entirely into thy divine hands; do with me what thou wilt. But what am I, O Lord? Is it really thou who hast thus spoken to my soul?' He replied: 'You will not be long in doubt.'"

"From that moment, it seemed to me that Our Lord, accepted the act of abandonment which I had made him, and I perceived that he was going to take possession of my entire being, in order that he, himself, would in some manner, suffer in me to appease his justice; then he commanded me to receive holy communion every Sunday, first as an honorable amend in reparation for all the servile work performed on this sacred day; second, to appease his justice ready to strike mankind, and to ask for the conversion of sinners; third, to obtain a respite from all manual labor on the Lord's day. Then it seemed to me that Our Lord invited me to offer his Holy Face to his heavenly Father, to draw down mercy."

"This is, as nearly as possible, reverend mother, what has taken place in my soul. Let us hasten to appease the wrath of our God, for I feel that his justice is ready to strike us, the arm of the Lord is raised! I abandon these things to your good judgment; but I pray you, reverend mother, to observe one thing which affects me sensibly, and is the reason why I desire more and more ardently to see the establishment of the Work of Reparation: that the communications which I have been receiving these three years, tend always to the same end my divine Master has always complained of these two things, the profanation of the Lord's Day, and the blasphemy of the most Holy Name of God."

"Oh, how much I desire the establishment of this work which Our Lord has so often demanded of me, for it will appease the wrath of God, and ward off the chastisements with which we are menaced."

Jesus had promised the sister that she would not long remain in doubt whether it were really he who announced the chastisements which the justice of God was preparing. Of this she was soon convinced by the inundation of the Loire, which threatened Tours with imminent peril, and caused the most frightful ravages, such as had not been witnessed for centuries. All the world was in consternation, and recognized therein the all-powerful hand of Him, who disposes of the elements at will, and whom none can resist.

"We should acknowledge," observes the pious Carmelite, "that Tours has been saved by a miracle. But alas, they are ignorant of the principal cause of this terrible disaster, — the profanation of the Sunday."

M. Dupont, in his letters, also speaks of this destructive calamity, and attributes it to the same cause. He therein beholds the fulfilment of the menaces made by the Virgin of La Salette. "These dear, little children," said he, "have prophesied but too well, when they announced that we were on the eve of experiencing great calamities, if we did not return to God. Famine was already making itself felt among the poorer classes who did not have sufficient means to purchase bread at the enormous price to which it had been risen. Public men are in consternation, fearing a revolution; in fact, there has been sufficient said to arouse the people and to fill them with the desire for blood and pillage. How often have they not been told that death is the end of all things, and that riches will render man supremely happy."

The Lord made known to his servant that his justice was preparingchastisements for mankind. We shall soon behold, not only the elements as the instruments of the divine wrath, but the malice of man in open rebellion against itself."

Some days after, another communication on the subject took place. In her report to the mother prioress, Mary of St. Peter exclaims: "Oh, if you could perceive all that my heart is undergoing at this moment! I cannot contain myself any longer. I weep, but my tears are tears of gratitude and love because of the words of mercy and peace which this amiable Savior has made me understand. O sweet Jesus, thou couldst not behold us sufferings from the chastisements of divine justice without being touched more than we, ourselves, at the sight of the punishments we have so justly merited by our sins!"

She then relates that Jesus Christ informed her that the torrents of divine justice were not yet entirely exhausted toward France. "I have seen," said she, "other chastisements prepared to satiate divine justice. At this sight I cried out: O sweet Jesus, if I could quaff the cup to the dregs that my brethren might be spared! Jesus replied that he accepted my good will, but that I was not equal to the task, that he alone was able to drain it to the last bitter drops."

"The Savior, beholding my sorrow, made me a sign to enter his Divine Heart; in his infinite mercy, he gave it to me as a sacred vase worthy of being presented to the Eternal Father, wherein to receive his just anger which, as I understood, would be changed into the wine of his mercy by passing through this vase. But the rights of his justice cannot be compromised; and if I may thus express myself, he desires to make an alliance between his justice and his mercy, and for this purpose, he asks for the establishment of the Reparation in honor of his Holy Name, for he would disarm the anger of his Father, if he could offer him a Reparatory Work. Is it not the least we might do, Osweet Jesus!to repair by our prayers, by our sighs and by our adorations, the enormous crimes of which we are guilty against the majesty of God! The following, reverend mother, is the prayer with which Our Lord has been pleased to inspire me, and which I would wish to repeat unceasingly."

"Eternal Father, behold the Divine Heart of Jesus, which I now offer thee, wherein to receive the wine of thy justice that it may be changed for us into the wine of mercy."

He gave me to understand that each time I made this offering, a drop of the wine of divine anger would fall into the Sacred Heart of Jesus, and there would be transformed into mercy. I beg of you, my good mother, to prevail on our sisters to make this offering frequently, for alas, what am I, but a miserable atom, incapable of arresting the anger of God! "

Mgr. Morlot had requested that information be sent him of all that would be manifested to the sister. Therefore, the mother prioress hastened to transmit the report which we have just read. On the same day, October 25, 1846, the prelate returned the following answer: "I thank you for this interesting communication. There is no doubt but that the calamities, we have just witnessed, are the chastisement of our sins and infidelities, and of the many crimes which inundate the earth. May this chosen soul use all her efforts to stay the torrent of evil. Let all who fear the Lord redouble their zeal and fervor! Pray for me that I may have grace to accomplish my duty on this point."

"Be assured, reverend mother, of my most devoted consideration in the Lord,
F. N., Archbishop of Tours.

In the communications which follow, it seems as if the Son of God were particularly occupied with France. He exhorted his little spouse to suffer and to pray, saying: "I am charged with all the sins of the world, but I desire that you will be responsible for those of France." He then encouraged her, adding: "I will suffer in you, in order to appease the wrath of my Father, and I will cede to you all my merits that you may acquit yourself of your assumed debts."

The faithful child of Carmel hastened to comply with the wishes of the Lord. "I beheld myself covered with crimes, and I asked pardon for them with the same confusion as if I had committed them myself." Another day, insisting on the special mission which he had confided to his servant, he spoke to her with the authority becoming the Sovereign Master of kings and of nations, who assigns to each a particular role as well in the spiritual order of grace, as in temporal and civil matters. It was with difficulty she persuaded herself that God would make use of so vile an instrument to perform such a grand mission. But Our Lord consoled her saying: "In the order of my providence, I appoint a certain king to govern such a country; can I not then in the order of grace assign a special portion to the care of a particular individual to look after its eternal interests? I have chosen you to care for France. Pray for her: —immolate yourself for her;—I give you again the chief and most important member of my sacred person to offer to my Father in order to appease his divine justice. Oh, if you knew how efficacious, how full of virtue is my divine Face! I have taken upon my head the sins of mankind, that my members might be spared. Therefore, offer my Face to my Father, for it is the sole means of appeasing him." He adds: "I desire this Work of Reparation, rest assured that it shall be established, but the fruit has not yet reached maturity."

The generous Carmelite followed the counsel of her superiors, and abandoned herself to her Divine Master, ready to do what would be most pleasing to him. "Then," said she, "Our Lord charged me anew with France, and I answered: I accept this charge most willingly, my adorable Master, but permit me to make one condition: that you will be the sovereign Ruler, for if your heavenly Father beholds you seated on the throne of France, most assuredly, he will stay his hand."

"I receive Our Lord in each of my communions in the name of the entire French nation, and I offer him my heart to serve as his throne; then I salute and adore him as Sovereign King, supplicating him not to abandon a nation which has been so generous in contributing to make his Name known to idolatrous lands."

"Whenever I suffer, I pray Jesus to suffer in me, in order to appease his Father, and I also beseech him to perform in me all my actions; thus I unite myself to him and suffer in union with him, in awaiting the moment appointed for the Work of Reparation. *Sit Nomen Domini benedictum.*"

From the mission consigned to the Carmelite virgin, we perceive that the salvation of France is intimately linked with the Work of Reparation. Consequently, Our Lord hastens to offer the same exterior sign of salvation to both, and the same efficacious means, namely, the worship of his adorable Face. This is the subject of one of the sister's letters, dated November 22nd, of the same year.

"I have received," said she, "a new communication on the subject of the Holy Face of our Lord, notwithstanding my unworthiness; the following is the substance of what my Divine Master has given me to understand. 'My daughter, I appoint you today as my agent, and I again remit my Holy Face into your hands, to offer it unceasingly to my Father for the salvation of France. Turn to good account this divine talent audit will enable you to transact all the business of my house. By this Holy Face, you will obtain the salvation of a multitude of sinners: in consideration of this offering, nothing will be refused you. If you knew how agreeable the sight of my Face is to my Heavenly Father!'"

We can understand the joy she experienced when she exclaimed in a transport of delight: "These favors redouble my zeal for the salvation of our country, and urge me to resort to the means which Our Lord has placed at my disposal, to offer without cessation to the Eternal Father the adorable Face of his divine Son for the salvation of France, and also to obtain the establishment of the Work of Reparation."

These three were never separated in her thoughts, the Reparation, the salvation of France and the Holy Face.

"I am occupied with all these," said she, "according to the inspiration of grace."

We perceived that her heavenly Spouse was most bountiful in dispensing his lights and instructions to this virgin of the cloister.

She writes to the mother prioress on the 21st of December: "How shall I express, reverend mother, all that has passed in my soul during the fifteen days that Our Lord poured torrents of graces, the most precious, on me a miserable sinner! Poor little worm that I am, I cannot find language to convey an idea of those heavenly gifts; nevertheless, I shall communicate to you all I can of what Jesus gave me to understand."

"This divine Director of my soul said to me: 'My daughter, be more pliable under my operations, and more simple, for I wish to nourish you myself with the milk of my consolations. The uneasy reflections you make on self, the fear you have of illusion, impede me from fully accomplishing my designs over you.' When I had acknowledged my fault, he assumed a greater power over me and revealed many admirable secrets of his infinite mercy. He called my attention to his justice and manifested his wrath as a great ocean, but at the same time, he commanded me to resist the impetuous torrent of his anger in union with his Divine Heart, that it might be lost in the abyss of his mercy."

"Another day, he presented to my view the multitude of souls who are daily falling into hell and invited me in the most touching manner to fly to the rescue of these poor sinners. He made me comprehend the real obligation of the Christian towards these unfortunate, blind creatures, who precipitate themselves into the eternal abyss; whose eyes would have been opened if charitable souls had interceded in their behalf. He said that if he would demand of the rich an account of the temporal goods confided them for the succor of the poor, with how much more reason would he not demand of a Carmelite, and of all religious souls, a rigorous account of the use they have made of the treasures of their celestial Spouse in succoring unfortunate sinners! Then my amiable Savior, opening to me the immense treasures composed of the infinite merits of his life and Passion, added: 'My daughter, I give you my Face and my Heart, I give you my precious Blood and my Sacred Wounds; draw from this treasury and scatter blessings around! Purchase without money, my Blood is the price of souls. Oh! what a sorrow it is for my Heart to see that the remedies which have cost me so much suffering are so wantonly despised! Demand of my Father as many souls as I have shed drops of blood in my Passion!"

"Again, on another day, he presented me his holy cross saying, that he had brought forth his children upon this bed of sorrow; making me understand that it was by the cross borne for his love, that I would obtain eternal life for the agonizing, for whose resurrection to the life of grace he was so ardent. Oh, what a longing desire I beheld in the Heart of Jesus for the salvation of sinners! What light I received from him on the efficacy of offering prayers in their behalf! But what shall I say of the sight Our Lord gave me of his Wounds and of his Blood! Ah, let us press these Divine Wounds by our ardent prayers and this Precious Blood will flow abundantly over poor sinners!"

"On another occasion, Jesus placed my soul at the gate of eternity, or rather at the gate of the end of the road called Time, in order to aid agonizing sinners to prepare themselves for this last important journey! Oh, when we reflect that the justice of God is always ready to pronounce sentence on the guilty, and that we can plead their cause and appease this Sovereign Judge, with what zeal should we not fly to the rescue of those who may be condemned to eternal death and who, perhaps, have still one more hour in which divine mercy, if implored, would touch their hearts! Oh, how I feel impelled to pray for these poor souls!"

"And now, reverend mother, with your permission, I shall speak of a wall of protection which Our Lord gave me to behold; a mysterious wall protecting France against the arrows of divine justice. Oh, with how much gratitude to the excessive mercy of God, have I not been filled on beholding this vision! He gave me to understand that this wall which reached up to heaven, was the exercise which I practiced every day, joined, no doubt, to the prayers and merits offered to God by so many holy souls for the salvation of France. This exercise consists in presenting the Face of Jesus a hundred times to his Father, in

honor of all the mysteries of the life and death of this divine Savior, and in offering him
the merits of each of these mysteries for the salvation of France. He told me that he gave
me this vision to encourage me to persevere in my undertaking."

The critical situation of the agonizing had visibly affected the servant of God; she was
brought back some time after to this same spiritual work of mercy, and was placed anew
between what she termed the "Gates of Time and Eternity."

On the 10th of January 1847, she writes: "For three weeks Our Lord has released me
somewhat from the important occupation pertaining to the salvation of France, that I
might apply myself solely and uninterruptedly to the service of the poor agonizing. I
accompany the most Blessed Virgin as her little servant on her visits to these travelers from
time to eternity. Jesus made known to me that he gave me to his august Mother to fulfil
this mission. Oh, what a glorious occupation, on which I have never much reflected; but
the moment has come, when I must work with more ardor than ever for the salvation of
souls. It seemed that Our Lord announced to me that I had only three years more to live. I
am now thirty years of age. I shall endeavor during the three years to come to try to imitate
Our Lord more closely, for at this age he was untiring in his efforts to bring back the lost
sheep to the true fold."

"These words give me new strength and light: 'If you but knew the gift of Grod!' He
enlightened me on their signification, and I commenced to penetrate the wonders of this
precious Gift of the Father. Oh, what could I not obtain for myself and for my brethren if
I knew how to make use of his infinite merits unknown to the majority of men! I sanctify
myself for them, Jesus has said to his Father. Let us then offer to this Divine Father, for
the salvation of souls, all that our Redeemer has suffered for us, and we shall thereby
enrich our extreme indigence. O blindness of men, who run with ardor after the treasures
of earth which together cannot purchase one single soul. The Gift of God is unknown,
despised; this vast treasure of Christians with which we can buy millions of souls by
presenting the infinite merits of Jesus at the bank of the Divine Majesty! It seems to me
that we should never present ourselves in presence of the Eternal Father without having
some of the merits of his Son in our hands to oblige him, in a manner, to accomplish
the admirable promise of Our Lord: 'Verily, I say into you, whatsoever you ask of the
Father in my Name shall be granted you.' If we have no virtue of ourselves to offer God,
let us present those of Jesus, our Savior, who has sanctified himself for us. Let us offer
his meekness, his patience, his humility, his poverty, his fasts, his vigils, and his zeal for

the glory of his Father, and the salvation of souls! Let us offer his divine and efficacious prayers. He has prayed during his mortal life; the Gospel relates that he retired at night to pray, he prayed to heaven, he presented his wounds to his Father, and he prays continually for us in the most Blessed Sacrament of the altar! Oh, ineffable mystery! A God Savior praying for his creatures! Let us unite our prayers to those of the Word Incarnate, and they shall be heard; let us again offer to the eternal Father the Divine Heart of Jesus, his adorable Face and his sacred Wounds; let us offer his tears and his blood, let us offer his journeys, his labors, his words and his silence, all he has suffered in each of the mysteries of his holy life; in fine, let us always have our eyes fixed on this 'Gift of God.'"

"Let us, if we are able, enumerate all the goods we possess in this treasure unknown to the world and we shall soon become rich ourselves and shall enrich poor sinners ; because we can offer the humility of Jesus for the conversion of the proud; his poverty for the avarious; his mortifications for the sensual; his zeal to glorify his Father, for the blasphemers, and all the accusations he has suffered at the hands of the Jews, especially that of violating the Sabaoth for the conversion of those who really violate the Lord's Day."

"O 'Gift of God,' so long unknown, thou shalt henceforth be my only treasure! How many new riches do I not daily discover in thee!"

We cannot help admiring these aspirations of love and these transports of zeal which gush forth from the pure heart of this admirable sister. It was not without reason that she concludes in these terms:—" You see, reverend mother, that if Our Lord has often charged me with the salvation of souls, he has taught me *how* to save them."

16

THE OBSTACLES

**"I am not known, I am not loved, my
very commandments are despised."**
(Words of Our Lord)

Three years had already elapsed since the time Mary of St. Peter had urged, in the Name of Grod, the establishment of the Work of Reparation, and had declared that the exterior symbol of the Work should be the sorrowful Face of Christ. In her ardent love, she composed the litanies, canticles and other prayers in honor of the Holy Face of Our Lord. After a long period of trial and contradiction, her superiors, more and more convinced that her communications were from Grod, made an effort to push forward the project, but no one dared take the initiative step. However, it was decided to make a collection of these divine communications under the title, *An Abridgment of Facts relative to the Establishment of the Work of Reparation for Blasphemy.* These were to be sent to some of the Carmelite monasteries and to a few pious souls. As soon as completed, they were submitted, in manuscript, for the approbation of the archbishop, who returned them to the mother prioress with the following letter: — "Reverend Mother, I fully approve of the propositions presented to me in reference to the inspirations respecting the Work of Reparation, believing as I do, that it is not only a meritorious but a most necessary work. The project of uniting Reparation for blasphemy with that for the profanation of the holydays, is entirely satisfactory: it has always seemed to me that the primitive object, Reparation for Blasphemy, was inadequate to meet the necessities of the times. I find the manuscript all that Could be desired."

In the same letter, the venerable prelate gave his consent for the publication of the little book entitled, *Association against Blasphemy.* He also granted a special authorization of the beautiful and pious litanies of the Holy Face, inspired to Sister Mary St. Peter, and permitted them to be published and distributed among the faithful. With regard to the "Abridgment of Facts," the superiors, through motives of prudence and discretion, had but fifty copies printed and given to the public anonymously.

M. Dupont distributed several among his intimate friends. The mother prioress, on her part, forwarded some to the various houses of her order with which she had any direct communication, particularly to the Carmelites of Rouen, and those of Rue d'Enfer, at Paris. The good sister, aware of what was being done rejoiced exceedingly, believing her desires were now about to be accomplished and her mission fulfilled; but in this the humble virgin was deceived. "I hoped," said she, "that Our Lord had granted my desires, and that I would have nothing more to write; but he has communicated to me certain things which he wished to be made known, and consequently I submit to his good pleasure. *Fiat voluntas tua.*"

The communication here mentioned was important, as we shall see, for it united two beautiful and holy devotions, each equally cherished by the sister, and essentially necessary to the Work of Reparation.

Let us see how the daughter of Carmel explains this necessity: "Our amiable and divine Savior," said she, "permitted me to hear his lamentations over his love, unknown in the most holy Sacrament of the altar. He most happily united my heart and my mind at his feet, that I might remain with him in his abandonment, adoring his most Holy Face, concealed under the sacramental veils. Verily, it is through this august sacrament, that Jesus our Savior wishes to communicate to souls the virtue of his most Holy Face. He has again promised me to imprint his divine features on the souls of those who honor him."

In presenting anew to the sister the mystery of his Holy Face, Our Lord enlightened her by a conception which, as she expressed it, disclosed a "beautiful horizon" on Reparation for Blasphemy, by manifesting the affinity existing between his most Holy Name and his most Holy Face. "Our Lord," said she, "by the aid of a comparison as simple as just, permitted me to comprehend how the wicked by their blasphemy attack his adorable Face, and how the faithful glorify it by the homage of praise rendered his Name and his person."

"The merit of an individual lies in his character, but the glory of his reputation rests on his name."

"The Holy Name of God expresses the Divinity, and contains all the perfections of the Creator; it follows, therefore, that the blasphemers of this Sacred Name insult God directly. Let us recall the words of Jesus: "I am in my Father and my Father in me." (St. John.) Jesus became man by the Incarnation; it is he who has suffered in his adorable Face all the outrages committed by the blasphemers of the Name of his Father. Our Lord has manifested to me, that there is something mysterious on the face of an honorable man, who has suffered contumely; his name and his face are particularly allied. Observe a man distinguished by his name and by his merits, in the presence of his enemies; these raise not the hand against him, but overwhelm him with injurious epithets, instead of the honorable titles which are his due, scoffing at him and mocking him."

"Again, notice the expression of his face, would you not suppose that all the derisive language of his enemies was imprinted thereon, causing him to suffer martyrdom? Behold that countenance covered with shame and confusion; he could support the most cruel pains, the most excruciating tortures without flinching; but the loss of his reputation, of his good name,—this is unsupportable, he can no longer control his emotions, which are soon depicted on his countenance. Such is a feeble portrait of the Divine Face of Our Lord, condemned by blasphemers."

"Now let us represent to ourselves this man once more, but in the presence of his friends, who being apprised of the insults he has received, eagerly present themselves to sympathize with him, offering the respect due to the greatness of his name. Shall we not then read in his countenance the consolation which these sympathies afford him? His brow again bespeaks peace, and his features become radiant with joy; happiness beams, from his eyes, and the smile of gladness is on his lips; loving friends have soothed that face outraged by enemies; opprobrium is forgotten, peace and happiness reign supreme. We can see in this feeble image, that which the friends of Jesus perform in the Work of Reparation. The glory which they render his Name encircles his august brow and is portrayed on his most Holy Face in the adorable Sacrament of the altar. Reverend mother, this comparison which Our Lord has given me, has greatly enlightened me. I now see clearly that blasphemers insult the Face of Our Lord, and that reparators rejoice and glorify it. I have never had occasion to make this remark, that the face of man is the seat on which is enthroned either glory or ignominy. Therefore, I shall apply myself anew to honor the Name and the most Holy Face of Jesus, who has so touchingly invited me to render him this service."

Notwithstanding the importance attached to these new favors by her superiors, the sister was still kept in her arduous office of portress. In the month of February 1847, a few days after the encouragements given by the archbishop, she felt extremely fatigued- Perceiving that her strength was failing she, with entire simplicity, asked for a sister to aid her in her office. The mother prioress told her that she could not spare any one at the moment and added that perhaps a little indolence and self-love had prompted her to ask for assistance; she directed her to pray for the restoration of her health, so that after two weeks she might be able to assist at all the regular exercises of the community.

Let us lend an attentive ear while she is relating to her superioress, what she experienced after this mortifying refusal: "I received your order, reverend mother, with respect, yet I confess that in my weakness, I was much pained, because I did not find in you, reverend mother, your ordinary tenderness; and the devil commenced to tempt me to murmur."

"Happily, I ran to expose my sorrow to Our Lord and while shedding many tears, I told him that this office of portress was a continual martyrdom, because it kept me away from him. Having explained to my good Master, all that was a cause of pain in this employment, I added: 'However, my dear Lord, I only desire that which will render thee the most glory and save the greater number of souls. Thou didst not descend from the cross, neither shall I, from mine!' And I then and there begged for my recovery in virtue of holy obedience."

"The next day, at holy communion, my Divine Lord said: 'My daughter, is not solitude your delight? During the first years of your religious life, when you were without any office, were you not supremely happy?' 'Oh, yes, my Lord,' I replied. 'Know then, my child, that a religious should be a living crucifix. If you had not these sufferings, how would you be able to serve the souls I have placed under your care? As a proof that I desire you to remain in this office, and also that you may know it is I myself, through the mouth of your superior, who have refused your assistance, I command that you be instantly restored to health. Be consoled, my child, I will give you immortal souls as the reward of your labors.'"

The Lord had not finished speaking, when all at once the loud ringing of the parlor bell called the virtuous portress to duty. This was the signal for sacrifice. "Ah, my Jesus," said she, "the bell calls me, I shall return to my post once more in the name of obedience."

In fact, the favor asked had been obtained; her health was perfectly restored, and she was able to keep her rule to the letter. In another communication, Our Lord said to her: "I wish you to honor my servitude, for I did not come on earth to be served, but to serve." Then he added: "In a time of famine, when bread is very dear, would not a father deserve the reproaches of his family, if instead of supporting them, he neglected to labor and was thus the cause of their sufferings? Well, then my child, this is your own portrait. — You have children to support; I have told you that you must earn bread for them; they need every morsel you can give them; do not expose yourself to the risk of being accused, on the day of judgment, of having neglected them."

On another occasion, he gave her this instruction on the duties of her office: "My daughter, you complain that you cannot lead a solitary life, because of your occupations; but do you not know, it is the soul that must be in solitude? The soul that controls her passions, by the continual immolation of self-will to the virtue of obedience, is truly a soul in solitude, for she participates in some manner, in the solitude of God by a life of conformity to his holy will. On the contrary, a soul, although in the silence of retirement, is not in solitude when the tumult of her passions agitates and troubles her, and when she delights in her own will; remember, my child, that the nourishment of all the passions is self-will." "These are the instructions which Our Lord has had the goodness to give me. Henceforth, I desire to have no other will than his; I will be portress all my life, if it be pleasing to God and to my superiors." And in fact, she was portress until her last illness.

These *children* given her to nourish, were the sinners whose salvation was confided to her. The Divine Master invited her frequently to this work of charity. "During the past two weeks," said she, (March 2nd,) "Our Lord has kept me in retreat. He has not communicated with my soul in any extraordinary manner; I have been solely occupied in renovating my inmost heart, and in humbling myself at the sight of my many infidelities. Having made yesterday the confession of all my faults, I approached holy communion this morning with the firm resolution of being more faithful to God. Like the prodigal, I humbled myself, repeating, 'I have sinned.' Then, as I was about to annihilate myself in the presence of the majesty of God, considering him surrounded with glory, he pronounced these words: 'Ah, my child, rather consider me covered with the wounds inflicted by sinners.' At that instant it seemed to me that I beheld him in a most sorrowful state, and he said: 'My daughter, approach and lend thine ear.' My Divine Savior then permitted me to hear these heartrending lamentations: 'I am not known, I am not loved; my very commandments are despised.' And he added the following words which made me tremble: 'Sinners, as clouds of dust borne on the wind, are whirled from this world and precipitated into hell. Have pity on your brethren and pray for them. Staunch the blood flowing from my wounds by. the ardor of your love, and fear not. When you elevate your heart to me by aspirations, I receive it in my hands, and I shall guard it safely.' After this, I understood that he was pleased with my little retreat and he added:—'If you have discovered in yourself so many defects, after having meditated on holy subjects, consider the unfortunate multitude who never reflect on the great truths of religion ! Therefore, my child, it is your duty to labor for them even as a mother who cannot take nourishment unless her children partake likewise.'"

This letter is concluded in these terms:— "This is what Our Lord has communicated to me. Oh, what sorrow I experience when I think of the eternal loss of so many souls! How ardently I desire to become a fervent Carmelite, to ransom numbers for God! Assist me I beg of you, reverend mother; spare neither my pride nor my self-will. It were full time that I should entirely immolate my perverse nature to clothe it with our Lord Jesus Christ."

Thus, it was that the Divine Master drew the attention of his servant to the one great object, the universal Reparation operated by his coming in this world, and by his death on the cross, that is, the salvation of souls. "He sent me to labor, now in one field, then in another, according to his own good pleasure. For fifteen days he has placed me in the retirement of retreat, forbidding me to withdraw until he would call me. During this time, he showed me the amount of tare in my own soul, and I sincerely confessed my faults." Our Lord was preparing her daily for the special work, the establishment of which had been previously announced to her. The project appeared to be dormant; there was no question of it, even at Tours, after the distribution of the notices of which we have spoken. But at the beginning of March in 1847:—"Behold!" exclaimed the sister, " the voice of the Lord has resounded in my ear, calling me and giving me anew the mission of the Work of Reparation for Blasphemy. This is the third time he has called me to this work."

"He assured me a short time ago, that it would be established, which has given me so much confidence, that if I saw the World and hell united to crush it, I would still hope in Him whose arm is all-powerful. From the outset, Jesus declared to me that he would permit the devil to counteract his designs, in order that the confidence of his servants might be proven. Today, he said: 'Rejoice, my daughter, the hour approaches, for the birth of the most beautiful work that has yet appeared on the face of the earth. Offer my divine Heart to my Father that you may obtain it the sooner.'"

Our Lord here means the work in reparation for blasphemy, to be offered through the merits of his dolorous Face. The redemption purchased for mankind by Jesus Christ on the Cross, is by excellence, the noblest and the most sublime manifestation of the wisdom and of the love of God. The mind of man can conceive nothing more astonishing than this act of the Word becoming incarnate in a Virgin's womb, and dying the ignominious death of the cross, for the salvation of sinners. Assuredly, then, this is the 'noblest work' that has ever been accomplished on earth and is continually renewed in the Church over every part of the globe from the morning watch even unto night. But since the consummation of this great sacrifice of the cross, generations have succeeded each other, new peoples have arisen; in our time, the spirit of evil, armed with pride and sensuality, has inflicted on society two wounds of such magnitude as have hitherto been unknown; deep-rooted impiety and absolute incredulity, these are the two loathsome wounds of modern society, which corrode all that is most sacred.

To combat this strange and satanical scourge and to expiate the abominations which result, the Word Incarnate, our only Mediator, and the Sovereign Reparator of degenerate society, offers us his Holy Face, this portion of his sacred humanity in which are reflected, both the thoughts of his mind and the affections of his Heart, and which give him an appearance like unto other men; and in which he has suffered the greater part of the ignominies of his Passion. He demands, therefore, a new work whose object is to repair these crimes of modern society. The Reparation is intimately allied to the great Work of the Redemption and is in reality *the most noble* and the most necessary work for our times.

As the sister was continually worrying over the many obstacles, Our Lord said to her: "You are now beholding the morning twilight of a beautiful day;" and he engaged her to abandon herself anew into his hands, to suffer both interiorly and exteriorly all the trials that he would be pleased to send her.

"He made me understand," said she, "that I was in his hands, as a feeble instrument which he used at pleasure. This is very true, for I cannot labor at this work but by a special grace, when he pleases and as he pleases. I feel convinced that I have received this grace in my soul, therefore, with the assistance of the Lord who directs me, I will do nothing from my own inclination. *Sit Nomen Domini benedictum!"*

However, the "Abridgment of Facts,' which had been sent to some of the Carmelite monasteries, and to some intimate friends in the city of Tours, had produced their fruit;—an ardent desire of seeing the Reparation established. It was the little grain of mustard seed sown in good ground, which increased and produced fruit a hundred-fold. Yet, notwithstanding all the precautions which had been taken in the distribution of these prayers of reparation, the subject was soon noised abroad and came to the ears of Monseigneur from various sources; he became alarmed in consequence of the political aspect of affairs, and wrote a hasty letter to the mother prioress, telling her they had gone too far, and had exceeded his intentions. In a word, he imposed absolute silence both on the Carmelites and on M. Dupont on the subject of Reparation. All submitted immediately, the command of the archbishop being received as if it were from God himself, and the distribution of the *Notices* was discontinued. But the first impulse in the right direction had been given in conformity to the will of God. Two great Works of Reparation would soon spring forth into life; of these we shall soon have occasion to speak: the work of Langres and that of Mlle. Dubouche. Despite this uproar, the "Instrument of God" remained in obscurity, as her name had not been revealed, save to M. Dupont and a very few intimate friends. Within the monastery itself, the secret was inviolably guarded. The religious, secretary to the mother prioress, was the only person who had any cognizance of what was going on. This sister was Mary Teresa of St. Joseph who succeeded Mother Mary of the Incarnation as prioress. She was an intimate friend of Mary St. Peter; both having entered the cloister about the same time and made a part of their novitiate together. The extraordinary graces bestowed on the latter could not long escape the discerning eye of this friend, ever at her side. When Sr. Mary Teresa was told of all that was transpiring, she was filled with astonishment; her esteem for her companion was boundless, and she rendered her many services which were acknowledged by an affectionate gratitude. In the designs of Divine Providence, it was this very sister who was to withdraw from their obscurity the manuscript containing the celestial communications of her old companion, the precious treasure which had been sealed from observation for thirty years.

The injunctions of the archbishop put a stop to any further action in the matter, on the part of the Carmelites. Nevertheless, in the interior of the monastery, the humble confident of Jesus continued to be the recipient of new favors. Rendering account of the sadness she experienced, the servant of God writes, March 14th: "Today, after holy communion, our Lord Jesus revealed to me that the evils which had been inflicted on us, were only the forebodings of what his justice was preparing, if we appeased not his anger. And he showed me the sins of blasphemy, and the profanation of the Lord's Day under the form of two engines by which the guilty drew down upon themselves the waters of his vengeance, exposing themselves to be submerged if this Work of Reparation given in his mercy as a means of salvation, were not established. Afterward, he said that the sectarians called Communists had only made an attempt to blindfold us. 'Oh!' said he, 'if you knew their secret and diabolical machinations! If you could comprehend their anti-christian principles! They are only waiting a favorable moment to set France in flames, therefore be earnest in your supplications for the Work of Reparation. Ask him who possesses authority to establish it, that mercy may be obtained.' 'But my Divine Master,' I replied: 'my superiors have already requested its establishment.' 'That is not sufficient,' replied Our Lord, 'you are the instrument whom I have chosen to accomplish this work, and you must demand it in my Name.'"

The pious Carmelite, having thus been twice ordered by the Lord to write to the archbishop, consulted the mother prioress to know if she should comply; the latter dissuaded her under the pretext that she ought not importune Monseigneur in the midst of his many occupations. "After holy communion this morning," said the sister, (March 19th), "I informed my Lord Jesus of the counsel I had received, not to write to the archbishop. My Divine Master answered me very nearly as follows: 'My daughter, the virtue of obedience is very dear to me. Be submissive, that all may recognize the spirit which guides you. I desire, however, that these communications which I give you, be transmitted to your first superior.' I replied as follows: "My Divine Master, permit me to ask you, with the simplicity of a child, what you desire me to say to Monseigneur when I ask for the establishment of the Work of Reparation, for you know he has already labored for it?' He answered: 'If this work is not built on a solid foundation, it can never be permanent; if it has not a special approval, it will only languish, and finally perish. But if approved of by a Brief, the Reparation will soon establish itself in all the cities of France; and it is proper that he who has been the first to put his hand to the work should complete it.'"

"As I seemed to fear being deceived if I demanded this work in his Name, he made me observe that I had not espoused the cause of reparation until he had inspired me, and that I should remain perfectly tranquil. He then informed me that he would explain his action in my regard by the example of a bow and arrow saying, it was a just image of my soul; that he aimed his bow and arrow in whatever direction he wished, for the accomplishment of his designs. He added; 'When I created you, I proposed that it should be through your instrumentality that the Work of Reparation be given to mankind. Therefore, be consoled; when this work shall be accomplished, I will leave you no longer on earth, and my mercy will compensate you for all your labor.'"

The admirable and courageous soul exclaims during an interview with the mother prioress: "Permit me, reverend mother, to beg the assistance of your prayers, for I stand so much in need of them; I bring forth this work by prayers and sufferings. When Our Lord charged me anew with the Work, he said:

Pray unceasingly for its establishment, and offer yourself entirely to me, ready to suffer in body and soul, all that I shall think necessary for the accomplishment of my designs.

"From that moment, I have been on the cross, but I dare not complain, I who have so many times asserted that I would give even the last drop of my blood for the accomplishment of his designs in this Work of Reparation! Oh, how unworthy I am to suffer for so noble a cause,—the glory of God and the salvation of souls ! I confess to you, reverend mother, that I have often had the weakness to weep and lament, but I implored Our Lord to pay no attention to my poor nature."

17

THE COMMUNISTS

**"Shelter France under the mystery of thy Face and
have mercy on her for the glory of thy Name."**
(Words of the Sister)

S ecret societies, the scourge of the French people and the sworn enemy of the Church
of God, had long been plotting their destructive machinations. The entire world
has been more or less poisoned by the pernicious influence of both political and religious
sects, diametrically opposed to all law and order. France, unhappily, has been the center,
and the most active agent in the formation and encouragement of these diabolical
institutions. It is from her midst, Paris especially, that the revolutionary and anti-social
spirit has spread all over Europe, assuming different names at different epochs to suit the
caprice of the moment; at one time styling themselves Socialists, then Liberals, and again
Nihilists.

Toward the end of the reign of Louis Philip, at the period to which the life and
communications of Sr. Mary St. Peter now lead us, they bore the appellation of
Communists. These by degrees had usurped the entire control of the press. They
numbered among their party, illustrious writers, men distinguished in the schools of
philosophy, and among the literati of the day, not a few of whom had endeavored to put
their dangerous chimeras into execution. This sect, by its secret maneuvers, had rapidly
increased. Silently and skillfully had they laid their subterranean mines; the moment for
explosion was near at hand, those entrusted with their country's welfare seemed totally
unconscious of the danger. France was asleep in the very mouth of a volcano. But the
watchful child of Carmel, with an attentive eye to the wants of her country and the

salvation of souls, raised the cry of alarm from the depth of her solitude and while pointing out the danger to the sacred sentinels, indicated the means of averting the catastrophe. The communications which she received on this subject form a series in themselves, with which the following extracts will make the reader sufficiently acquainted. On the 29th of March she writes:

"God has imposed on me a new mission, at which I would be disturbed were I of any consequence, but as I am nothing but a feeble instrument in his all-powerful hand, I am not alarmed. He has commanded me to cross swords with the Communists, who, as he told me, were the sworn enemies of the Church, and of his Christ. He gave me to understand that the greater number of these renegades were born in the bosom of the Church, of whom they now declare themselves the most bitter enemies. Then he added: 'I have already made known to you that I hold you in my hands as an arrow, now I will shoot forth my arrow upon my enemies. To combat them, I give you the arms of my Passion, my Cross, of which they are the enemies, as also all the other instruments of my sufferings. Wage war against them with the simplicity of a child but with the courage of a valiant warrior. For this mission be signed with the blessing of the Father, and of the Son and of the Holy Ghost.'"

Then I besought the Blessed Virgin, she who is compared to the Tower of David with a thousand bucklers, to take charge of these arms which I had just received. Our Lord gave me more information on this subject, but it is too difficult to explain. —I exclaimed: 'Prepare me for the combat, O Lord, and instruct me how to use these holy arms.' He replied: 'The arms of my enemies inflict death, but mine restore life.'"

"I frequently recited the following prayer: Eternal Father, to oppose thy enemies, I offer thee the cross of our Lord Jesus Christ, and all the instruments of his holy Passion, that thou mayst counteract them by divisions and discord; for thy well-beloved Son hath said: 'Every kingdom divided against itself shall perish.'"

It is now that our little sister has entered the arena: her arms are the cross and the instruments of the Passion. "With these she resists the attacks of the enemies of God. To encourage her in this mystic combat, the Savior reveals to her the designs of the Sectarians, and their anti-Christian principles.

On Holy Thursday, April the first, he said: "The soldier who knows the object of the war in which he is engaged, aware of the insult offered his prince, arms himself fearlessly to avenge the affront. Well, my daughter, it is the Communists who have dragged me from my tabernacles, profaned and despoiled my sanctuaries, and have even dared to raise their hands against the anointed of the Lord, but their designs shall be frustrated. Have they not committed the crime of Judas! Have they not sold me for silver! This knowledge should not remain sterile in your soul, for I give it you to help you in the combat. Be actuated with a spirit of simplicity, for if you reason too much, you will not be a fit instrument in my hands. Think rather of the glory which the heavenly court will render me for having made use of so worthless a creature in so noble a cause!"

"Observe, if you please, reverend mother, that Our Lord made me understand this yesterday; and today, Holy Thursday, a most memorable day, for it was on this day that he instituted the ineffable sacrament of the altar in which he is exposed to the outrages and the profanations of his enemies, I wish to make again an honorable amend to my Divine Savior in the sacrament of his love, in reparation for these sacrilegious outrages, which he so forcibly recalled to my mind and which, alas! I had too soon forgotten."

Some days after she writes: "I have entered the arena to combat the enemies of God; my soul has recovered its calmness since I have received the banner of obedience if I can thus express myself. I am secure under this standard, and I no longer fear the evil spirit. Jesus gives me grace and courage to remain firm at my post; today after holy communion, he encouraged me to the combat and pledged himself to give me a cross of honor, which would open Heaven to me, if I were faithful. He also assured me that he would give me the gold of charity: I understood that he meant by this, tribulations which he in his mercy reserved for me, and that he would grant me the grace to suffer with patience and love. May his Holy Name be blessed! But reverend mother, I have some remorse after having combatted the enemies of God with all my strength, during these three days. I shall explain myself: I am afraid that I have made use of imprecations against the enemy, although I am certain that the holy king David has done likewise, as we may perceive from his psalms: yet I am in doubt whether it be permissible for me to do the same. But I have said all that Our Lord seemed to inspire, if it be wrong, I shall do so no more."

"I begin by placing my soul in the hands of God, then I ask him to bend his bow and to shoot forth his arrows on his enemies that I may combat against them with his cross and with the instruments of his Passion in virtue of the holy Name of God. On this point arises my uneasiness with regard to the imprecations, for I have repeated the same words a hundred times, but I had no evil intention. These Communists are so malicious and vindictive that I wished to destroy their vices and I pray that virtue may triumph where vice has reigned. I said: Let God arise, let his enemies be dispersed, and let all those who hate him be scattered before his Face! May the Name of God thrice holy upset all their schemes! May the Sacred Name of the living God bring disunion and dissention in their designs! May the terrible Name of God wipe out their iniquity!"

"I also repeat many other invectives and having fought them thus I add: 'I desire not the death of the sinner but that he be converted and live. Father, forgive them for they know not what they do.' I perform this exercise with great facility and without any disturbance of mind for I allow myself to be conducted by grace."

It may be of interest to know the state of her interior during this period of generous labor for the salvation of souls, and the spiritual welfare of France; we shall most certainly find that she has rendered an account to her superior. We quote the following: "The way by which Our Lord now conducts me is most .painful to nature, for my Divine Savior continually exacts from me the most absolute interior mortification. I rarely experience any spiritual joy for the communications which I receive, are more of a nature to cause much suffering, as they unveil to my view the justice of an angry God, and the eternal loss of so many immortal souls, as well as the sight of France on the verge of the abyss. This Work of Reparation, I have now borne for nearly four years, and God alone knows how much suffering it has caused me, he himself being the author. Alas! It has not yet appeared upon the earth, and yet terrible calamities are menacing us. O my God, arise and defend the cause which is thine as well as ours. Shelter France under the mystery of thy Face and show her mercy for the glory of thy Name!' I most firmly believe that the future of France depends on this work. It is always shown to me as the means of salvation which God, in his infinite mercy, has designed for her. I would shed even the last drop of my blood to obtain its establishment, for then, the anger of the Lord would be appeased, and a multitude of souls would be saved. Such are the sentiments with which he inspires me, and which I make known to you, reverend mother, to unburden my conscience. I declare that none other than God has given me this idea, and that I was perfectly ignorant of the establishment of a similar association at Rome, which I did not know until long afterwards, and only by a special permission of Providence. I also declare that I have never been influenced by any one in demanding its establishment, but on the

contrary, and thanks be to Grod, I have had the good fortune to receive from my worthy
and prudent superiors, nothing but reprimands and humiliations because of this work. I
likewise declare, that the unity of idea prevailing among these successive communications
is due solely to God; and not to me, for I make a short note of each communication that
I receive and present it to our reverend mother, then I feel relieved and think no more
of it, except to pray God to accomplish his designs; I dare not converse about them with
our mother superior for I am covered with confusion when I speak of these heavenly
communications. When Our Lord first confided this mission to me, I begged of him the
following graces which he has had the mercy to grant:—first, that of never entertaining
sentiments of vanity because of the communications with which he favored me; and
second, that of not being known as the instrument of the divine mercy."

"Our Lord, himself, who conducts my soul in this way, convinces me of my misery and
my utter nothingness, so that it would be impossible for me not to be covered with
confusion at the sight of the extraordinary graces which I receive from his divine hand,
notwithstanding my repeated ingratitude. To my worthy superiors, I leave the care of
establishing this work; as for me, my mission is to tell them all Our Lord says to me, to
submit to their decision and to pray for the accomplishment of his designs for the glory of
his Name. For this object, I have copied the letters containing these revelations. *Sit Nomen
Domini benedictum.*"

Shortly after, she adds: "The object of this work is twofold: Reparation for blasphemy,
and Reparation for the profanation of the Lord's Day by manual labor, consequently it
embraces not only reparation for the outrages committed against God, but likewise the
sanctification of his Holy Name. Here it will, perhaps, be asked if the devotion to the
Holy Face should form a feature in the work? I answer, yes; for it is its most precious
ornament and the source of its riches. Our Lord, himself, has given his most Holy Face to
the associates, in order that this divine Face which is, so to say, outraged and despised anew
by the blasphemy of sinners, as he himself complains, that this Holy Face be respected,
honored, and revered in a most particular manner. In the second place, Our Lord makes
us a present of his most Holy Face, that we may thereby be all-powerful before the throne
of God, by means of the offering which we would thus be able to make of this most august
and sacred Face, the sight of which is so agreeable that it will infallibly appease his anger,
and draw down his infinite mercy upon poor sinners. When the Eternal Father beholds
the Face of his well-beloved Son, bruised and covered with ignominy, when he looks upon

this Sacred Head crowned with thorns, emblem of the sins of mankind which Jesus has taken upon his divine head to save his members (as he one day told me) this sight moves the very bowels of his mercy. Let us try to profit from such a precious gift and beg of our Divine Savior to conceal us in the secret of his Holy Face, during the wicked days of calamity about. to befall us. O God, our Protector! Look upon us and cast thine eyes on the Face of thy Christ!"

Grod did not break off his communications with the humble Carmelite on the principal object of her mission. The divine Master, from time to time, suggested new motives of encouragement.

One day, May 5th, 1841, when she was asking him for the establishment of the Reparation, he replied that he would grant this grace through the intercession of the Blessed Virgin.

"Our Lord," said she, "informed me that he had placed all things in her hand, and that she would obtain the Brief from the Sovereign Pontiff. This Work of Reparation is so necessary for France and fraught with so much glory for God, that he desires his Holy Mother to have the honor of giving it to this kingdom, as a new pledge of mercy. Let us then have recourse to the most Blessed Virgin who is the treasurer of the graces of Grod.

Let us continually recall to her mind that France has been consecrated to her, consequently, that it belongs to her. Let us redouble our zeal for this work and let us not be disheartened. Our Lord has given me boundless confidence. *Sit Nomen Domini benedictum*"

On the feast of Pentecost, May 23rd, while before the most Blessed Sacrament, the sister asked what more she had to do, and manifested her willingness to make any sacrifice, even to shed the last drop of her blood, were it necessary, for the establishment of the Reparation.

"Our Lord gave me to understand," she writes, "that his sole desire was to possess my heart and my will; that the more I would love him, the more grace I would obtain for the accomplishment of his designs. Soon this Divine Savior took possession of all the powers of my soul, favoring it with a most admirable perception of the beauty and excellence of this reparatory. work which I beheld as a mine of gold. Our Lord told me that it required much patience and care to work in this mine, for it was only by dint of hard labor that we could obtain the gold. He also said: 'Oh, if the world could only behold the immense treasure to be reaped by those who work my mine, I would not be without laborers. Make known this communication.' Then my good Savior, to console me, showed me that the work performed in this mine for four years, had not been without fruit; and I saw that indeed the numerous prayers already distributed, for instance, the little Manual and the other prayers relative to the work, were like gold discovered in this precious mine, and Our Lord addressed me these consoling words, regarding the reparatory prayers: 'This new harmony has charmed my ears, delighted the angels, and appeased my wrath, but I shall not repeat again what I have said before; *I want the Work finished.*'"

"This encouragement has filled my heart with joy, while the tears covered my face, but they were tears of joy; then I answered: — 'My sweet Savior, if I say you are no longer angry, I am afraid that your cause will be injured and the zeal of those who are as yet not very much interested, will be cooled.' Our Lord answered: 'Oh, my daughter, what have you just said, the contrary to what you imagine will happen; that soul must have very little love who would not be more inflamed with ardor to perfect a thing so agreeable to me that it subdues my wrath.' Then he gave me wonderful light on the sublimity of this Association and the preference with which he esteems it more than all others established in the Church, because of its object, to make reparation for all the outrages offered against the Divinity by blasphemy and by the profanation of the Sunday. He compared the first to the common wine used at the wedding of Cana, and the latter, to the miraculous wine served at the end of the supper. I told him that there were many obstacles to his designs; but he consoled me and assured me that all this opposition would only make it shine forth with a more resplendent glory, and that I should tell our mother prioress to continue to labor in its cause when she found a favorable occasion; he gave me to understand that it required prayer, ardent desires and suffering."

"Behold, as nearly as possible, reverend mother, what has transpired in my soul. In conclusion, my Divine Savior said: 'It is to my holy Mother that you are indebted for the communication you have just received; she has obtained it. Live Jesus and Mary forever!" The day following the sister wrote: "The letter which I remitted to you yesterday about the grace which I received from Our Lord concerning the work by excellence consecrated to the glory of his Name, does not satisfy me, for I still feel urged to speak; the effects of this communication are so great, and have fortified my soul to such a degree, that earth and hell armed together against the work (if such a thing were possible) could not diminish my confidence. *If God be with us, who shall be against us?* When the moment appointed by God will have come, all things will yield to his sovereign power. Oh, how excellent is this work! How sublime! What immense benefits are reserved for the defenders of the Holy Name of God! Would that I could publish to the entire world all the truths my soul has learned on this memorable day of Pentecost by means of this celestial light which it is not given to mortals to express!"

"Why have I not the eloquence of a St. Bernard that I might win all men to enroll themselves in this holy crusade! In the early ages of the Church, the Lord raised up an army of courageous soldiers to combat the enemies of the Holy Land; and his faithful servant St. Bernard preached this holy Crusade with marvelous success: but in our times, the same Lord demands courageous soldiers to defend his Holy Name, blasphemed and despised by his enemies. Alas! Shall he not find one! It is not necessary to go to foreign lands and arm oneself with breastplate and buckler, nor to endanger one's life. In our sacred militia the cross of Jesus Christ will be our arms, both offensive and defensive with which to attack, and to defend ourselves against these enemies; and his sacred Name, full of virtue and power, will be our buckler of defense."

"But to succeed in this pious undertaking, we must address ourselves to the glorious Virgin Mary with boundless confidence. Beg her to place herself at the head of this holy army, she the General of the armies of the Lord, more terrible than an army set in array! It is this amiable Mother who has obtained for me, notwithstanding my unworthiness, the unheard of favor which I received yesterday from her dear Son. May she be forever blessed! Being at the feet of this august Mother, I felt inspired these two days, to invoke her under the title of Our Lady of the Holy Name of God. Then I composed a crown of seventy-two invocations, to honor the precious years of her holy life. At the end of each decade, I recalled to her these words which she pronounced in her divine canticle: *Quia fecit mihi magna qui potens est, et sanctum nomen ejus.* (He who is mighty hath done great things unto me, and Holy is his Name). After these words, I added: 'O most holy and most worthy Mother of God, most powerful advocate of Christians! I place the cause of the Holy Name of God into thy hands.' I believe this little prayer touched the tender and compassionate heart of my Blessed Mother, for while offering it, I felt convinced that she accepted it."

"O holy Virgin!" said I, "deign to receive this new title for thou art really Our Lady of the Holy Name of God, since thou art the Daughter of the Father, the Mother of the Son and the Spouse of the Holy Ghost, and that thou dost thyself proclaim that he has done great things unto thee and that his Name is holy! Verily, O Blessed Virgin Mary! thou art the honor and glory of the Holy Name of God, for thou art the masterpiece of his hand, of him who has operated such wonders in thee. Therefore, I style thee, Our Lady of the Holy Name of God. Thus, reverend mother, I say all that I can think of, to the most Blessed Virgin in order to win her favor for the Work of Reparation, if I can thus express myself, respectfully reminding her, that she, more than all others, is obliged to work for the honor and glory of Him who has favored her more than all his other creatures, and that I doubt not she will obtain for us the establishment of this work, which Our Lord has compared to the delicious banquet at the wedding of Cana. Let us remember that it was the most Blessed Virgin who obtained from her Son this miraculous wine. In the meantime, I humbly beg you to invite all who have at heart the establishment of this work, to salute with me this Holy Virgin under the title of *Our Lady of the Holy Name of God.*"

As a sort of "Remark on the glory of the most Blessed Virgin," the pious sister adds: "Our Lord made me approach his most Holy Mother, to receive from her blessed hands the grace which I had been soliciting for such a length of time for the glory of the Holy Name of Grod. I placed myself with all confidence in the heart of this Mother of Mercy, begging her to be my advocate in the cause of God, earnestly recommending to her this great object, during the beautiful month entirely consecrated to her. I did not invoke her in vain; she beheld the tears of her little servant, she listened to her sighs and entreaties and soon inspired her servant, the Bishop de Langres, who heard the project spoken of, to take the most lively interest in it. His zeal for the Holy Name of God urged him on to establish the Association. The rules were formed, June 28, 1847, on the vigil of the feast of the most holy Apostles, Sts. Peter and Paul; and what is quite remarkable, was that it was solemnly and canonically erected into an Association on the 16th of July, feast of Our Lady of Mount Carmel."

"O powerful hands of Mary, it is you who have performed all, men have been but your instruments. I thank you a million times! Mayst thou be forever blessed! Let us admire another trait of Divine Providence and of the mercy of Mary; Mgr., the Bishop of Langres brought the plan of this Work in Reparation for Blasphemy and the violation of the Sunday before the Sovereign Pontiff, to obtain a Brief which would enrich this Association with the blessings and the indulgences of the Holy Church. Our Holy Father signed this Brief on the 27th of July 1847, and a second the 30th, erecting the Association for Reparation into an Archconfraternity. I look upon the Church with admiration bringing forth this work during those three days of sorrow. I behold the mercy of God, superabound where sin hath abounded. Be forever blessed, O my God! All this has not occurred by hazard; thy Providence has conducted and directed all for the glory of thy Holy Name and for the salvation of France. Protect this work, which is thine, and defend it against its enemies. Propagate it in this kingdom consecrated to the glorious Virgin Mary."

We have not wished either to interrupt or abridge this pious and simple narrative of the sister, relative to a fact which has so happily crowned all her desires. There remains to us to relate some of the details connected with the principal circumstances of the formation of these societies.

18

THE ARCH-CONFRATERNITY

> ***Sit Nomen Domini benedictum!***
> **May the Name of the Lord be blessed!**
> *[Archconfraternity for Reparation]*

The confraternity for Reparation sprang up, as it were, miraculously by the sole will of God, without the intervention of man. In our brief account of its establishment, we shall follow exactly the notes furnished us by the Carmelite annals, likewise those of M. Dupont.

One of the "Abridgment of Facts" fell into the hands of a fervent Christian of Rouen, M. le Brument-Jeulin, a man like M. Dupont, renowned for his zeal and for his many works of charity. It was through one of his friends, Rev. P. Veilcazes, former director of the Grand Seminary of Tours, and at the time of which we are speaking, superior of the Grand Seminary and of the Carmelites of Rouen, that he first heard of the said Abridgment; shortly after, being obliged to undertake a journey to Paris on business, he went as far as Tours on purpose to ascertain the truth and importance of these "Facts." From what he there learned he did not hesitate to become the courier, and so to say, the travelling agent of the Reparation, resolving to plead its cause whenever Providence would give him the occasion, which was not far distant, as the designs of God were nearing their fulfilment.

On his return from Paris, M. le Brument met at the hotel were he was stopping, M. Tabbe Favrel, vicar general of Langres. During a short interview, the latter informed him that Bishop Parisis was staying at the same hotel, and invited him to visit this illustrious prelate, which he did the same day. During the conversation, the pious gentleman spoke of his journey through Tourraine, and related what he had heard of M. Dupont relative to the work of Reparation, which he warmly advocated. The Bishop of Langres was forcibly impressed by what he had just heard and told the pious gentleman that for some time he had been very desirous of establishing in his diocese a confraternity to meet the need of reparation.

On his return home, the Bishop of Langres wrote to the Archbishop of Tours on this subject; the latter, who did not deem it advisable to take any steps of himself toward the establishment of a confraternity, through fear of giving any ostensible proof of his belief in the revelations of Sister Mary St. Peter, allowed the bishop of Langres to take the initiative, which he could do the more plausibly, as Langres was his own native city. After having received the prelate's reply, Mgr. Parisis, by a mandate, dated June 28, 1847, vigil of the feast of the holy apostles, Peter and Paul, established in the parish church of St. Dizier, *a Confraternity in Reparation for Blasphemy and for the Profanation of the Sunday* under the protection of St. Martin. He sent M. l'abbe Marche, pastor of the parish, as his deputy to Rome to solicit the title of Archconfraternity for the association, and also that it be enriched with special indulgences. Pius IX., then but two years raised to the pontifical chair of St. Peter, received this petition with enthusiasm, and exclaimed: "The Reparation is a work destined to save society," which words have become the watchword of the zealous associates. The Holy Father granted the desired indulgences, and by a brief dated July 30, 1847, raised the Reparatory Association of St. Dizier to the dignity of an Archconfraternity, desiring that his own name be inscribed the first on the register: an inestimable privilege and a source of benedictions for the new work.

Thus, were realized the wishes of our dear sister conformably to the inspiration she had received from heaven.

Before going to Rome, the parish priest of St. Dizier, by order of the Bishop of Langres, kept up a regular correspondence with the Carmelites of Tours relative to the work of reparation. The rule for the Confraternity was long a subject of discussion between them; at last by their joint efforts, the society was molded into form; and though not comprising all the minutiae dictated by Sister M. St. Peter, yet Reparation was the prime object, all the rules and regulations of the association verging to this one point. The said association was consecrated to the adorable Trinity and to the Holy Name of Jesus, and placed under the patronage of St. Michael, St. Louis and St. Martin, protector of France. A cross bearing on one side these words, *Sit Nomen Domini benedictum* and on the other *Vade retro, Satana*, was its insignia; as also a medal, bearing on one side a triangle with rays, symbolical of the adorable Trinity, and on the other, the Holy Face of Jesus. The words of the inscription were to be repeated by the members every time they heard blasphemy, or that they witnessed the profanation of any of the feasts of obligation.

Being a confraternity, it had the privilege of aggregating to itself all other associations formed for this object, and adopting the rules, to which an express clause had been added, reserving to bishops the power of modifying this rule according to the necessities of their respective dioceses, provided that the fundamental points be not interfered with.

The object pursued by Sister Mary St. Peter was thus attained; but it was ever a subject of regret to her that this association had not been established at Tours, that a minor church in a small city of a distant parish, would have this glorious privilege of being the headquarters of a work destined to spread all over France. Another source of regret, then as now, is that perfect silence has been maintained in the episcopal decrees relative to the devotion to the Holy Face of our Lord Jesus Christ, specified by the sister as the visible object of Reparation.

Necessarily, this must be attributed to the ignorance of those at Langres with respect to the special lights on this point accorded to the humble virgin of Carmel; and perhaps, also, to the apparent necessity of not seeming to act in virtue of a revelation not yet sanctioned by the authority of the Church.

However, as a substitute, the *Ecce Homo* was engraved on one side of the cross, and the Litanies of the Holy Face, composed by Sister Mary St. Peter were inserted in the Manual of the Archconfraternity. Evidently, there was much more to be done, to fulfil the desires of Our Lord, according to the revelations of the Carmelite of Tours; but we must bear in mind that the devotion to the Holy Face of Our Lord, had not then the eclat it has today. The sister seemed satisfied with what was achieved; it was also a great subject of joy to M. Dupont, who for many years had been so actively occupied in seeking the glory of the Holy Name of God by Reparation for blasphemy.

The Arch-confraternity of Reparation is perfectly adequate to the necessities of our times; and because it was so manifestly desired by God, it has spread with marvelous rapidity from city to city. From the very first moment of its existence, Reparation for blasphemy and for the profanation of the Sunday, until then concealed in the hearts of a few saintly souls, became the object of general attention; entire parishes were inscribed under its banner and the faithful from all parts of the globe solicited the honor of membership. It may be said that the project communicated to the Carmelite, and by her to the entire Church, has been the fountain-head of the manifold works of reparation since established in France.

One of these deserves a particular notice, for it contains both Reparation and the devotion to the Holy Face: the Reparatory Congregation with perpetual adoration, founded at Paris by Mlle. Dubouche, in religion Sister Mary Teresa.

This pious lady, a distinguished artist, (portrait painter) and at the same time a person of uncommon strength of mind, and of high moral worth, heard of the Abridgment of Facts when on a visit to Mother Isabella of St. Paul, prioress of the Carmelites at Rue d'Enfer. She was struck by what she read in this little notice and was full of admiration for the beautiful litanies of the Holy Face which she had just received and commenced to recite them with great devotion. "The night following (Friday)," said M. Dupont, "Our Lord appeared to her in the same suffering condition as during his Passion. The next morning Mlle. Dubouche, full of holy ardor, undertook to reproduce on canvas the disfigured and bleeding Face of Our Lord which she had beheld in her vision. She was inspired to work at this painting only on Fridays and on her knees: for four successive Fridays she toiled at this labor of love, and at the expiration of the fourth week a picture was produced such as would be creditable to our best artists. Mlle. Dubouche, laden with her precious burden hardly finished, set out for Tours, and presented herself unexpectedly at the Carmelite monastery, where she found souls ready to appreciate and understand her noble heart, for Our Lord had previously said to Sister Mary St. Peter:

"I will give you my Face and every time that you present it to my Father, my mouth will open to plead your cause." Mlle. Debouche was received in the parlor by the mother prioress assisted by her secretary Sister Teresa of St. Joseph; and in presence of Sr. St. Peter, at the time portress, Mlle. Dubouche opened the box containing the picture set in a black frame with a gold star in each corner. Sister St. Peter was called upon by the lady to know if the picture corresponded to what she had seen; she humbly replied that the Face of Our Lord had never been shown her in a sensible manner, but that the picture was a good expression of the idea she had conceived of the suffering countenance of our Divine Lord.

To give the Community the pleasure and opportunity of beholding it, the picture was placed on the novitiate altar, and whilst the sisters were piously contemplating it, Sister

Mary St. Peter approached and regarded it with such an expression of sorrow and love, that many of the sisters remained profoundly impressed thereat.

M. Dupont desired to behold this wonderful picture, and to gratify his wish, the pious artist had it brought to his house, and presented it to him herself. She very willingly gave the permission to have it copied, of which favor he was not slow in taking advantage; the first hasty but faithful copy was given to the Carmelites. It is preserved with great care in the chapter-room, above the spot where our good Sister St. Peter now reposes. Mlle. Dubouche, herself, recopied the picture several times; one of these copies is now in the chapel of St. Ursula at Tours.

From this time forth, as we would naturally suppose, friendly relations sprang up between this lady and the Carmelites; nor was she forgotten when the circulars announcing the death of Sister St. Peter were sent to the friends of the community. At the moment the death letter arrived, Mlle. Dubouche was seriously ill; after reading the notice she suddenly conceived the idea that she ought to make a novena in union with the dear deceased, promising if restored to health that in thanksgiving she would go on a pilgrimage to her tomb. Only ten days had elapsed, when full of joy and gratitude, she went to fulfil her vow. "On her return from the cemetery," says M. Dupont, "I heard her exclaim with enthusiasm: 'I was sick, given up by the physicians, but through the powerful intercession of this venerable servant of God, I am now perfectly restored to health.'"

On her return to Paris, Mlle. Dubouche put into execution the project with which she had been inspired. On the 6th of August, just one month after the death of Sister Mary St. Peter, she retired from the world, and together with a few chosen souls founded the "Congregation of Reparation" with the perpetual adoration of the most Blessed Sacrament. At the end of three months, the young community, although but few in number, commenced the nocturnal adoration once or twice a week, in the chapel of the Carmelites on Rue d'Enfer. It was on one of these occasions of perpetual adoration that the celebrated Hermann, a recent convert from Judaism, and later called Father Marie Augustin, conceived the idea of assembling the men together, that they might render their nightly homage of adoration to Our Lord in the most Blessed Sacrament of the altar.

One afternoon, this pious neophyte, who frequently visited the churches in which the Blessed Sacrament was exposed, entered the Carmelite chapel where he prostrated himself in adoration before Our Lord, concealed under the sacramental veils. There he knelt in prayer, heedless of the flight of time. It was in the month of November, one of the sister tourieres gave the signal for departure; a second was rung, yet Hermann, unconscious of the approach of night, made no movement; then, as if suddenly coming to himself he said to the sister: "Yes, yes, I will go when those near the altar rise to depart." "But they will hot leave here tonight," replied the sister. This answer was the precious seed which fell from the hand of the sower on good ground. Our fervent convert, whom we shall soon call, the Angel of the Tabernacle, left the holy place and with all haste repaired to the house of Mgr. de la Bouillerie, then Vicar General, to whom he said: "I have just left a chapel where there are ladies who will remain in adoration all night before the Blessed Sacrament!" Mgr. de la Bouillerie, who had been one of the founders of the Reparatory Order of Mlle. Dubouche, replied: "Well, what of that? If you find the men, we shall authorize you to imitate these pious worshippers, whose lot at the feet of the Lord, you so much envy."

The next day, with the assistance of the good angels, Hermann awoke a responsive echo in many holy souls; he was soon enabled to count twenty fervent adorers, and before the end of the year, the men's nightly adoration was organized at Notre Dame des Victoires.

The first night of adoration was on December 6th, 1848, at the very moment of the news of the departure of Pius IX from Rome, fleeing from before the face of a revolution which had changed France to a republic, and had shaken the mighty thrones of Europe to their very foundations.

We perceive that the nightly adoration for men in France has always been characterized by these two principal intentions; first, for the expiation of the outrages committed against God, second to obtain mercy for France. We thus behold that the work of reparation by the adoration of the Blessed Sacrament, when still in its cradle among a congregation of pious women, gave rise to the nightly adoration by men, while both were but the offspring of the communications made to Sister Mary St. Peter; the designs of the Divine Master manifested to his faithful servant, could not have been better carried out than by uniting together the perpetual adoration of the Blessed Sacrament and the devotion to the Holy Face. We remember that in the year 1844 (Feb. 27th) Our Lord had nominated our little Carmelite of Tours as his ambassadress to France and had commanded her to remain continually before the most Blessed Sacrament, at least in spirit, praying for France and for the establishment of the work of Reparation. From that day forth, she felt called upon in a most particular manner by her Divine Master never to lose sight of his Sacramental presence on our altars. At the beginning of 1847, when the co-relationship between the Divine Majesty blasphemed and the veneration of the Holy Face had been manifested to her in the extraordinary manner we have portrayed, Our Lord allowed her to hear his lamentations over his love unknown in the most Blessed Sacrament, and then, as she said, "he had happily united at his feet both the heart and the mind" of his servant, in order that she might keep him company in his abandonment, adoring his most Holy Face concealed under the eucharistic veils.

In founding this Reparatory Congregation with perpetual adoration, Mlle. Dubouche fulfilled to the letter the will of the Lord communicated to the sister. Mother Isabella of St. Paul, who rejoiced at the success to which she herself had contributed, had no hesitation in attributing (after God) all the honor to the Carmelite of Tours. In one of her letters to Mlle. Dubouche, we find the following remark: "Sister Mary St. Peter is certainly the foundress of this work, and I believe that from the highest heavens she aids us with her powerful assistance and fills with fervor and generosity those who are the cornerstones of this edifice." M. Dupont, aware of the origin of all the works of reparation, did not hesitate to say that Mlle. Dubouche was inspired with the project of her congregation at the tomb of Sr. Mary St. Peter, during her pilgrimage of thanksgiving. After the foundation of the nightly adoration by men at Paris he, himself had nothing so much at heart as to have a similar established at Tours (February 1849) as if it were the mission of this great servant of God to see realized in a public and ostensible manner, the most secret designs communicated to the virgin of Carmel.

19

THE DIVINE MATERNITY

"O Mother of God! Remember thou art my mother, and that I am the little sister of the Holy Infant Jesus."
(Words of the Sister.)

The Work of Reparation is now canonically established: at last Sr. Mary St. Peter has attained the essential object of all her desires. Our Lord will now spread out before her vision a new horizon and cause her to behold a series of communications so extraordinary and mysterious, that before exposing them to our pious readers, we must point out their precise import and their nature. They form, in the history of her visions, a chain of revelations in themselves, of the highest interest. Indeed, they could not be omitted from these pages, without leaving in the shade the most hopeful and the most consoling part of this great work of Reparation. The Lord granted them to the virgin of Carmel for two reasons, clearly discernible in her own account of these favors. One seems to have been to recompense her here below for all the sacrifices which the accomplishment of her mission had entailed; our good Master often acts in like manner toward the souls who serve him with fidelity. The other motive, more general, relative to the work of Reparation itself, was to prefigure the graces of mercy and salvation by which the realization of this work was to be followed. This future effusion of grace, promised to the world, will be the result of the merits and of the intercession of the Blessed Virgin, the august Mother of Jesus, (at the same time the Mother of Christians), a foretaste of which was given to the pious servant of her Divine Son in causing her to participate in a spiritual and heavenly manner in the virginal food which he, himself, received in the arms of his Mother during his infancy.

A favor so surprising is not an exception nor a novelty in the history of the saints. No one is ignorant of the miracle which took place in favor of St. Bernard, Abbot of Clairvaux. In a celebrated vision, the Queen of Heaven, as a recompense for the many volumes he had written with so much learning and piety in her honor, caused to descend on his lips some drops of heavenly milk. This prodigy has not unfrequently occurred, it has even been a favorite subject of study among artists. According to the learned Baronius, (1028), St. Fulbert, bishop of Chartres, a devoted servant of Mary, was once favored with a similar privilege, when reduced to the last extremity by illness. By virtue of the divine milk which the Blessed Virgin made him taste, he instantly recovered his health, and was at the same time blessed with the gift of prophecy.

No one will contest that the foundation on which these extraordinary details rest, is perfectly in keeping with the teaching of faith and with the doctrine of the Church. The divine maternity is a dogma of the Catholic Church, essentially connected with the Incarnation of the Word; in all ages it has furnished to ascetic writers and to the holy fathers themselves, the most elevated and ravishing considerations upon the mystery of the Infancy of Jesus, and upon his first relations with his most Holy Mother. Let us, for example, glance over the writings of St. Athanasius, of St. Augustine, of St. Bernard and of St. Vincent Ferrier; these illustrious doctors extol the maternity of Mary in most admirable terms of faith and piety, bearing the very same signification which we observe in the writings of Sr. Mary St. Peter.

We must, likewise, not mistake the nature and the method of these divine operations in this daughter of Carmel. We have already affirmed and here affirm anew, that nothing has transpired in a visible or sensible manner. In explaining to the mother superior what passed, she has been obliged to employ expressions and images which strike the senses, while in reality all passed in a sphere purely intellectual. It is well known that theologians distinguish three kinds of divine communications; those which strike the senses physically, such as visions and other external apparitions; those which take place in the imagination with the aid of representations and interior, invisible images; and thirdly, those which pass in the understanding, the superior part of the soul, without any images whatever, either visible or invisible. These last, according to the masters of the spiritual life, are the most elevated and the most perfect. Now this is precisely the kind of communication with which Sister Mary St. Peter was favored. Consequently, in all that she has described so ingeniously, she has beheld nothing with her eyes, heard nothing with her ears, touched nothing sensibly, not even in imagination, which has had no play whatsoever in her celestial communications. "Our Lord caused me to understand," such is her ordinary expression; she saw, heard, felt, and tasted, but as the pure spirits, by a means intellectual and angelic, satisfactorily explained by theology, but understood only by the chosen few who have had the experience of this most perfect mode of revelation.

We shall cite here the testimony of St. Theresa, so well versed in these matters; the following are her own expressions: "The vision of the intellect is the most elevated, the most sublime, and that to which the devil can have the least access. We behold neither with the eyes of the body, nor with those of the soul, understood that the vision is not imaginary. It is a light which, without striking the senses, illuminates the understanding that the soul may enjoy so great a flood. Truth is there imprinted by a knowledge sovereignly clear, excluding all doubt, even producing a certainty more positive than that afforded by the testimony of the senses, for oftentimes in that which strikes the latter, it not unfrequently happens that a doubt arises whether it be an illusion. In our case it may happen that a doubt presents itself at the first moment, but there is a firm conviction that this doubt is without any foundation.... The language is so heavenly that no human effort could succeed in causing it to be heard if the Divine Master himself did not teach it us by experience. He places in the depth of the soul what he wishes to make known to her, and while conversing with her makes her attentive to all that he says, despite herself; he forces her to hear him, and prevents her withdrawing her attention. She is then in the condition a person of excellent hearing to whom another, quite near, would speak so loudly, without allowing her to stop up her ears, that willing or not, she must hear... By this kind of conversation, the Lord wills to give the soul a faint idea of what passes in Heaven; he initiates her to speak without words, and this is the language of her heavenly home. That such language existed, I was in entire ignorance until it pleased the Lord to give me evidence in an ecstasy."

"While in this valley of tears, God and the soul understand each other by this means, for he makes her comprehend all that he wishes her to know and comprehend; they have no need of any other art to express their secret thoughts. Even on earth, two people of intelligence can express their mutual love without making signs, only by looking at each other. This is precisely what passes between God and the soul; but it is not given to see in what manner they cast their eyes one on the other, nor the glance in which they read their mutual love..."

"And again, God in this manner causes the soul now to understand some great truths, again some profound mysteries. 'By means of this divine language, truth is infused in us iii the same manner as an aliment which is incorporated in us without the trouble of masticating it, ignorant of the way it has become a part of our substance, but quite positive of the fact that it is in us. There is, however, this difference; here the nature of the aliment remains unknown to us, whilst as regards this infusion, I know what is its substance, and that it comes from God, but I know not how he has given it to me, for I have not seen it, I cannot comprehend it." These are the expressions of the illustrious reformer of Carmel; what she has experienced, what she has so admirably explained, has been worthily exemplified in one of her saintly daughters, the Carmelite of Tours. In perusing what is about to follow, let us not lose sight of these preliminary reflections; and instead of being scandalized, we shall rather be edified, and rejoice to behold such precious and rare favors accorded as a reward, for her fidelity and her generous sacrifices.

Likewise, let us not forget that this good sister had long been prepared for the reception of these heavenly gifts by a precocious and tender devotion to the Blessed Virgin, and also by the particular attraction to the infancy of the Word Incarnate that we have remarked from the first moments of her religious life. This sweet mystery was, indeed, the principal cause of her rapid progress in religious perfection and the primary source of the wonderful lights lavished upon her.

According to the method hitherto adopted, we shall take her own simple and candid narration of the marvels of grace of which she was the object. Her letters on the divine maternity of Mary are preceded by the following" preamble: "A woman of the Gospel, speaking of our Divine Lord, cried out: 'Blessed is the womb that bore thee and the paps that gave thee suck!' According to the testimony of the holy fathers, this woman, full of faith and piety, represents the Church; she recognized and confessed before the world both the divinity and the humanity of Christ, adoring in him a Man-God."

"The mystery of an Infant-God nourished with the sacred milk of the Virgin Mary, his Holy Mother, is a hidden, unknown mystery, which the divine Infant Jesus discovers to whomever he wills. He has deigned, notwithstanding my unworthiness, to apply me to the contemplation of this mystery for five months, by giving me lights and ineffable consolations to rejoice and recreate my soul after the little labors and sufferings I have undergone in working for the glory of his Name. Yes, most amiable Infant Jesus, at the birth of thy Work of Reparation, thou hast spread a grand banquet before my soul, in which she has tasted the most delicious viands!"

"My sins have merited nothing but the rigors of thy justice; but thy mercy is above all thy works, and the admirable familiarity which thou dost display toward some souls, surpasses the understanding of man."

In speaking of a "hidden and unknown mystery," the sister undoubtedly does not wish to lead us to infer that she imagines it has never been revealed to other than herself: but rather that it contains hidden and reserved lights, treasures above the knowledge and comprehension of the majority; then, to the eyes of the worldling, it will always be a "hidden mystery." In a first letter to the mother prioress (June 24, 1847). the servant of God writes thus on the subject: "It is with the greatest confusion that I behold myself obliged to say something of the favors which I have received from the Divine Jesus and his most holy Mother. I have long hesitated before undertaking to write this letter, for I would much rather write my sins; however, I must cooperate with the will of the Infant Jesus, who wishes to engrave his innocence in me, and in all simplicity, I will narrate what has passed in my soul."

"A few days ago, the Infant Jesus strongly applied me to consider the honor and the homage of perfect praise he rendered his heavenly Father during the period he was nourished with the virginal milk of his most holy Mother; he gave me to understand that he willed I should adore him in this humble condition in union with the angels, in order that his mercy might fill me with innocence, purity and simplicity, and that I might collect the precious graces which flow forth from, this ineffable mystery of an Infant God. Then, my Divine Savior ravished my soul to a most sublime state, and in a high contemplation I beheld this prodigy of love and humility. He, who is conceived eternally in the bosom of the Father, amidst the splendors of his glory, is nourished with the virginal milk of his Holy Mother! The Holy Ghost has caused me to penetrate the depth of this mystery, which until that moment I had never understood. Oangelic spirits, you who are continually in adoration in his presence, tell me, which, think you, is the most charming, to see a virgin holding her Creator and her God in her arms to nourish him with her virginal milk, or to behold a God becoming a child, the Word reduced to silence, the All-powerful enveloped with swathing bands in the lap of his Virgin Mother! Ah, I imagine I hear you answer that the humiliations of the Infant-God in this profound mystery, constitute the grandeur and the glory of Mary, whose most august privilege was to have been the mother and the nurse of a Man-God."

"Today, feast of the holy precursor, St. John the Baptist, joyful day of the happy birth of this friend of the Word Incarnate, the Divine Infant Jesus has prepared a feast for my soul."

"I relate it with the greatest confusion, for such a favor were due only to a St. Bernard and not to a miserable sinner as I; yet I am obliged to avow it in the simplicity of my heart; it is not mere imagination, but a grace which I know not how to express, having no words at my command fit for so sublime a subject. Oh, would that it were given me to make known all the lights I have received!... The treasure I have found!... The Infant Jesus, if I may thus express myself, from the virtues of his holy infancy, has made up a bouquet with which he has adorned the chaste womb of his Mother; these are the virtues of meekness, humility, innocence, purity and simplicity, which the brothers of Jesus, brought forth by Mary at the foot of the cross, ought to come and seek from their adopted Mother. Oh, what a grand mystery I perceive! Mary the nurse of a God! but she is also the nurse of man! What great things my soul has conceived here at the feet of Mary during this high contemplation which has ravished my soul! It took the entire hour of recreation for me to return a little to myself."

"This is but an abridgment of the operations of the Divine Savior in an unworthy sinner. He desires to embellish my soul with the virtues of his Holy Infancy before I appear at the tribunal of God. I must become a little child, in order to enter the kingdom of heaven; for this reason, whatever time remains for me to pass on this earth, must be consecrated to honor and imitate his infancy, in order to receive its divine impress."

"These, reverend mother, are the dispositions of my soul, which is entirely concentrated, as you perceive, on the Infant God and his Virgin Mother; I experienced a shower of graces falling gently on me. Nevertheless, I do not forget the Work of Reparation, for it is from the mouth of the Infant Jesus that God truly receives perfect praise and glory."

Let us notice here the relationship she establishes between the "Reparation" of the outrages offered God by blasphemy, and the mystery of the "Infant Word." This comparison seems to have been suggested by the passage from the psalms in which the prophet proclaims: "Out of the mouths of infants and of sucklings thou hast perfected praise because of thy enemies, that thou mayst destroy the enemy." (ps. viii.)

The first time that the pious Carmelite was drawn by the Lord to contemplate his divine infancy under this mysterious aspect, she was much surprised, and sought to ascertain if any of the saints had treated of this subject in their writings.

"Already," said she, "had I consulted two priests distinguished for their knowledge and piety. I was told that the spirit of God was acting in my soul, that I should follow the attraction of grace and correspond to it with fidelity, as God would draw forth his glory therefrom; also that I ought to despise the devil and pay no heed to these extreme repugnances with which he filled me, seeking to withdraw me from a path apparently so extraordinary."

"I was assured that there was no danger for me, that I must continue my exercises in peace; yet this did not entirely satisfy me, for I still sought to find the doctrine of some of the saints in harmony with these communications, but I did not know where to look for such, and I implored our Divine Lord to grant my request. My simple little prayer was not in vain, for I soon felt urged to ask our mother for the life of Father d'Argentan, which she gave me. What was my surprise and my gratitude to God, when on turning over the pages, I found a conference on the Maternity of the most Blessed Virgin, Mother of the Word Incarnate! my admiration continued to augment when in reading this conference, I observed the esteem in which the Fathers of the Church have held this grand privilege of Mary. What I read was an echo repeating letter for letter, all that had been imprinted on my soul touching this mystery during the operations of the Holy Ghost. Oh, with how much respect, with how much joy I kissed those sacred pages which Our Lord and his august Mother placed under my eyes, to enlighten my mind and reassure me against all disquietude! Convinced that this devotion was neither novel, nor visionary, since St. Augustine, St. Athanasius and St. Bernard have spoken of it with so much piety and eloquence, I became established in perfect peace of mind, abandoning myself into the hands of the Infant Jesus that he might perform his most holy will in me."

To explain this pious transport of our dear sister, it may be well to state that the spiritual book of which she speaks was held in great repute, among those competent to judge, for its solid theological and ascetic principles. Father d'Argentan, one of the Capuchin Friars Minor, was one of the writers of the seventeenth century. With the exception of a few trite expressions and certain eccentricities of his oratorical style peculiar to himself, his works are not unworthy of the literary period in which he flourished. His conferences, on the greatness of Jesus and Mary, are well known and highly appreciated in the monasteries of his order.

The Carmelite of Tours, therefore, had good reason to rely on the authority of such a writer; she has even done more, we need not be astonished, for she is so imbued with the doctrine and even with the very words of the book she had in her hands, that she makes use of the most striking passages in her own narration, which she ingeniously avows.

"These thoughts of the holy Fathers have been so instructive to me, that I proposed making use of them in my own account, in order that those who read it afterward, may find it more intelligible. I shall write in a spirit of obedience and charity, according to the light which the Lord deigns to bestow upon me, in reference to a work so entirely consecrated to the Incarnation of the Word, and to the Divine Maternity. I shall speak in all simplicity. The Lord has transformed me, (pausing me to become as a little child to perform in me operations which surpass my understanding. 'If you become not as little children,' said he to his apostles, 'you shall not enter the kingdom of heaven.'" These "Operations" began the day of the feast of St. John the Baptist, June 25th.

She writes: "Having received the holy Infant Jesus in my heart in holy communion, and adoring him in the mystery of his birth, on which I meditated today, I beheld in spirit the most Blessed Virgin nursing her divine Infant; suddenly I found myself confined in the heart of the Infant Jesus. He caused me to understand that I should remain there in silence, in order not to disturb him by the acts I wished to perform. I obeyed his command. Soon after, the Blessed Virgin turned from her Divine Son, to converse with me, if I can express it thus, to make me understand the designs of mercy which her Divine Son had formed over me."

"The following is what she said: 'My child, my Divine Son desires to contract a most intimate union with you. Acknowledge that you are most unworthy of such a favor, for it is a prodigy of his love, for which he has charged me to prepare you."

Then she avowed her past infidelities, and whilst asking pardon of Jesus, her soul was interiorly occupied with her extreme indigence, and the Blessed Virgin informed her that her Divine Son had charged her to nourish the humble sister with the spiritual milk of grace and virtue; that she should beg for these graces twice a day with the simplicity of a little child, a favor which would always be granted her, not in a sensible manner, but by the influence of grace lavished on her soul, which would render her more worthy still to contract an intimate union with the Infant Jesus.

"Then," said the sister, "the most Blessed Virgin gave me to understand that I should honor her maternity by some practices of piety. I obeyed, and the Holy Ghost inspired me to compose a little exercise on the incomprehensible mystery of a God becoming man in the womb of a Virgin."

This "little exercise" of the pious Carmelite was composed of invocations taken from the prayers and hymns of the Church, or else from the pious colloquies, with which the reading of "Father d'Argentan" seemed to have inspired her. The following is a small extract: Hail Mary, full of grace, the Lord is with thee blessed art thou amongst women and blessed is the fruit of thy womb, Jesus, whom thou hast nourished with thy virginal milk for fifteen months."

"Thanks be to thee, Omost Blessed Virgin: Mary, for the immense love with which thou, hast nursed the King of heaven; mayst thy maternal tenderness ever be blessed."

"Eternal Father, we offer thee the Word. Incarnate at the breast of his divine Mother, rendering thee by this infantine action, a perfect act of praise in honor of thy Holy Name."

"O most holy, and most worthy Mother of God! remember thou art my mother and that I am the little sister of the Infant Jesus, nourish me with the spiritual milk of grace; thy most holy child has blessed thy maternal heart with the charming virtues of his infancy, and today he sends me to collect this heavenly dew which will fill my soul with the lovely graces of purity, innocence and simplicity."

"O favored Virgin, and most Blessed Mother! receive, I implore thee, these fifteen salutations in honor of the fifteen months thou didst nurse the Son of God, born in the stable of Bethlehem."

"O divine, O august Lady! what art thou doing?" "Of my substance I am giving nourishment to him who has given me life. It will be incorporated into his being, becoming the very blood in his veins, which will be shed on the cross for the salvation of mankind."

"O angels of heaven! What think you of this prodigy? You who have been commissioned to nourish creatures of this earth with the delicious manna from heaven' And this was accounted such a stupendous miracle! Behold the Virgin Mother, your Queen, giving nourishment to God himself, her Creator, and yours!"

"O most precious milk of Mary! O Blood divine of Jesus, water the earth that it may bring forth legions of elect!"

Shortly after, the sister was consoled to find in the life of a Carmelite of Beaune, venerable Marguerite of the Blessed Sacrament, devoted to the holy infancy, an analogous trait, similar to that which she herself had experienced. It is related of this venerable sister that Jesus revealed to her he had been nursed for fifteen months by his Holy Mother, and that he desired her to honor him for the same length of time, to adore him in this stage of his holy infancy. At the termination of the fifteen months, the holy Child promised that he would grant many graces to the soul who would honor him thus, that she would be most specially assisted by the Blessed Virgin, his mother, and that in consideration of how lovingly she had nourished him with her precious milk, he would grant whatever grace would be desired through her intercession.

Our Carmelite of Tours says: "It is no more difficult to the holy Infant Jesus to make me a participator in the virtues of his infancy, than to have communicated them to one of our sisters two hundred years ago; for he is all-powerful. But what does astonish me, is that this sister was a saint, whilst I am but a miserable sinner, divested of either virtue or talents, a poor worm of earth meriting but hellfire, yet of whom the Infant Jesus wills to make use, because of my abject misery; I have abandoned myself to him entirely for the accomplishment of his designs."

The whole month of July was passed in the contemplation and the enjoyment of the humble and sweet mystery which had just been revealed to her. On the first of August, she wrote another letter to the mother superior.

"Notwithstanding my repugnance to write of the present dispositions of my soul, I will do so willingly, to practice the obedience and the simplicity of the Infant Jesus whom I wish to imitate. I will speak to you with the simplicity of a little, child, in giving you an account of what has passed in my soul from the feast of St. John the Baptist until today."

"Reverend mother, my soul has been all absorbed in the contemplation of the Word Incarnate in the arms of his Holy Mother. Oh, what an ineffable mystery! My soul is ravished at the sight of such a prodigy. A God, the child of a Virgin! He who has spoken by the prophets, who has given his law to man in the midst of thunder and lightning! He by whom all things have been made, the Word of God the Eternal Father! He, there in silence in the arms of his Mother, in obedience to God his Father, offering him the homage of his absolute power, by reducing himself to the helpless condition of a little babe nursed with the milk which will soon be changed into his most precious blood, and be shed for the salvation of the world!"

"There is this Lamb of God, marked out for sacrifice, helpless in the arms of his Blessed Mother through the same obedience which will soon attach him to the cross. Oh, what a ravishing contemplation! After having considered this divine Infant, my heart turned toward his Blessed Mother. Oh, what must have been the sentiments which filled her heart in beholding God, her Creator, partaking of her substance! How much do I thank her for her tender care of the future victim for our salvation"?

The sister then explains that to correspond to this ineffable mystery, Jesus demanded of her perfect innocence of heart and a complete detachment from creatures. "I must now," she writes, "imitate the virtues of his infancy. For having once been a little distracted, I lost sight of the presence of the Blessed Virgin, and the Infant Jesus for nearly a week, but I humbled myself before God at the remembrance of my manifold miseries and he pierced my heart with lively contrition; I wept bitterly over my past sins. Soon, like the father of the prodigal, he gave me the kiss of peace and of reconciliation, communicating himself to my soul in the most intimate manner. Then he made me understand the purity and the perfection which I ought to have before uniting myself to him, for he is my God, my all."

"Afterward, he showed me the favors which he destined for me if I were faithful to follow the attraction of his grace. This communication has entirely changed the disposition of my soul. I found the Infant Jesus once more in the arms of his Blessed Mother. Our Lord declared to me several times that he wished me to adore him in this state, because but few souls are capable of this holy application which demands a great purity of heart."

"The devil came to torment me, trying to make me give up my devotions in honor of this mystery; but when I had submitted my inquietude to the guide of my soul and had put his counsels into practice, the Evil One took to flight."

The pious Carmelite continued, therefore, to follow this divine attraction. In contemplating the sweet object presents to her interior vision she united herself to the angels, to the Holy Innocents, offering to God the Father for the salvation of sinners, this Lamb without blemish, in his condition of absolute dependence and helplessness. Jesus made her a child like himself and gave her to receive from his Holy Mother a part of this spiritual food; the happy sister was inundated with delights and filled with purity and innocence.

"My soul," said she, "is lost in this ineffable mystery, I think of it day and night. Once, when I awoke at one o'clock in the mornings, I felt the presence of the Blessed Virgin near me; she gave me to behold the treasures of grace contained in her maternal heart, inviting me to draw forth graces from this source with full liberty, urging me to share these riches with poor sinners. During holy communion, on this same day, the Infant Jesus admonished me to pray for the impure 'I have prepared and purified thy soul,' he said, 'therefore, arise, go and seek souls for me that I may reign over them.'"

"Then he operated something in me which I cannot comprehend; I experienced a weight of sorrow, inexpressible. 1 was as if in fire, my senses were bound up as if by a divine power. I understood that the Infant Jesus wished me to combat the demon of pride and of impurity, with the virtues and the graces of his holy Infancy. Live Jesus and Mary."

The sister makes the following reflection after the above letter, which is well worthy being copied: "Perhaps some will be surprised after having seen me occupied for four years in meditating the Holy Name of God, to behold me now so much absorbed in a mystery which may seem in the eyes of some Christians, to be the most insignificant, the least worthy of attention in the life of our Lord Jesus. I do not pretend to condemn those who may hold this opinion, because last year I would, perhaps, have shared it with them as I was without the lights which the Infant Jesus and his Mother have since granted me. But today it is not thus, I declare that this mystery unknown and comprehended as it may be to the world, is nevertheless grand admirable, ineffable; its depth and sublimity are only penetrated by the Infant Jesus and his most Holy Mother."

"May God grant that I may never imitate the rebel angels, who after having contemplated the awful majesty and the perfections of the Divinity, refused to acknowledge the Word made Flesh, or to adore him in this state of annihilation. Verily, O divine Child, thou art as worthy of our profound adoration in the arms of thy Mother as seated at the right hand of the majesty of thy Father; Thou art and hast even been the Eternal God!"

Mary of St. Peter, as we see, would not that "Christians" be scandalized after the perusal of her account of the action of God in her regard. For four years she had been occupied in redeeming the honor of his Holy Name, and in appropriating the fruit of his most sorrowful mysteries. And now, we behold her entirely lost in the contemplation of a circumstance in his mortal life which seemed to be the last and the least worthy of consideration. Is it that he has less love, less grace to offer his servant than formerly? Is not the susceptibility of man shocked at the thought of a Man Grod being nursed by a Virgin? Is not this abasement unworthy of the majesty of God, and of the superiority of man? Moreover, what good can accrue to the soul from the assiduous contemplation of this mystery?—The sister will give a satisfactory reply to these objections.

"There are, in the economy of the Incarnation, mysterious secrets, treasures of wisdom concealed from view which the world despises or ignores, but which for all, are none the less necessary for its instruction and salvation. Man, naturally independent and proud, cares not to recall to mind his origin, his nothingness; willingly does he cast off all remembrance of the early necessities of his nature, desirous only of contemplating himself in the full vigor of his manhood, when arrived at the age of maturity, he wills to recognize but his absolute independence, and his power over all other creatures. His pride, offspring of original sin, finds a lesson and a sovereign remedy in the humiliations and annihilations of the Son of God who in descending in our midst, willed to be born and brought forth in the world like himself, with the same necessity for the first tender cares of a Mother. By this means has he been pleased to instruct our proud humanity, and to correct our unfortunate spirit of independence."

According to St. Paul, this is that which the wise and prudent of this world have not understood; what even Christians themselves do not understand enough in our day. This, likewise, was the rock on which the pride of the evil spirits was shipwrecked. According to the teachings of theologians, Lucifer and his accomplices, in the hour of trial, placed in the presence of a God humiliated and abased even to become the Son of a humble Virgin, refused to offer him the adoration which is his due; —their revolt consummated their reprobation. Reflecting on these rebellious spirits and on the infinite number of proud unbelievers who in their self-constituted grandeur of mind refuse to submit their feeble intelligence to the mystery of the Incarnation of the Word, and the Divine Maternity, the daughter of Carmel exclaims in a holy and laudable transport: "Thou art as worthy of our adoration in the arms of thy Mother as seated at the right hand of the Eternal God." The sister here imitates the language of the Fathers and Doctors; of St. Bernard, among others, who speaking of the Word Incarnate, says: "The viler and more despicable has he made himself for my love, so much the more beautiful and worthy of all glory has he become." The Church in the hymns of her office publicly sings to her ministers and to her children: "A little milk has nourished him by whom all creatures are sustained and nourished." And again, "O glorious Mother, elevated above the highest heavens, he, by whom thou hast been created, has become a little child, whom thou dost nourish with thy most pure and virginal milk'"

Et lacte modico pastus est,
Per quem nec ales esurit!
(Hymn for Lauds, Christmas.)

O gloriosa virginum
Subliinis inter sidera
Qui te creavit parvulum
Lactente nutris ubere.
(Office of the Blessed Virgin at Lauds.)

These, as we have seen, are the sum and substance of the thoughts which have filled the heart of the Carmelite of Tours in her pious contemplations of the Word made Flesh.

It was not only for the spiritual enjoyment of Sister Mary St. Peter alone, that she had been admitted, as we have seen, to the participation of the sweet and mysterious fruits of the infancy of the Word made Flesh. In this, as in all the preceding communications, she had with regard to the Church and immortal souls, a higher and more general mission to fulfil. God the Father, irritated against the world which blasphemed and outraged him, had menaced his people with his wrath; his justice had announced scourges and chastisements. But a Mother, full of mercy, the Blessed Virgin Mary, has interceded in favor of the guilty; she has bewailed the sins and wanderings of her people. She has appeared at La Salette, the tears 1 lowed silently from her eyes, and covered her face; her hands were concealed, for the moment had not yet come to distribute grace and mercy on sinful man. But a beginning of Reparation takes place, she appears serene and compassionate, her eyes are raised to heaven, her hands are elevated to intercede and to bless her maternal heart sends forth a fruitful stream of grace, to which souls may come and draw forth pardon and life.

This was the aspect, as novel as consoling, under which the mystery of the Divine Maternity was presented to the Virgin of Carmel. "I was," said she, "in continual contemplation of the Infant Jesus in the arms of his Blessed Mother, reposing on her maternal breast. Then he gave me admirable instructions upon the Maternity of the Blessed Virgin toward men, whom he had given as her children on Mount Calvary at the foot of the cross."

Mary, having been called by God to be the Mother of Christians, received at the same moment the ('barge of nourishing them and of training them to a spiritual life; consequently, she must procure for them the milk of grace for their souls even as she has procured the natural milk for Jesus, her first-born. The following communication will develop this idea. The sister opens the subject by excusing her incapacity. (August 13, 1847). She writes to the mother prioress: "Where shall I find words to express ideas so incomprehensible? With the aid of the Infant Jesus I shall try to lisp forth a few words which, although imperfectly uttered, will nevertheless give you some idea of the present state of my soul." Then she exclaims in her enthusiasm: "Oh, if I could only speak! If I could only write! Never until now have I understood the value of the precious gift which Jesus dying has bequeathed us in the person of his most august Mother! O mystery of love and clemency! At the very instant he was bringing forth the human race, to a heavenly life on the cross in the midst of the most excruciating tortures, he placed these new-born children in the arms of Mary, the tenderest of mothers, to nourish and bring up to eternal life. With this object in view, he has filled her maternal breast with the milk of grace and mercy; he has made his Divine Mother legatee of the immense riches he has acquired for us during his laborious life, and his dolorous Passion, that she might become the admirable channel through which all his infinite merits would flow to the Holy Church, his spouse."

How is it that Mary has been constituted the "legatee," of the riches of redemption? This is precisely what Our Lord will explain to his servant. She writes: "I have again been enlightened on this mystery: the Holy Ghost, from the most pure blood of Mary, formed the adorable body of our Savior Jesus Christ. This body was, therefore, of the substance of Mary; consequently, she possessed certain rights over it; for this reason, it was deposited

in her maternal arms after his death My amiable Jesus caused me to understand that he
wished to return to her all that he had received to operate the redemption of the world.
She had nourished him with her most pure milk; Jesus, to thank her, remitted his blood,
of which he made her the treasurer. There she remained, standing at the foot of the cross,
to receive this precious deposit in the sacred vessel of her maternal heart. Mary had given
to Jesus his most adorable body, and Jesus, after his death, returned it to her covered with
his glorious wounds, that she might draw forth, from these sacred fountains, eternal life
for the new children confided to her watchful care at the very last moment of his life.
Verily, Jesus belongs to Mary together with all his treasures of grace, and Mary belongs
to mankind, with all her tenderness. Oh, how magnanimous is this merciful Mother! She
stretches forth her maternal arms inviting us to come and repose on her motherly heart,
always open to receive us, that she may lavish on us the most heavenly favors."

These communications, bestowed on the sister, were but a preparation for the reception
of a knowledge more precise and more intimate. The Infant Jesus and his Blessed Mother,
will in turn, manifest themselves, to instruct this child of Carmel. Jesus said: "Man, while
on this earth, is in a state of infancy; in heaven alone will he be arrived at his perfect age
of manhood, for this reason should he have continual recourse to his mother, as a little
child."

Our good Carmelite exclaims: "Verily, I behold this truth clearly in the light of God: man
should have continual recourse to the most Blessed Virgin, his Mother, if he wishes to
arrive at the perfect age of manhood in eternity. Behold the two grand mysteries of the
Maternity of Mary, which the Infant Jesus wishes to teach me: Mary, Mother of God, and
Mary, Mother of man. For this reason, it is, that he keeps me in constant contemplation
of himself as Infant in the arms of his Mother, being nourished with her virginal milk, to
teach me by his example to have recourse to her, that I may be fed with the heavenly clew
of her virtues."

The Blessed Virgin, likewise, revealed herself to the pious confident of Jesus. "She made
known to me," said the sister, "'that as she had chosen certain hallowed spots, wherein
to bestow her favors in great profusion, so would she now make choice of my soul to
lavish on it her boundless mercies. I was not long waiting for the accomplishment of this
promise; for today after the holy communion, I beheld the Infant Jesus reposing in the
arms of his Divine Mother. This great mystery is a hidden treasure, buried in the field of
the Church, which he discovers to whomsoever he wills. There have been souls appointed

to honor him in the mysteries of his Passion, and who consequently, have been favored with the sacred stigmata; but for me, notwithstanding my unworthiness, he has bidden me to bear the state of his infancy, and for this favor he has already prepared me himself. Today, he has condescended to unite me to himself during the holy communion, and to make me penetrate even to his adorable heart, that I might draw the nearer to his Virgin Mother, He it is who has led me to this source of grace and benedictions, bidding me draw forth the milk of divine mercy in the same spirit of charity with which he himself had imbibed the virginal milk of his tender mother; for he was nourished with this milk for the salvation of mankind, and for mankind had he shed it in such profusion on the cross. Therefore, in imitation of his example, I ought to imbibe this mysterious liquor from the maternal bosom of Mary in the name of all my brethren, to lavish it afterward over the entire world as a heavenly dew, to refresh and purify the earth desolated by the fire of concupiscence and filled with the debris of sin and corruption."

Then the sister seemed to hear Our Lord saying to her: "I wish you to be very simple and childlike, but that you have a large heart." She added: "The following is a short prayer which was inspired to me, by which I can collect this mysterious liquor of mercy from the maternal heart of Mary:"

"O most holy and most worthy Mother of God! send down in life-giving showers the milk of grace and mercy upon all men, thy children." The Blessed Virgin told her that she ought to be very grateful for this inestimable privilege granted by the bounty of her Divine Son. Closing this narrative the sister says: "O reverend mother! How can I express what I experienced during this operation of grace! Oh, I how incomprehensible the favor of beholding oneself as a little child in the tender arms of Mary, reposing on her maternal breast! This source of grace and mercy is inexhaustible. But, alas, what am I, miserable and unworthy as I am, to be thus deputed to draw forth at this fountain of mercy for the salvation of sinners! I prostrated myself on the ground, confessing before God my unworthiness for such a mission; but the Lord has ever chosen the weakest among his creatures to show forth his power and glory. *Sit Nomen Domini beneditum.*"

20

INTERVIEW WITH THE SECRETARY

"Your pilgrimage is drawing to a close!....
The end of the combat is nigh!..,
You will soon behold my Face in Heaven!"
(Words of Our Lord)

The establishment of the archconfraternity for Reparation was a source of joy to Sister St. Peter. "But," said she, "I am not yet perfectly satisfied, because the Church of Tours, the inheritance of the great St. Martin, has until now remained sterile. When shall this seed which she has so long borne, spring forth?"

Another attempt was about to be made. On the 11th of November, feast of St. Martin, the virgin of Carmel experienced an operation of grace which, as she said, "was a signal for combat. After my soul had been inundated with ineffable graces for six months, Our Lord confided anew to my care, the Work of Reparation." The following Sunday, November 14th, day on which the feast of the Thaumaturgus was celebrated with great solemnity at Tours, she was inspired to renew her supplications to the archbishop. "O God," she exclaims, "how impenetrable are thy judgments! Let us adore them in silence! All our plans were futile, but I was not on this account discouraged, for the most Blessed Virgin had given me the hope that a work so necessary for the salvation of France would take root and spread over the entire kingdom, and that she would bestow upon us innumerable graces. The child Jesus, on his part, promised me that if this devotion were established in accordance to his wishes, he would bestow upon France the kiss of peace and reconciliation. At another time, the most Holy Virgin again recommended to my prayers this new-born Confraternity, just approved by the Church and enriched with precious favors. Our divine Mother seemed to be so full of joy at the birth of this association, that she demanded of God extraordinary graces for France."

The future welfare of her beloved fatherland was always uppermost in the mind of the servant of God, and thus we behold her praying for it unceasingly. On the 2nd of December, Our Lord appeared to her all covered with wounds, saying these sad words: "The Jews crucified me on Friday, but Christians crucify me on Sunday! I implore you to solicit the establishment of the Reparation in this diocese of Tours, that my friends may embalm my wounds by their expiatory prayers and obtain mercy for the guilty. My daughter, the heavens are overcast, the storm is threatening to burst forth, but I shall keep my promise if my will be done. Speak with humility, but at the same time with a holy liberty." She made no delay in informing Mgr. Morlot of this communication. He was warned of the "storm" which was threatening, and apprised that the last hour for action had come.

If the sister was disheartened with her want of success on one hand, she was encouraged on the other by a vision so much the more pleasing as it was unexpected. Let us listen to her relating the cause of her joy: "Our holy Mother St. Teresa," said she, "appeared to me this morning. She has been appointed by God to combat the enemies of the Work of Reparation which the powers of darkness are trying to overthrow. She told me that this holy work would be the honor of Carmel for it was truly in conformity with the spirit of our holy vocation, whose sole object is the glory of God and the relief of the necessities of the Church; for this reason, she urged me to devote all my energies to this work, and to pray with untiring fervor. Then she recommended me to be scrupulously obedient, giving me to understand that Jesus would work miracles for the soul obedient to her superiors, that she herself had always submitted the lights and communications, received from Heaven to the decision of obedience. She showed me with what fidelity I ought to acquit myself of all our religious observances, which are so agreeable to Our Lord that the fulfillment of them alone is sufficient to enrich the soul with merit. In fine, I understood that God gave to this work a most powerful protectress in the person of our holy Foundress, and to me a most powerful consoler in my afflictions. From this moment, I felt united in a most particular manner to our holy Mother, so remarkable for her zeal for the glory of the Most High. It is she who will succor me in my weakness and help me to pursue my thorny path."

The "storm" of which the Lord had spoken, was threatening in the distance. About two months later, it was on the point of bursting forth. The Divine Master had foretold it in unmistakable terms.

"During my evening meditation," said the sister, "Our Lord intimated that he had something to communicate. I resisted several times, for I feared an illusion. But at last, Jesus, having recollected all the powers of my soul in his Divine Heart, told me to recall to mind that I had given myself entirely to him, to labor for the accomplishment of his designs; for this reason, he wished to confide to me a new mission. Presently he warned me of the terrible blow which was menacing us: *The Church is threatened with a violent tempest; pray, pray, pray!* He repeated this several times on different occasions. It would be impossible to express the touching manner in which Our Lord said: 'Pray, pray!' He taught me what prayer to say in order to shelter his Church in virtue of the most Holy Name of God: it was the same prayer he had offered to his heavenly Father for his Apostles and for the Church, before quitting the earth. 'My Father, keep in thy Name those whom thou hast given me.' (St. John.) This prayer is more efficacious than any I could compose of myself and since he chose me in his mercy to render glory to the Holy Name of God, I have, in some manner, the right to ask grace in virtue of this Holy Name, the refuge of the Church."

"My adorable Savior made me understand that his justice was roused by the sins of the world, but particularly by the crimes which are an outrage to the majesty of God. At this moment, I beheld Our Lord in the most Blessed Sacrament, and I saw that the prayers of the just held captive the arms of divine justice. Our Lord recommended me to pray for the Sovereign Pontiff. Lastly, I beheld what seemed to me a thick black smoke rising toward the heavens; it did not, however, obscure the sun, and I was somewhat consoled. This smoke was the figure of enemies, and the sun symbolized the Church. Jesus continued: 'The affects you will experience in your soul will make you understand that it is I who have spoken.' And soon my heart was transpierced with a sword of sorrow. I then commenced my mission of prayer, saying: 'Holy Father, guard the Church of Jesus Christ in virtue of thy salutary Name, for this was the last will of thy Divine Son, his last desire. Remember the last loving prayer he offered for our holy Mother the Church, Holy Father, keep in thy Name those whom thou hast given me; while I was with them, I kept them in thy Name. Most Holy Name of God, refuge of the Church and of France, have pity on us and save us.'"

"Sunday, 20th of February, having offered my holy communion in reparation for the outrages committed against the Divine Majesty, I saw that all was over! — Guilty France was about to be chastised; a celestial ray caused me to observe that the Lord has drawn his bow, he is ready to aim his arrows. On beholding him arming himself against sinners who so shamefully outrage him, I was penetrated with a holy indignation, and entering into the designs of his justice, I cried out: Strike, Lord! I panted for the glory of God to be avenged, for I saw that the blow would not be mortal. Although I prayed to the Most High to strike, that he might retrieve his glory, yet I begged him to strike as a father and not as an angry judge. Let us adore the justice of God and at the same time invoke his mercy. It is now more than four years that the arm of the Lord has been raised in anger over our guilty heads!..."

In fact, the hour for chastisement had come; an unexpected revolution had broken out in Paris, the effects of which were experienced all over Europe.

Louis Philip had been under the impression that a reign of nineteen years had secured his scepter, but alas, he was obliged to fly with his family into exile. The Church, however, was not openly persecuted, at least in France, for she is still respected even in the midst of the greatest social disorders It will not be until later on that the secret emissaries of impiety, will try to tyrannize over her by their diabolical intrigues.

On the 26th of February, after having received holy communion, our Carmelite was much consoled, the Lord having said these words relative to the Community: "Fear not, little troop, thou art reposing under the salutary banner of my Name. No evil shall befall thee, for all power is in my hand, and I will not suffer thee to be wrested from my grasp."

"Verily," cries out the pious virgin, "the Lord will recognize and protect all those who invoke his Holy Name; it is an all-powerful rampart, shielding our house, for the members are united by the bonds of charity."

"Our Lord gave me to understand that the clergy, likewise, will be spared; troubles and vexations will doubtless arise, but the hierarchy will not be openly persecuted; the blood of priests will not be shed as in '93, because he has not as much reason to complain as in those unfortunate times. I am confident that the Church of France will be protected in virtue of the Holy Name of God."

"Holy Father, keep in thy Name those whom thou hast given me. This is the prayer which we must continually recite for the Holy Church, in union with our Lord Jesus Christ."

"Permit me, Rev. Mother, to tell you the words which Jesus said to me after holy communion on the 21st of November; they caused me to shed tears in abundance. He was at the time speaking of the Work of Reparation and said: "When I shall shake the throne of France to its very foundations, what, think you, shall be her distress!'"

"With good reason was I overwhelmed with grief, for I saw that the terrible moments of God's justice were drawing nigh. Alas, the hour has sounded, and in the twinkling of an eye, he will execute what he has sworn. I adore thee, O justice of my God; yet I invoke thy mercy, O Lord most high."

The sister felt inspired to invoke mercy with renewed fervor. Listen to her supplicating cries: "My soul is sorrowful even unto death, and I feel the necessity of confiding my troubles to you, reverend mother. When I consider the predictions which Our Lord has made, I say: Soon, too soon, shall they all be fulfilled! My God, have I not reason to fear, when I think I have been charged with such a formidable mission! when I recall these terrible words: 'If through your fault, my designs are not accomplished, I will demand a rigid account of the loss of these souls at your hands.' Several years have now elapsed, since I made known that the Lord demanded a Reparatory Work, in order to stay the threatening arm of his Father; for Reparation would appear as the rainbow in the heavens. Happily, the work has been founded and even now sheds around its beneficent influence, but it is still too feeble to arrest the arm of the Most High. Oh, if this work were spread in the entire diocese, I would be without fear, for God is faithful to his promise. For some time, I have implored my good Master to give Monseigneur an indisputable sign of my mission, so that he would do something to establish the Reparation. I have set forth the present difficulties of his Lordship to Him who can do all things, and I have supplicated him to give some proof of his will. O Lord, I implore thee, send him a sign so marked and certain that entire France, beholding, will recognize this work as thine. Grant this great sign I implore thee."

"Our Lord, seeing that I begged this favor solely for the glory of his Name and for the accomplishment of his will, heard my prayer. On the 13th of February, I had the vision of which I have spoken. It was in confirmation of what I had announced to Monseigneur in the communication of December 2nd. My Divine Master at that time told me to inform his Lordship that the storm was threatening in the distance, that it was time for action. On the 13th of February, I saw that this storm was about to burst forth, and I beheld a black, cloud rising from earth to heaven which did not, however, obscure the sun (the Church) because the Church of France had then invoked the Holy Name of God, this Name, her refuge during the tempest. The Lord told me that in consequence of this work, France would not be humiliated as she deserved, but would be only slightly chastised."

"Our Lord has done what he has promised; yes, indeed, he has shielded his Church in virtue of his life-giving Name. Before striking the awful blow of his justice, he said: 'Holy Father, keep in thy Name those whom thou hast given me.' Therefore, have those who belonged to him been spared. Oh, how I desire to make known this consoling truth to all bishops:—that the Holy Name of God is the impregnable fortress of the Church of France! How I would beg of them with all the earnestness of which I am capable, to propagate this Work of Reparation! I have always said, and I still repeat, that Reparation alone can disarm the justice of God and save France. Happy shall we be if we know how to use this plank of salvation."

If unable to proclaim this truth to all bishops of the world, it would be expedient that at least she should be allowed to make it known to the prelate who, from the year in which she submitted her communications to him, appeared convinced of the truth and of the heavenly origin of her revelations. On the 3rd of March she addressed the following letter to the mother prioress: "At the conclusion of my thanksgiving, I hasten to write what Our Lord has communicated to me during holy communion. He positively commanded me to speak to Monseigneur, or to his secretary, telling me that I should boldly proclaim what has been revealed to me during the past four and a half years. My good Master assures me that he will place the proper words in my mouth. He added: 'I have again taken the rod of justice in my hand, if my people wish to avoid it, let them put in its stead the Work of Reparation. For your part, be faithful to fulfil your mission. How noble to be chosen to manifest my will! If you remain deaf to my voice, you will expose yourself to the blows of this rod; use all your efforts to withdraw it from my hand.'"

"Behold, as nearly as possible, reverend mother, that which Jesus has communicated to me. I must continue to recite this prayer in union with him: Holy Father, keep in thy name those whom thou hast given me! According to what I have beheld, it is he who says this with me and I who say it in him. Oh, what tenderness he has for his Church! It seems that he has no other thought but for her welfare; he desires to save her, to shield her by the adorable Name of his Father. If the Church of France could speak, she would implore the establishment of the Work of Reparation. I demand it in her name, for it is her only rampart against the assaults of her enemies."

"Reverend mother, in obedience to my Divine Master, I very humbly beg you to solicit the favor of a visit from Monseigneur. If his lordship be too occupied, beg him to send his secretary to record all that I feel it my duty to reveal on this matter."

The request was forwarded to Mgr. Morlot, and the object of the desired interview was explained to him. The prelate sent his secretary, l'abbe Vincent, who held the following conversation with Sr. Mary St. Peter; we shall give it literally, according to the account written by herself.

"Reverend mother, I shall give you a short extract of my pleadings with the archbishop's secretary on the subject of the Work of Reparation. I assure you that Our Lord assisted me as he had promised; for I was neither troubled nor intimidated and spoke with the greatest facility. I will now relate, as nearly as possible, what passed during the interview."

The Secretary: "Sister, I have come to tell you from Monseigneur, that he has presented your letters to the members of his council, and that all, unanimously, have pronounced against the establishment of the work you demand. Monseigneur has seriously examined the matter before God and finds it impossible to take any part in it; we do not recognize the validity of your mission."

Sr. St. Peter: "I do not pretend to importune Monseigneur, nor to uphold my own opinion of the mission which I believe has been imposed upon me by Our Lord for the salvation of France. My intention was to fulfil my duty conscientiously. When I had the honor of speaking to his Lordship about the communications which I have received from God, he said to me at the time: 'My child, be tranquil; there is no illusion here for I discern the finger of God.' It was on the authority of those words, which I received as coming from the Holy Ghost himself, that I persevered in my mission."

The Secretary: " My good sister, Monseigneur told you this at the time, because he knew not to what lengths this affair would go; but since then he has minutely examined all the particulars; he has prayed:—this cannot be."

Sr. St. Peter: "Very well, reverend sir, that is sufficient. All I desired was to have the decision of his Lordship. My conscience obliged me to do as I have done for the work of Reparation; now I am in perfect peace. But allow me to tell you that the reason why I desired to speak to Monseigneur, was to discharge my duty. Since you are his representative, I shall depose my mission in your hands, leaving the responsibility to the authorities of the Church. They will answer for it before God."

The Secretary: "But my good sister, the association of which you speak is already established."

Sr. St. Peter: "It is true, but the Church of Tours should have had the honor of being the mother of this association. I begged it from Monseigneur, but he did not deem it advisable to establish the work, and I submitted! What proves the Reparation to be really the work of God, is that without any concurrence bn my part it has been established."

The Secretary: "But there are many members here in Tours. And has not Monseigneur approved a little book of prayers on Reparation?"

Sr. St. Peter: "Yes, very true, reverend father, but there must be at Tours an association aggregated to the one at Langres. The work has need of the patronage of the archbishop, all eyes are fixed on him because it is in his diocese that the idea was first conceived."

The Secretary: "Sister, I tell you quite candidly that this work established at Langres is not very prosperous, it has even been the subject of comment in the daily papers."

Sister Mary St. Peter: "That is not very astonishing, sir, for Our Lord has warned me that the work would be opposed by all the powers of darkness. Have you not observed that the devotion to the Sacred Heart met with nearly the same opposition? And that there were many difficulties to be overcome before the feast of Corpus Christi was established? The Lord has imposed similar missions on souls more worthy than I, it is true, but they also have suffered from unjust accusations and persecution."

The Secretary: "All the works of God have suffered from persecution, among others, the archconfraternity of the Sacred Heart of Mary. This is a most admirable project embracing all good works, for its primary aim is the conversion of sinners."

Sister St. Peter: "Our Lord was fully aware of its existence when he demanded another confraternity; for he made me understand that the first was not sufficient; because if we wish to obtain pardon from a person offended, it is but just that we offer reparation of honor. The Lord has given me to understand that it is the transgressions against the first commandments that have aroused his wrath against France. If these disorders cannot be prevented by the authority of the Church, or that of the State, they should at least be atoned for by a suitable reparation."

The Secretary: 'Very true, but there lies the difficulty, my good sister. How are we to be assured that God exacts reparation? You may be deceiving us."

Sister St. Peter: "That is very possible, yet I hardly think that the imagination could invent anything like unto this, lasting for five years, without the influence of any mortal being. My prudent superiors have not countenanced me in my ideas; they have even forbidden me to think of the subject, yet they have not wished to pass any judgment. Our father superior has always referred me to the decision of the archbishop."

The Secretary: "Very well, my good sister, be perfectly tranquil; you have done your duty in making known these communications to the archbishop. Now I say to you in his name, think of these things no more, cast them entirely from your mind."

Sr. St. Peter: "Monseigneur, doubtless, does not forbid me to ask of God the accomplishment of his designs?"

The Secretary: "No, but do not pray for this work."

Sr. St. Peter: "Reverend sir, I pray you to assure Monseigneur of my obedience to his orders."

The sister was faithful to her promise. A few days after, she writes: "Our Lord has entirely divested me of the desire of beholding the Work of Reparation established in Tours. Were but one-word requisite for its erection, I would not pronounce it, and this through obedience to ecclesiastical authority which I shall always respect. I have been not a little grieved over these last refusals, but Our Lord consoled me, notwithstanding my unworthiness, for he gave me to understand that his work would take root and flourish, that it would remain firm in the midst of storms, and that if it were not planted in one soil, it would thrive the better in another. This latter promise was fulfilled two days after, for we learned that the Reparation has been established at Lyons, where it has been pushed forward with great zeal."

As if to receive from his servant some compensation, the Divine Master applied her anew, with greater intensity than ever, to the contemplation of his Holy Face. There is no more powerful means of appeasing the irritated justice of the Almighty, than to offer the most Holy Face of him who has borne the thorns of our sins on his sacred head, which became as a rock under the blows of his divine justice."

"He has paid our debts, he is our security, this is why our most amiable Savior has commanded me to remain unceasingly before the throne of his Father, offering him this divine Face, the object of his complaisance. My tender Savior gave me this consoling promise: 'Every time that you present my Face to my Father, my mouth will demand mercy. My good Jesus promised me that he would have pity on France. Let us then be filled with confidence; his all-powerful Name will be our buckler, and his adorable Face, our rampart. But he gave me to understand that he desired to see the devotion to this adorable Face take root in the hearts of the faithful. O good Jesus, conceal thy people in the secret recesses of thy Holy Face, that it may be to them a tower of defense and an impregnable fortress against the attacks of thy enemies."

After communion, the Lord appeared to the sister as "Ecce Homo." "He desired that I should contemplate his Holy Face. But soon, he drew my attention, in a very special manner to the reed which he held in his hand, this he presented to me as a sword with which to fight the enemies of the Church, promising that they would smart from its blows. He also helped me to understand that this feeble reed was the figure of my soul. Verily, I am indeed but a weak little reed, yet in the hands of Jesus Christ, my Spouse, I shall become all-powerful against his enemies, I shall say with faith and confidence: May the malice of the devil become powerless before the reed of Jesus Christ; like young David, I shall behead the giant Goliath in the name of the living God with my javelin, I mean with the adorable Face of our Lord Jesus Christ."

Nothing is more conformable to the holy scripture than this idea of the "rock," applied to the Face of Christ. As we have seen, it is the expression used by the prophet, Isaias; and St. Paul says, that Christ is the "rock" by excellence. The Prince of the apostles, in one of his epistles, uses a similar figure, calling Our Lord the "corner-stone." He predicts that this stone will crush to atoms the enemies of God. Thus, we behold how appropriately our simple little Breton applies her comparisons!

"These, reverend mother, are the projects with which the Lord fills my soul. Eternal Father, I offer thee the most Holy Face of Jesus. This is the mysterious coin of infinite value which alone is capable of discharging our debt. I offer thee the most Holy Face of Jesus to appease thy anger: remember that it has been pierced with the thorns of our sins; that it has become like to a rock under the blows of thy justice. Look upon these divine wounds of which I would be the voice to cry out incessantly: 'Mercy, mercy, O my God, mercy for poor sinners!' Another day, March 30, 1848, she proposed to receive holy communion to honor the most Holy Face of Our Lord, to comfort him in the sufferings caused by his ghastly wounds She implored him to imprint this adorable Face upon her heart so deeply that it would never be obliterated. "Before communion," said she, "a celestial light dawned on my soul and I beheld that the Face of the mystical body of Jesus Christ is the holy Church, which is now covered with wounds by the wicked!"

"Then, I was inspired to offer to Our Lord the virginal milk of his Holy Mother as a precious and fragrant balm wherewith to heal the wounds of his most Holy Face; my soul experienced great joy in performing this act of simplicity and love."

"After communion, my divine Savior, in his infinite goodness, was pleased to show me that this exercise was most agreeable to him and that I should continue it. He told me that in return he desired I would taste the milk of his divine consolations to alleviate my sufferings. Then I beheld Our Lord resplendent with glory and all my senses were ravished with joy. Soon he caused me to hear these sweet and consoling words: 'Your pilgrimage is drawing to a close! The end of the combat is approaching! You will soon see my divine Face in heaven'"

"At these words, I prostrated myself on the ground, saying: 'Lord, I merit only hellfire? But my good Master replied: 'The virtue of my Holy Face has restored the image of God in your soul. Those that contemplate the wounds of my Face on earth will one day behold the glory and majesty with which it is surrounded in heaven.' I was then on Thabor, and like the apostle St. Peter, I would willingly have cried out: 'Lord, it is good to be here; let us erect three temples for the three powers of my soul, that they may always enjoy this sweet repose which surpasses all the pleasures of earth. But our Divine Lord gave me to understand that his true spouse ought to prefer the heat of the combat to the repose of contemplation, that to defend his glory she need not fear casting herself in the midst of the battle. I told him that I would combat the enemies of his Church with the instruments of his Passion, and I perceived that my design was agreeable to him."

"This is the substance of what passed during this last communication; I say the substance, because it would be impossible to find a literal conveyance for these interior words, still less to describe what my soul experienced. How unworthy and despicable it is to fix our heart on creatures! Eternal Father, I offer thee the most Holy Face of Jesus to appease thy anger. Look upon his wounds, behold his humiliations! He is the only worthy reparation for our crimes; He is the glory of thy Holy Name! Eternal Father, I offer thee the most Holy Face of Jesus to pay our debts! This is the coin of infinite value stamped with the effigy of the King of kings."

The next revelation is short, and bears the same impression of simplicity, as do all the others. With a feeling of piety and veneration which we doubt not will be shared by our readers, we shall transcribe it entire, as it is the last penned by this good sister.

"For several days," said she, "I have perceived myself preoccupied with the holy infancy of the Word Incarnate. You are aware, reverend mother, that my soul is vowed to this mystery. Our Lord invites me from time to time to contemplate the other mysteries of his holy life; but the stable of Bethlehem is, so to say, my refuge and my home."

"Our Lord gave me to understand last Sunday, that many pious souls devoted themselves to the contemplation of the humiliations endured during his dolorous Passion, but that few thought of the annihilations of his Holy Infancy. He desires that I should contemplate this phase of his life, with the intention of fighting against the spirit of pride, of ambition and of independence, being armed with the humiliations, the poverty of his manger, and the captivity of his swathing bands. I think that the Eternal Father would not be the less pleased with the Face of the Infant Jesus in the lowly manger, covered with tears on account of our sins, than with the Face of Christ covered with blood and forsaken upon » the cross; for he is the august victim for our sins both in the manger and on the cross. Therefore, I offer this divine Infant to the Eternal Father; I place him between heaven and earth to appease the anger of the Most High. The Holy Ghost directed me anew to contemplate Jesus reposing in the arms of his Holy Mother, and toward the end of my prayer, the most Blessed Virgin deigned to appear to me, notwithstanding my unworthiness. She told me that she was the Queen of Carmel, that she would protect its houses during the days of calamity, and that we should have great confidence in her and in her Divine Son. She also told me that we should labor with zeal to attain the end of our institute, that is to pray for the necessities of the Church, and to offer violence to heaven for the conversion of sinners. This tender Mother desired me to say the hymn *O Gloriosa Virginum,* in honor of her divine maternity, as many times as we have houses in France, promising me that she would bedew the flowers of Carmel with her virginal milk, emblem of mercy."

"She also told me that the more the army of God would be augmented (here she meant the defenders of his Holy Name) the more the army of Satan would be weakened (the enemies of the Church and of the State.)"

"Behold, as near as possible, reverend mother, what has passed in my soul. Seventy-two times I repeated the hymn indicated by Mary, in honor of the years of her blessed life, and I prayed St. Joseph, our good father, and our holy mother St. Theresa to offer them to the Queen of Carmel for the preservation and perfection of our dear monasteries of France."

"Oh, Divine Mary, water the flowers of Carmel with the mysterious milk of grace, that they may be strongly rooted in this ground of benediction and that they may never be touched by the devil."

In recommending the "flowers of Carmel" to the "Divine Mary," the dear sister was inspired with the purest sentiments of gratitude towards a blessed ground where for nine years she had been favored with numerous graces, and blessed with abundant benedictions. How could the Mother of the Infant Jesus refuse to grant a prayer so worthy of her maternal heart!

21

HER VIRTUES

**"What gives me the greatest consolation now,
at the hour of my death, is that I have always been obedient."**
(Words of the Sister)

I t may not be uninteresting to our readers to retrace our steps succinctly, to cast a rapid glance at the virtues of Sister Mary St. Peter, and at the same time to sketch the outline of her religious life, before undertaking the account of her last illness and death. We shall thus cull whatever flowers may have escaped our notice hitherto, besides those which her good sisters, the Carmelites, have treasured up in their religious esteem and affection.

Let us not expect to behold those of rare or brilliant hue, such as may be found among the precious few of earth's immortal sons and daughters. As we have already remarked, nothing could have been simpler than the life of this servant of God. We have been assured by her superiors that it would have taken an acute and attentive observer to detect the least sign of the marvels of grace with which she was favored by the Holy Ghost. The details we are about to narrate may seem trifling and commonplace, yet they are not without their due importance, for they will disclose the hidden beauty of the saintly life that we have been admiring. Pious souls of the cloister, even seculars, will here find a subject of edification, well worthy of imitation. Would that we could cause the rich treasure bequeathed us in Mary of St. Peter to be more appreciated!

We must first say a word about her physiognomy, that mirror of the soul, the mystery of which she has so eloquently developed in the passage on the Holy Face of Our Lord.

She calls herself a "little Breton," although she was about medium height. Her appearance at first glance, was far from prepossessing because of the irregularity of her features; her forehead was narrow, her eyes and nose small, and her mouth projecting, but these defects were amply compensated by a clear, fresh complexion, but more especially by a sweet and calm expression which bespoke the hidden beauty of her soul. Her glance was modest and cautious; her grave deportment announced a mind absorbed send concentrated on the one theme, God and his glory. Her beautiful, clear voice was of great assistance in the choir. Skillful and adept, she was remarkable for her taste in needlework, and for her assiduity in the performance of all her duties.

Her literary education, as we have already remarked, was very incomplete; but unknown to herself she possessed, besides harmony of style and an almost poetic instinct, a great perspicuity in her conception of the sublime and supernatural operations of which she was at times obliged to treat. Figures abounded under her pen, and although many might have been revealed to her, yet we find them so plentiful, that we must conclude the greater number evidently resulted from her own natural ability.

The same happened when she explained these marvels by word of mouth, yet she knew how to make use of them with as much simplicity as modesty. The only desire of her heart was to advance in the science of the saints, the knowledge of God, desiring only to know, to love and to serve him.

She was endowed with good judgment, and a candid mind easily open to conviction; her imagination was fully under her control: her natural inclinations, moderated and guided by divine grace; her passions were subdued and almost extinct, giving her slight cause of resistance. Her disposition, particularly adapted for community life, was naturally sweet, gentle, amiable, and gay. She was quick at repartee, but was never betrayed beyond the bounds of justice and charity; firm in her opinion, especially where there was question of duty, yet she never maintained it with contention or obstinacy.

She possessed so much self-control that it required a penetrating eye to detect the first sallies of nature, for she knew how to restrain her emotions before they were betrayed exteriorly. She was naturally of a loving and sensitive disposition, although not demonstrative, possessed of much tact and perfect discretion. She usually spoke little, and that little on Grod, never on self. She practiced the most heroic virtues without affectation, avoiding all singularity.

Sometimes she seemed concentrated in self, and this from various causes; first, the influence of Grod who frequently held her captive; then, perhaps through respect or deference for those with whom she was in conversation. She was at times a little absent-minded, but this might be attributed to her application to the things of Grod. The virtue of simplicity animated all her actions, and the rectitude of her judgment gave her uncommon liberty of mind, although to behold her, one would have judged otherwise.

She took so many pains to conceal her virtue that a just appreciation of her merit could only be acquired after a long and attentive observation. Possessing none of those brilliant qualities which naturally inspire esteem and preferment, her beauty was not exterior: *Omnis gloria filia regis ab intus.* It would be difficult to state the particular virtue in which Sister Mary St. Peter excelled. Without enumerating all, we shall mention in preference those which have contributed to make her a perfect religious and a saintly Carmelite.

She possessed the virtue of charity in an eminent degree, her tender and solid piety inspiring her with most ardent and effective love for God. The glory of the Lord and the salvation of souls were the only objects of her desires, the sole end of her prayers and of all her actions. This zeal for the glory of God animated her during her entire life; we may even say that she was consumed by it from the moment, when in 1843, she perceived by a supernatural vision, that divine wrath was about to descend on mankind because of the heinous crimes committed against the three first commandments. Inspired by grace, she offered herself to God as a victim to satisfy his justice.

The eternal loss of immortal souls made such a lively impression on her sensitive heart, that she could not contain her sorrow but often gave vent to it in torrents of tears. Her heart became dilated in the love of Jesus; she honored his sacred humanity in all its mysteries, but those of his birth and of his hidden life possessed inconceivable charms for her. Her devotion to the Holy Infancy and to the Holy Family manifested itself on all occasions. When she was portress, it was a pleasure for her to open the doors for the carpenters, who recalled to her mind the labors of Jesus and of St. Joseph. Oue day, a wagon, driven by an ass, entered the yard; approaching this animal, the good sister commenced to caress it in remembrance of the services rendered to Jesus and Mary by the humble beast which transported them to Egypt.

At Christmas time, she manifested her lively piety in every conceivable manner; with a radiant countenance she contemplated the Infant Jesus in the manger, taking him in her arms, making illuminations round the crib and singing pious hymns in her "best voice." Sometimes, like David before the ark, she would commence to dance and rejoice, inviting her companions of the novitiate to join with her; at which the Mother Prioress expressed her surprise, telling her to beware of levity. "Oh, no mother," replied she, "I do so as an honorable amend to the Infant Jesus for all forbidden dances of lukewarm Christians."

Jesus in the Holy Eucharist was the object of all her affections. In the choir, in presence of the Blessed Sacrament, her countenance, her entire deportment would lead one to believe that, piercing the eucharistic veils, she really beheld Jesus on the altar. Did she quit the sanctuary, she left her heart at his feet; in whatever part of the house she was employed, she would turn in this direction, transported with joy when she could perceive the chapel windows. The holy place was her repose; she would willingly have passed there her entire days and nights; if she had a few spare moments, her steps were immediately directed to the chapel; on Sundays and feasts, she made it her dwelling. There, absorbed in God, she seemed a stranger to all that passed around her.

When she spoke of the Holy Eucharist, she laid aside her habitual reserve and yielded to the vehemence of her love. A hundred times a day, and perhaps more frequently, she went in spirit to offer him her homage. She assisted at the most holy sacrifice of the mass with the utmost reverence and was more than once observed to shed torrents of tears; it was especially at communion that her faith became manifest. She prepared herself on the eve with extraordinary fervor, inviting the Blessed Virgin and the holy angels to prepare a dwelling place for the celestial Spouse whom she expected to entertain, but when she possessed him, lost and absorbed, she forgot all else, to enjoy his divine presence.

Her ordinary dwelling-place was in the Sacred Heart of Jesus; it was from this furnace of love that she drew forth so many graces for herself and for others. It was her place of refuge in all her troubles, and to the Sacred Heart in the most Blessed Sacrament she had recourse in all her necessities. We are aware of her devotion to the most Blessed Virgin before her admission to the religious life; her love for this divine Mother was ever on the increase, especially since she beheld herself consecrated to her forever as a child of Carmel. In her fervor, she conceived many pious practices in her honor and spoke of her frequently, endeavoring to enkindle in every heart the devotion to our Blessed Lady, through whose intervention, she had received so many innumerable favors. Abundant light was given her on the prerogatives of the Holy Mother of God. She called St. Joseph her good father.

The seraphic St. Theresa was also tenderly loved by this fervent child of Carmel. We might say as much for her love of her Angel Guardian. One day, during her novitiate, she was in the garret sorting clothes for the wash. It suddenly recurred to her mind, that at the death of her grandfather, whom she venerated as a saint, she had preserved a lock of his hair, and not remembering what she had done with it, she became uneasy and begged her good angel to take care of this precious souvenir which she believed to have left at home. On turning round, she beheld at her side a lock of white hair which she immediately recognized as being the missing treasure... For fear of making a mistake, she inquired of the sisters if anyone could give her any information about the lock of hair she had found, but no one knew anything about it.

She had attained a high degree of humility; even in the world she had been well exercised in the practice of this, the mother of all virtues. Her soul, nourished with the bread of humiliations, found in it more delight than worldlings experience in praises and acclamations. We find that her superiors were ever lavish of the food for which she constantly hungered, and this not only to second the designs of God and to secure their fulfilment, but to preserve in her soul the precious virtues with which she was enriched. Sincerely believing herself the last and least in the community, the most unworthy, the most miserable sinner, she chastised herself for the smallest imperfections. She had arrived at such a degree of perfection that self-love and self-seeking found no place in her heart. She ingeniously avowed that neither the graces with which she was so wonderfully favored, nor all the praises she could possibly receive, would be able to excite in her the least sentiment of vanity. Thus, the gifts of God only served to humble her the more, and to disclose her weakness and unworthiness. Far from being vain of the favors accorded her, she trembled at the remembrance of the account which one day she would be obliged to give.

Once, when still a novice, the mother prioress told her during recreation, to sing for the amusement of a newly arrived postulant, the same hymn she had sung on her arrival: "Let us bless the Lord, &c." She sang so sweetly and with so much feeling and piety, that her young companion was charmed. At the conclusion the mother prioress said: "Well, Sister St. Peter, how many vain thoughts have you had while singing?" "Mother," she replied, her eyes modestly cast down, "If I have had any, I chased them all away." In this answer she showed her true spirit of humility, avoiding to acknowledge publicly that she had been exempt from all sentiments of vanity, which would have been only too natural on such an occasion.

Her obedience was most perfect, without delay or excuse; she submitted with the simplicity of a child to all that was desired of her, imitating the example of the Infant Jesus at Nazareth. She repeated without ceasing, these words of the Gospel: *He was subject to them,* suggesting the same to her companions with so much gentleness, that the influence exercised on those around her, can scarcely be imagined. She made the holy virtue of obedience her food, and daily derived new strength from its practice. Her opinions, her will, her interior lights, all vanished the moment she was aware of the intentions of her superiors. She had such a lively spirit of faith that she spoke to them as to God himself, receiving as from him all their commands and counsels. She used to say: " If my superiors were to order a postulant or novice to take the direction of my conduct, I would submit to her for the love of God without any difficulty."

She blindly obeyed, not only her superiors, but also the sisters with whom she was employed, regarding them all as her superiors, and making it a duty to acquiesce in their least wish.

She was like an infant incapable of either action or movement but by the will of those who conducted her. The obedience of this dear sister was so perfect, that she was able, during her last illness to say: "That which consoles me now at the hour of my death is the thought that I have ever been obedient."

Her detachment was that of a true Carmelite. She loved in God all those linked to her by the ties of kindred, of religion and of gratitude, but no unregulated affection ever found any place in her heart. Her parents were very dear to her and she prayed for them always, but beholding all things in God, she left in his hands the care of all that concerned them, without allowing herself even a thought on the subject.

Her immolation to God was entire and without reserve, according to the counsel of the Psalmist: "Forget thy people and thy father's house, and the king will recognize thy beauty." We find that she never spoke of those whom she had left in the world, she was even observed to burn some letters before reading them, for fear lest they might pre-occupy her mind. She was wont to say that one of the greatest obstacles to religious perfection was irregular affection for parents; although it was an obligation to pray for them, yet we should commit them to the care of an all-wise Providence, without being pre-occupied with their temporal affairs.

Her spirit of recollection was so profound that it was sufficient to behold her, to feel one's heart elevated toward God. So absorbed was she in Him that even after her profession, she was ignorant of the places occupied by the sisters in the choir and refectory, and often listened with surprise to the account of what had passed under her very eyes. Calm, silent and modest, one became aware of her presence only by the edification of her whole bearing, and by the manner in which she accomplished the smallest actions. To belong entirely to her heavenly Spouse, she abstained from all that could flatter the senses.

If, on the one hand, she concealed from creatures the virtues she practiced, her simplicity and obedience caused her to reveal them at the first question from authority.

After each celestial communication, she was pale, trembling and covered with tears, more especially when God announced the misfortunes which threatened France. Calmly and silently the tears flowed from her eyes. She appeared at these times absorbed in profound contemplation; this lasted for entire hours at a time, without however deterring her from the performance of her obligations. Sometimes it was noticed that she bore the impression of great sufferings; she seemed to be occupied with some subject that entirely captivated her thoughts.

Her union with God was almost continual; she never lost sight of his divine presence, and according to her own expression, her soul, closely united to Jesus, was "a happy prisoner at his feet." But this life, to all appearances so heavenly and sweet, was not exempt from great trials and sufferings, which she bore with heroic fortitude; the mother prioress was convinced that these had contributed to shortening her days. Is it then astonishing that her prayers were sometimes miraculously heard?

How admirable was her love of silence and regularity! So vigilant and exact was she at all times that she might have been regarded as the living rule of the house; at the first sound of the bell, her work fell from her hands; she would not have made one movement which could have retarded her. It was sufficient for her companions to observe her attentively to know, love and practice all their duties. This dear sister possessed, in an eminent degree, the spirit of her seraphic mother St. Theresa, being gifted with that sweet liberty of mind which distinguishes a true Carmelite; to the interior virtues she knew admirably how to unite the charms of perfect charity and even at times the sallies of wit.

One day, a friend of the house, offered some cake; Sister St. Peter, who was still portress, being extremely fatigued, received the present, and brought it immediately to the mother prioress, saying: "How fortunate!" and adding with her usual simplicity: "The Ass is hungry!" The good mother smiled, and gave a piece of the cake to the little portress who ate it gayly, rendering thanks to God. During the recreations, she spoke but little, always preferring to listen; yet she was ever lively and amiable, taking part in all that was said and done, although obliged to offer extreme violence to herself to interrupt her interior conversation with God. Her companions loved to pass the recreation with her, as they always drew some fruit from her conversation.

Her reserve, when there was question of charity, was particularly remarkable; she excused all, palliated the defects of others with as much tact as cordiality. She never refused a service to others for she figured herself as serving Jesus and Mary in the persons of her sisters. We have noticed how she fulfilled the office of first and second portress, even discharging the duties of both for a considerable length of time. She was prudent, discrete and attentive, of easy access, affable toward all and spreading round her the sweet odor of Jesus Christ. Her devotedness was of great service to the house; she acquired the esteem and affection of all who had any intercourse with her. Although this office was very repugnant, it did not in the least interfere with her habitual recollection, nor with the tranquility of her soul, fruit of her purity of heart. It was even amidst the most fatiguing and annoying occupations that she obtained from Our Lord the greatest graces.

Her soul, firm as rock through her union with our Lord Jesus Christ, was sheltered from all those disquietudes which agitate the heart and trouble the mind. She acted without precipitation, how numerous soever her occupations. In general, she was so pleasant and joyful in the midst of all the self-renunciation which she practiced, that no one was aware of the violence she offered herself. The following is an example. When the community removed to their new monastery, it was not completed, and the workmen being obliged to go in and out continually, gave grand occasion for patience to our virtuous portress; but her habitual serenity never deserted her. When her rule permitted her to speak, she said laughingly, with her natural taste for poetry to those whom she accompanied:

Now since obedience
Rules our actions,
Let us go in diligence
To conduct our masons.

M. Lebroument, whom she called "the courier of the Infant Jesus," and who in turn called her his "godmother", desired to have a pious souvenir of our Carmelite after her death. He wrote to the prioress who replied: "Observing, by your letter, that you wished to possess some little souvenir of your poor godmother, I thought of an object which she made under very singular circumstances; and I was surprised, when without any intimation on my part, she, herself, begged me to keep the same object for you; I confess you are her only heir, for it is the sole article she asked me to dispose of. What then is your legacy?"

"It is a drum,—but a drum resembling none other than in its form, it is fashioned so ingeniously. The following is its history. When the poor sister fell ill, it happened to be at the very time that the elections were taking place. I said to her somewhat in fun: Since you are no longer able to pray, you must be our spiritual drum, and when you hear the National Guard beating the call to order, you must invite the angels to our succor. She accepted her new mission and the next day presented me a little drum on which was drawn the nine choirs of angels, the Holy Name of God, etc. She kept it beside her on her bed to call to our assistance all the heavenly hosts by striking this little drum with her fingers."

"Worldlings would laugh heartily at this trait of childish piety, but you, sir, who are not of the world, you, as I, will no doubt, behold in it the admirable simplicity of a soul transformed in the science of the manger and in the virtue of obedience. This drum is, therefore, destined for you. It will be a pleasing toy, I think, for your little Charles; we also include some other little souvenirs for Madame Lebroument."

M. Lebroument, *a man not of this world,* far from giving this precious drum to his little boy, had it richly enshrined under a glass case, desiring that this object which he regarded as a relic, should never pass from his family.

To these details, which we have taken from the private annals of the monastery, we shall add the testimony of one of the religious.

"To speak of Sister Mary of St. Peter," said she, "to render homage to her virtue, is both a duty and a happiness. She entered religion several years after I did. At the time, although professed, I was still in the novitiate, which gave me an opportunity of observing her closely, and consequently of admiring her greatly. We already perceived her to be a soul fully formed to all virtues; those which I particularly remarked on were her humility, her recollection, and her obedience. She received the trials and the humiliations to which she was subjected with, as much joy as gratitude, so much so, that we were all edified; far from ever excusing herself, on the contrary, she was always accusing herself, ever seeking new occasion of humiliation."

"She was so recollected that she did not behold what was passing before her very eyes. Until her profession, I had no other relationship with her than that of the novitiate; but soon after, I perceived her special devotion to the holy Infancy of Jesus, toward which I also experienced a great attraction; this bound us closely to each other and gave me an occasion of becoming better acquainted with this beautiful soul. Her piety was so meek and loving that I was enchanted with her."

"Our practices of devotion were always directed to honor the mystery of the Holy Infancy. The holy child Jesus was the subject of our conversations. With what tenderness she spoke of him! How well she knew how to imitate the virtues of this Divine Child! For her rule of conduct, she had taken these words, *He was subject to them,* I am confident that she practiced them with the greatest perfection."

"The office of portress, to which she was appointed a few years after her profession, gave her a wide scope for the exercise of virtue; I was a witness of her promptitude to obedience and her perfect self-abnegation. At our removal, her occupations were redoubled, and although over-burdened, yet she never for an instant lost her habitual recollection. She was very diligent and edified all by her remarkable zeal and charity. Being at the time treasurer, I was often in embarrassment to settle the bills, but when she perceived me depressed, or impatient, she would quietly repeat these words: 'And he was submissive to them,' adding, 'Come, let us submit ourselves to the will of the Holy Infant, we are his little servants.' She had to bear sufferings and trials from all sides; but she was ever meek, patient, and resigned, and was never heard to murmur or to repine. Our dear sister was a great edification to me in all the corporal infirmities she had to support. She was taken ill nearly a year before her death. I was then, infirmarian, I cannot describe the consolation I experienced when beside this pious invalid. She never refused any remedy how disgusting or bitter it might be, content with all that was done for her, she seemed to forget her sufferings to be occupied solely with God. To such a degree did she carry her spirit of submission, that she would not have taken one step outside the infirmary without my permission. Her recollection seemed to be continual; in a word, I seemed to behold an angel rather than a suffering mortal. I was inconsolable when I ceased to take care of her."

This picture will be completed by one more remark: there was a conviction, almost amounting to a certainty among the Carmelites, that this pure soul had preserved intact her baptismal innocence; she lived in the world as not belonging to it, and from the moment of her arrival in religion, she was never seen commit a single voluntary fault. This is the unanimous testimony of the entire community.

22

HER ILLNESS AND DEATH

"I wish for nothing but my crucifix;
it is my treasure, my strength, my consolation."
(Words of the Sister)

In narrating an account of the last illness and death of Sister Mary St. Peter, we shall simply reproduce the account written by order of the venerable prioress of the Carmelites, Mother Mary of the Incarnation. This faithful testimony of the sanctity of our holy religious, will be received with respect by the pious reader, which will warrant its insertion in these pages.

"Our dear sister foresaw her approaching dissolution; in several of her letters she plainly stated that Our Lord had made known to her the time of her death; although not aware of the precise moment, yet she spoke of it as a thing near at hand. However, she enjoyed very good health, and we observed no indications that her career was to be so short. She was frequently subject to headaches, and we noticed that she suffered particularly on Fridays. From the moment she made an entire abandonment of herself to God for the accomplishment of his designs, she gradually pined away. The fire of divine love and her zeal for the salvation of souls slowly consumed her; the responsibility of the work which she bore as she said, with incredible pain, contributed still more to immolate the victim; but very little of all this was apparent, as Sister St. Peter, ever exact and fervent, continued to fulfil the duties prescribed by the rule. In the summer of 1847, to the great joy of our dear sister, the work of reparation was canonically established.

"Discharged of the burden which rendered her existence so painful, her soul was inundated with delight; happiness beamed from her eyes, her health seemed to improve, she even became sufficiently strong to observe the fast of the ensuing lent; but at the very moment when the Church celebrated the Passion of Our Lord, a long martyrdom began for this dear sister, whose life so full of merit, was fast drawing to a close. On the 30th of March, Jesus announced that she was nearing the goal. From this moment she thought only of heaven; she loved to converse on this subject; burning words escaped her lips proving the ardor which consumed her."

"The events which had just taken place in France had excited her to new zeal, and the appearance of the evils which she had announced and which now threatened her country, induced her to the performance of a most heroic act of charity. On Good Friday, at three o'clock, she prostrated herself on the ground to adore Jesus Christ expiring. At that very instant she perceived that the enormous weight of divine anger was about to fall heavily upon mankind; immediately renewing her act of perfect abandonment, she offered herself as a victim to ward off the dreadful blows of divine **justice."**

"Our Lord seemed to have been waiting for this last generous act, before immolating his courageous victim; a cruel malady immediately declared itself, which reduced her to the last extremity. We hastened to lavish the most assiduous care on our dear sister; the doctor was called and pronounced the disease mortal. Our dear invalid herself suspected the gravity of her condition, therefore, we could warn her of the imminent danger without fear; there was only one thing capable of causing her regret: 'The sorrow of leaving you, and of quitting this dear community forever; but I shall pray for you in heaven. I must sacrifice my life for the Work God has confided to me.'"

"Before leaving her cell for the last time, she begged a sister to go before the Blessed Sacrament (not being able to do so herself) to ask the blessing of Our Lord that she might suffer worthily all that it would please him to ordain. Arriving at the infirmary, she cast a glance around the apartment which seemed to say: 'I shall never go forth from here.' And in truth, this spot was to be the last stage of her virtues and her sufferings. One of the sisters desired to bring some little objects of piety from her cell in order that she might continue to enjoy them, but she refused saying; 'It is now that *all* must be sacrificed.'"

"However, we had some faint hope; the desire of prolonging so holy a life urged us to use every means within the power of science to preserve it. The resources of art were unavailing in her case, so we had recourse to the Blessed Virgin. Our dear sister on hearing of this, in her humility, said: 'I am of so little use and my health is so poor, why do you pray for my recovery? I will never get better.' As she was suffering much corporally someone said to her: 'Beg Our Lord to relieve you somewhat.' 'No,' she replied, 'as regards sacrifice and sufferings I have never asked anything in particular from God, neither have I ever refused anything.'"

"When she took to bed never more to rise, she Was deeply penetrated with the judgment of God. Forgetful of the favors by which she had been overwhelmed, she thought only of her sins and of imploring pardon for them. This sentiment of humility in a soul of such purity is easily explained, if we consider the light she had received on her own misery. She was frequently beheld shedding tears. On being asked the cause, she replied: 'O Mother, when I think of the judgment of God, I cannot but weep for my sins.'"

"Her disease was hasty consumption, but other complaints added to the intensity of her sufferings and made the most frightful ravages. A burning and continual fever devoured her; her throat was ulcerated, and her tongue and mouth as if pierced with thorns, (we must recollect that Our Lord had told her she must suffer for blasphemers)."

"The nights flew by one after the other without bringing her the slightest repose; every position on her bed of agony became a new source of torture; she was therefore obliged to keep the same posture for a length of time together, consequently large wounds were formed in her body, and her sufferings were almost incredible."

"During the two months and a half that her illness lasted, she took no food, a liquid substance in small quantities, was all that she could retain. Twice a day she took a little milk which she offered to the Blessed Virgin before drinking; this never caused her any pain. She became quite emaciated, her face alone retaining its natural hue; her skin shriveled up as though she had passed through fire. The frightful state to which she was now reduced seemed to indicate a speedy end. Her patience was ever unflinching, her union with God uninterrupted, and her spirit of sacrifice as entire, as unreserved as ever. In the midst of her suffering, her docility, innocence and childlike simplicity appeared in every movement."

"To encourage her in these sentiments, we spoke to her of the Child Jesus and of all the graces she had received through the mysteries of his childhood. To which, she said: 'Our Lord was then instructing me in the science of the Cross.' Alas, our poor sister had until now, but tasted of the bitter chalice which she was to quaff even to the dregs. She was animated by the most tender confidence in God and an ardent desire for heaven; at the thought of her death, she was overcome with joy. 'My hour has come!' she repeated, 'soon my chains will be broken. When shall I behold thee, O celestial abode! When, O my God, shall I see thee face to face?"

"If any one spoke to her of heaven, her whole figure became animated: 'O heaven, my home, my eternal dwelling-place! thou art the only object of my desires! Ah, when shall I take my flight from this dreary earth!'"

"These, and other beautiful passages from the canticles, she frequently repeated. On beholding her one would have thought that a ray of beatitude had already penetrated her soul. Her brow was serenely tranquil, and a pleasant smile played about her lips, which only opened to murmur the name of God. Long would we stand observing her, before she raised her eyes, so absorbed was she in profound recollection.

"At the beginning of June, she was so much worse that she, herself, asked for the last sacraments; the danger was imminent and all haste was made to comply with her request. She received the Holy Viaticum and the Extreme Unction with the greatest piety, and asked pardon of the community in the most touching manner. After the last rites had been administered, several sisters remained praying beside the bed: her countenance was radiant: she seemed to be in a sort of ecstasy, we could not behold without being penetrated with devotion, and moved even to tears. After some minutes had elapsed, we approached the bed and asked if she were not sleeping: 'Oh, no,' she replied, 'I am entertaining myself with Our Lord.' 'Are you then, very happy?' 'Oh, yes, mother, I desire nothing more. I now possess my All!'"

"On Friday, the 16th of June, she passed through a terrible crisis: the community assembled in the infirmary to recite the prayers of the agonizing. The dear, sick sister, who was in full possession of her faculties, united with us by fervent aspirations, but she suffered most cruelly. Suddenly, she passed into a supernatural state, the effects of which were very evident. When our sisters pronounced these words: *Maria mater gratia, mater misericordia,* she spontaneously raised her hands to heaven, as would a child perceiving its mother. She remained a long time in this posture, although, a few minutes before, her arms were so stiff and powerless that we could not succeed in making her form the sign of the cross. Then, at two different times she extended her arms in the form of a cross, to die as a victim, and when a sister tried to prevent her, she exclaimed: 'Oh, Let me remain thus, it is a duty I must fulfil.'"

"She took alternately her crucifix and a little statue of the Infant Jesus, which she never let out of her sight, and covered them with kisses, pressing them to her heart. Then holding up the Infant Jesus as high as possible, she solemnly but quietly pronounced these words: 'Eternal Father, I once more offer thee this adorable Infant, thy Divine Son, in expiation of my sins and those of all mankind, for the needs of our holy mother the Church, for France, for the Reparation. Amiable Jesus, I remit this work into thy hands, for it I have lived, for it shall I die!' Then she placed the little statue on her head, saying: 'Divine Infant, cover my guilty life with the merits of thy precious blood: renew my soul in innocence and grace; clothe me with thy robe of purity, thy spirit of humility. Oh, come with me when I shall depart this life; come, O my Jesus, come, tarry no longer! Mary, my tender Mother, come to claim my soul!' She pronounced these and other ejaculations with so much love, that it were vain attempting to convey an adequate idea to the reader; they were like sparks of fire escaping from a furnace. She begged pardon of God for all her sins, then of the community, shedding torrents of tears, thanking the sisters for all the care they had lavished upon her and adding: 'Oh, my sisters, how happy, to die a Carmelite!'"

"Then addressing us: 'Adieu mother,' said she, give me your blessing. I shall soon appear before God. I am so happy to die in your arms.' She testified to her gratitude for the care we had taken of her soul; after which she said: 'The hour has arrived. O Jesus, come!' Shortly after, crossing her arms on her breast, she said: 'Father into thy hands, I commend my spirit.' She remained for some moments recollected, and then returned to her ordinary state. During this touching scene, it was evident that something extraordinary was passing in her soul."

"During her illness, Sister St. Peter received the Blessed Sacrament as often our holy rules permitted. She longed for this favor, finding in the Eucharist all her strength, all her consolation. According to her custom, she prepared for its reception from the eve, and as she was deprived of sleep, passed the entire night in amorous colloquies. Several of the sisters who watched by her bedside during the night, assured us that that they have never passed the time more profitably. Once, our pious sister was unable to contain her joy when it was announced to her that she was going to communicate the next morning."

"Tomorrow morning, my divine Spouse, full of tenderness, will come to strengthen my weakness!' and from time to time she added: 'My well-beloved appears not yet: O night, too long, wilt thou last forever!' She then took the statue of the Infant Jesus, and while embracing it, begged pardon for her faults, conjuring him to purify the heart of his little servant; then, as if offering him to the Eternal Father, she held it up high, and remained one full hour in this fatiguing position without making the least movement.”

“Another time, we hesitated in having the Holy Communion brought her for fear that her conscience might not be well at ease, for she had passed a most miserable night and seemed much depressed: but Sister St. Peter had not forgotten the promise made her. In the morning, from the moment she perceived me, she said: ‘Mother, I am waiting for my Grod: when will He come? Oh, how I long for him! How much need I have of Him!’ We were obliged to yield to her entreaties and had the holy communion brought her.”

“One day, after receiving the Holy Eucharist, a sister remarked an expression of sanctity on her face which struck her forcibly. She could not look at her for any length time because of the rays of glory which she beheld on her countenance. Our dear, sick sister received anew the holy viaticum on the feast of the most Holy Trinity, patronal feast of the archconfraternity of Reparation. She had a great desire to die on that day, but Jesus decided otherwise. Sometime after, I went to the infirmary to see her. ‘Mother,’ said she, ‘I shall remain a little longer on earth, for my soul is not yet purified; but during this time, I shall suffer most cruelly, for Our Lord has attached me to the cross, and I shall remain there until my last sigh. Give me no more care, no more consolation, I must now suffer; I desire to think of nothing but eternity.”

“I wish to remain alone with God, for I can scarcely speak any more; they think I sleep, but I am occupied solely with him. Soon shall I contemplate his adorable Face, soon I shall be singing his praises for an entire eternity. Oh, how fervently I shall then pray for the Church, for France, for the Reparation!’… ‘But’ said I to her, ‘have you no fear of having been in illusion, or have you no disquietude for having followed your own ideas rather than those of God?’ ‘No, not at all,’ she replied in a grave and solemn manner. ‘I might have been deceived, as I have always said, but I can certify now, as I am soon to appear before God, that I have never acted of myself in this matter. It has cost me dearly, but I have never taken one step but in obedience to the will of God!’”

“‘In all that I have written by order of my superiors, I have always spoken in the sincerity of my soul. By the grace of God, I have nothing to reproach myself on this subject, and I am perfectly tranquil.’ Have you any hope for the future of France? ‘I have the greatest confidence; the wicked will not succeed in their evil designs, peace will be restored; it is for this purpose that reparation has been established. My course is run, as Our Lord has declared to me, for the Work of Reparation is established. It was for this Work that God placed me in the world, it is this Work which will save France.'"

"'O God, how good thou art! How boundless is thy mercy! He wills not that his little servant be separated from him after her death, and he purifies her entirely before admitting her to his presence. Never, never could I have believed that he would have given me this grace if I had not heard it from his own lips. The holiness of God is so great that I thought I would have remained in purgatory until the end of the world. But now I must suffer, I must fulfil the designs of God. Oh, how true it is that his justice has means of satisfying itself far beyond the reach of our poor comprehension!'... In effect, this generous soul soon entered on a new path of suffering."

"No", she used to say, "nothing now but suffering, let God act as he will." If anything were suggested, she would say: 'I shall take it if given me, but I shall not ask for anything. Yet she yielded more through love for obedience, than to the necessities of nature, following the common path, taking whatever was prescribed her. But henceforth, we could give her no remedy or relief for her ills, on the contrary all that was prescribed seemed to add to her sufferings. Not a single complaint ever passed her lips. Sometimes the excess of her sufferings would cause her to break out into plaintive sighs of resignation, as for instance: 'My God, how I suffer! I have pity on me, aid me, abandon not thy little servant. Thou knowest, O Lord, I am thy victim, but I beg of thee to forget me not. How admirable are thy ways. O God! Let us adore his holy will! How long the time is! How ardently I sigh for my well-beloved! My sweet Jesus art thou not going to let me die! Come, Lord Jesus, come, and tarry not!' During her worst hours of agony, she said in a tone and manner impossible to portray: 'How terrible is the severity of divine justice! My God! thou art so rigorous! What agony I endure! Oh, my divine Spouse how bitter to me art thou who hast always been so sweet and loving!'"

"In order to sustain and encourage her during these moments of desolation, we recalled to her mind that she had offered herself to God for the accomplishment of his designs. 'Yes,' she replied, 'and I do not repent of it; my God, I desire all that thou dost desire, and if it were necessary, I would be willing to suffer even to the end of the world.' Being asked where she suffered the most: 'In all parts of my body, I am undergoing a universal martyrdom: my bed is a purgatory where I burn! the fire consumes me, every instant seems a century.'"

"I do not ask of God to abridge or alleviate my sufferings, but I call upon the hour of my deliverance. Oh, my sweet Jesus, when shall I be united to thee forever!' She also loved to repeat: 'I die a daughter of the Church, and of Carmel.' During the most violent pains she used to say in a suppliant tone which drew forth tears from those around: 'I implore you to demand patience for me, I can no longer suffer, speak to me of heaven, speak of God." She would seize her crucifix and kiss it unceasingly. 'I desire nothing but my crucifix, it is my treasure, my strength and my consolation; I keep my eyes continually fixed upon him, for he encourages me to suffer; yes, my Lord is crucified, and I am crucified with him.'"

"She often asked us to offer her sufferings in union with those of Jesus, and when once she was desired to apply them for a particular intention, she said: 'I do not know if I can, for I am entirely consecrated to the Reparation, I am a victim, but, obedience will decide the question."

"In the meantime, the innocent soul, over whom Satan seemed to be unable to gain any power, was suddenly assailed by all the powers of darkness; it was necessary that her entire being should be offered as a holocaust, and that she should undergo all kinds of temptation. She said, 'It is but a part of my penance.' During the last days of her life, she was a victim to all the malice of the devil, she believed that there was one of these infernal spirits continually at her side, urging her to murmur and impatience, uttering blasphemies in her ear, even suggesting thoughts of despair. She seemed to be extremely uneasy and would not remain alone for an instant; she had recourse to the Blessed Virgin; but soon the enemy redoubled all his fury against her. 'Oh!' exclaimed she, 'how I suffer! My God, I can resist no longer, have pity on me.' As a last resource she prayed to the holy Infant Jesus, the tender object of her devotion, and she placed on her neck the "Little Gospel" of the circumcision. The virtue of be Holy Name of Jesus dispelled all the illusions of the enemy; the devouring fever, the terrible temptations—all ceased at that instant, and she became most wonderfully calm."

"Toward the end of her illness she was honored by the visit of Mgr. Morlot : the venerable archbishop was anxious to come and see her to give her his benediction for the last time; a great consolation which the dear sister fully appreciated! She was also assisted by our ecclesiastical superior and was most earnest in testifying to her joy and gratitude for this privilege. A benefactress of the house, who as such, was privileged to enter the cloister, begged the mother superior one day to allow her to receive a last blessing from Sister Mary St. Peter. This favor could not be granted as the mere mention of it would have frightened the humility of our pious invalid. However, she was admitted and soon reached the sick bed. Sister Mary St. Peter was apparently sleeping, but she was profoundly absorbed in God. After having regarded her for some time without wishing to disturb her, the pious benefactress prepared to withdraw, when suddenly, the sister seized the little statue of the Infant Jesus, and without a word, made the sign of the cross over the venerable lady, thus giving the blessing which had been vainly implored. The lady, beholding the spontaneous act, was deeply touched."

"The pure soul of our languishing victim had recovered its peace and tranquility, yet her body was a continual prey to excruciating sufferings which became more and more poignant as the time of her dissolution approached. On Friday, July 7th, her death agony began, but she was in full possession of all her mental faculties to the last. As it was thought she would not survive the night, we recited the prayers and recommendations for the dying. This last night was passed by our dear sister in the most acute sufferings; she frequently called for holy water and kept united to God by fervent aspirations. I remained at her side, for she seemed to feel great consolation when I was present, she even implored me with tears not to leave her. However, at dawn I withdrew for a few moments. During my absence, she wished to change her position, and needed help; (for many days she had been unable to make any movement) she was told I had recommended she should not be moved, but that if her sufferings were too intense, they would presume my permission and try to change her posture. But she would not consent. 'No, no,' said she, 'we must obey to the last. "

"She responded to all the prayers we suggested, kissing her crucifix continually, pressing it to her heart repeating: 'He is all mine, and I am all his. What happiness!' I returned to the bedside of Sister St. Peter and she exclaimed: 'Mother, when?' I replied: 'When the Spouse, comes, is it not?' She answered by an affirmative sign, and I continued: 'Soon, my child, in a very few moments.' She appeared satisfied and composed. Recollecting that Our Lord had promised in one of her communications to reestablish in her soul the image of God at the hour of her death, she begged to renew her baptismal vows, and as a symbol of the grace which she desired to receive, asked for some holy water, and made the sign of the cross on her head saying: 'Child, I baptize thee in the name of the Father, and of the Son and of the Holy Ghost.' Then joining her hands, she added: 'I renounce Satan with all his works and pomps. I desire to belong to Jesus Christ forever.' A few moments before this, she seemed to undergo a painful combat, but after this little ceremony, her countenance beamed with peace and happiness; one would have said that she was a child just after being baptized, or an angel about to wing its flight to the realms above. From this moment till her last sigh, she never ceased praying; the sweat of death covered her face, her body was already cold and stiff, yet her livid lips kept repeating: 'Jesus, Mary, Joseph. Come, Lord Jesus.' *Sit Nomen Domini benedictum!* These were the last words we were able to distinguish, the movement of her lips continued, but in an unintelligible manner. Soon she heard nothing more, her eyes closed, and as if in a last resemblance to her Divine Master, she uttered a cry and calmly expired, in the presence of the whole community."

23

HER BURIAL—HER WORK

"She will protect your house, the diocese and France."
(Words of Mgr. Morlot)

"Sr. Mary St. Peter died on Saturday, day consecrated to Mary, the 8th of July, near mid-day: our dear sister had often begged of the Blessed Virgin to present her soul to God, and we see that her request was granted. From the moment the servant of God breathed forth her last sigh, the conviction of her beatitude filled all hearts; each felt more like praying to her than for her; each recalled her virtues, and loudly proclaimed that she was a saint."

"We must remember they were still ignorant of the rare favors and celestial communications which the Lord had bestowed on her. In the community she became the object of general veneration; the ambition of each was to have a particle of something belonging to her; they touched her with objects of piety: nor could they be separated from her precious remains. Her countenance bore a peaceful and happy expression; her limbs, which during her illness were stiff from the excess of emaciation and suffering, became flexible immediately after death."

"There was one sister who did not share in the general opinion of the sanctity of Sister Mary St. Peter. She had never beheld her commit any fault, it is true, but her life so simple and ordinary, did not seem to her to merit so much praise. Annoyed at the difference of opinion existing between herself and the other religious, about a month before the death of the sister, she had earnestly addressed to Grod the following prayer: "My God, if Sr. Mary St. Peter be as holy as they say, make it known to me, I beseech thee by giving me some relief (this sister was ill) so that I can join in the community exercises."

"She was heard, and was able to follow the rule minutely, to the great surprise of all; yet she was not convinced by this first proof. But at the death of the sister, she had a dream which gave her subject for reflection. It seemed to her as if she were with the other nuns, round the bed of the dying sister, who expired before her eyes. She saw her immediately resuscitated under the figure of a most beautiful child, who descending from the bed went to embrace each of the sisters except herself and disappeared out of sight forever."

"The day following at communion, she felt entirely changed. The life of her pious companion appeared in all its holiness, and she was filled with regret for not having recognized the sanctity of her companion."

"During the time our dear sister was laid out in the choir, a great number of seculars came to pay their last respects to the dear departed. Many exclaimed: 'How like an angel! Oh, may she pray for us!' A considerable number of people attended her funeral."

"It was remarked during the solemn requiem service which lasted nearly an hour and a half, that the large candles placed at the corners of the coffin, burned without being consumed. They remained burning brightly, although there was such a strong draft in the chapel that the candles held by the sisters were quite wasted away. This was proved by a fifth candle which had not been used because it was shorter than the other four: the same difference was found to exist between them when measured after the ceremony."

"Heaven also gave signs in favor of the humble Carmelite; several had recourse to her intercession and have assured us that they experienced in an extraordinary manner the effects of her power with God. When the news of her death was spread abroad, the people came from all parts to ask for little souvenirs of the dear departed.

"It was noticed that little particles of her clothing, exhaled a delicious fragrance which did not resemble any known perfume, it was a celestial odor penetrating even to the soul, exciting the love of God and virtue."

"Both seculars and religious have attested the fact: one in particular assured us, that on opening a box which for some time had contained little pieces of her habit, a delicious perfume was noticed, like the fragrance of a beautiful bouquet of flowers. A lady of Ingouville, in the diocese of Rouen, was taken ill with a violent fever, for which the doctors could prescribe no remedy; a piece of Sister St. Peter's veil was forwarded her. Scarcely had it been applied than she felt an interior process being performed within her which lasted four hours. The dreaded crisis, the first symptoms of which had already been announced, was averted; she passed a quiet night, and the next day was proclaimed out of danger."

To this pious narrative, literally transcribed from the Carmelite annals, we shall add what we have gleaned from authentic documents. Mgr. Morlot, who as we have said, came to give his blessing to the dying sister, having received information of her departure from this life, wrote in the following terms to the mother prioress: "It is with the liveliest sympathy I read of the death of this good sister, but we must rejoice with her rather than weep over her. Let us hope that she will continue in heaven what she has so well begun on earth. She will protect your house, the diocese and France'... Of this I am convinced; tomorrow, I shall offer for her and for your community the august sacrifice of the mass."

When the circular, composed according to the custom, after the death of Sister St. Peter, was forwarded to the prelate, he wrote: "I have read the notice of the death of Sr. M. St. Peter with the deepest interest, and I doubt not of the good impression it will produce in all the houses of your Order. I am confident, that this chosen soul, now in the possession of eternal glory, will efficaciously plead our cause before the Lord, after having prayed on this earth with so much faith, and practiced here below the beautiful virtues which distinguish the true spouses of Christ."

Such were the personal sentiments of the archbishop of Tours, and they were shared by all those who had any relationship with the pious Carmelite; but there was no one more impressed than M. Dupont. To him the day of such a saintly death was a day of joy, the beginning of glory for the humble virgin, and for her work of predilection. He had assisted with a radiant countenance at her funeral obsequies, and as if in triumphant procession followed her mortal remains to the cemetery of Saint Jean des Corps, a place already hallowed in his eyes, as six months previous he had deposited the last remains of his only and dearly beloved daughter, Henrietta. When he received the obituary notice from Carmel, ho read it with transports of admiration. *Sit Nomen Domini benedictum!* He wrote the mother prioress: "I believe we are nearing the realization of the wishes of the venerable sister, apostle of the Work of Reparation. It is impossible that the circular will not produce a great effect in the hearts of Christians who will use all their efforts to demand grace and mercy. May God be blessed, and may his Holy Name be forever glorified!" M. Dupont desired that a number of copies be sent to his friends.

From this time, one of his pious practices, was to go frequently to pray over the tomb of this venerable sister and keep it in perfect order. He directed his steps alternately to the tomb of his daughter and to that of the Carmelite, recommending to her all his affairs. Those who came from afar to confide to him their difficulties, he frequently sent to the cemetery of St. John to pray. On his way, thence one day, he said to a priest who accompanied him: "This is one of my secrets: that I address myself to this saintly soul when I desire to receive any particular grace from God." Under the impression thus given, the grave of the Carmelite received many visits.

To perpetuate this kind of pilgrimage, and to testify his veneration for the memory of the deceased, he determined to buy a more suitable burial-place. He took the necessary steps and bought in his name and at his own expense, thirty lots, the deed of which he presented to the community on the 27th of September 1854.

"But," said he, "God will yet do more to glorify his faithful servant. For a reason only known to Him, the remains must be removed to Carmel." It was not long before this pious desire was fulfilled. Three years later, immediately after the great inundation of the Loire in 1856, the cemetery was transferred without the city limits and M. Dupont took advantage of the circumstance to have the remains of Sister St. Peter exhumed and restored to her monastery. On the 13th of November 1857, the anniversary of the day the sister had entered religion, he accompanied the inspector before sunrise to open the tomb. A walnut coffin lined with zinc had been prepared. M. Dupont, with the utmost care and religious respect collected, and placed in it the hallowed remains, even the smallest particles of dust; and to the great joy of the mother prioress and all the religious, he obtained permission from competent authority to have the precious remains deposited in the interior of the monastery. They still repose in the chapter room, which is at the right of the chapel on entering. A slab near the holy water font bears this simple inscription:

Here reposes
Sister Mary St. Peter of the Holy Family,
Professed of this Monastery,
who died on the 8th July, **1848,**
AGED 31 YEARS AND 9 MONTHS.

"Conceal her, **O** Lord in the secret of thy Face."

M. Dupont, who often came to hear mass in the Carmelite chapel, never entered without pausing a few moments at the spot, above which the tomb of the revered sister had been deposited, and in his simple faith, holding converse for an instant with the dear departed.

A more intimate and fruitful union was still to draw these two souls more closely together. In the designs of God, M. Dupont's mission was to develop the work, revealed to Sister St. Peter as the means of salvation for France, the Work of Reparation for blasphemy and for the profanation of the Sunday, by the worship of the Holy Face. More than any other, the pious layman had received more knowledge of the wonderful favors granted to the virgin of Carmel.

He was already admirably prepared by the piety of his life, to devote himself to "Reparation." What struck him most forcibly in the revelations of the sister, was the means, indicated by Our Lord to his servant, of repairing the outrages committed against his adorable person; namely, the devotion to his Holy Face. Completely enraptured with this idea, he labored to propagate this devotion without any premeditated object, solely for the glory of God and the salvation of souls, wishing to be, as he said, "the voice" of the revelations of Sister Mary St. Peter. A circumstance, very simple in itself, soon gave a decisive character to his pious enthusiasm.

Lent was drawing to a close. The mother prioress, who was perfectly aware of M. Dupont's opinion with regard to the devotion of the Holy Face, offered him a present of two pictures of the Holy Face, copies of Veronica's veil which is preserved in the Vatican. These the prioress had received from the Benedictines of Arras, with whom she had corresponded for several years on the subject of the Work of Reparation. These holy pictures came from Rome and were soon copied and spread among the faithful by the zeal of the religious of Arras, who, from the time of their establishment in 1816, had a lively devotion to the Holy Face, inspired them by the writings of St. Gertrude; these religious took a marked interest in the revelations of the Carmelite of Tours. They possessed a certain number of pictures with authentication. At the request of Mother Mary of the Incarnation they sent her several copies, two of which she gave to M. Dupont, who framed one and hung it in his parlor. It was before this venerable image that he passed the last twenty-five years of his life, thus becoming the apostle of Reparation. The most extraordinary cures, conversions miraculously brought about, peace and harmony restored to families, in fact, so numerous were the wonders performed through the prayers of this saintly man before the "Holy Face" that his house soon became the favorite resort of pilgrims from far and near.

M. Dupont looked upon these miraculous graces as so many manifestations of the will of God; this explains why he attached so much importance to the certificates brought him, which he preserved with the greatest care, as a faithful guardian, to place them in the hands of the ecclesiastical authority, when inquiries would be made relative to the mission of Sister Mary St. Peter.

"Verily," says M. Dupont, "if the communications of Sister St. Peter were acknowledged as revelations, what a blow would be given to the infernal spirits!"

"The prodigies, operated by the oil of the lamp burning before the Holy Face, will naturally draw the attention of the authorities of the Church to this subject, and she will be called upon to give a decision relative to the writings of the pious Carmelite. We find among her revelations the most consoling promises made to those devoted to the Holy Face. She proclaims in every letter that the Holy Face ought to be the external object of Reparation. What is the conclusion? Every day we are here witnesses of the remarkable cures which have taken place under our very eyes, cures so extraordinary that if we sought to establish the facts they could be called miraculous. Every day at least two or three are operated here before the Holy Face, after the application of the oil; without mentioning the wonders wrought by the application of the oil demanded by the sick, too ill to be brought hither. These facts authorize us to believe that there is here a clear manifestation of the will of Our Lord, to procure our salvation by the work which he himself, demanded from Sister Mary St. Peter."

His joy was extreme when, on his deathbed, he learned that the archbishop of Tours, Mgr. Colet, had at last broken the seals, and that the examination of her precious writings, so long condemned to secrecy, was confided to the learned Benedictines of Salamanca, the worthy sons of his illustrious friend Dom Gueranger. On hearing this news, his countenance became illuminated, he raised his eyes to heaven and exclaimed: *Nunc dimittis servum tuum, Domine.*

A weight seemed to have been raised from his heart; shortly before he expired, on the 18th of March, 1876, turning his eyes toward the cloister of the Carmelites, where thanks to his zeal and devotedness reposed the body of Sister Mary St. Peter, he exclaimed: "How brilliant is Carmel! It glitters with rubies and emeralds."

He made no mention of the " Holy Face" in his will, saying to those around his bedside: "God will provide for it." His confidence was not unfounded. God had placed on the archiepiscopal throne of St. Martin, a most worthy prelate, who, at the first glance had recognized the providential mission of our Carmelite, interpreted and followed up by M. Dupont. An archiepiscopal decree transformed the private oratory of the holy man of Tours into a public chapel. The venerable prelate himself presided at the ceremony of consecration, on the 27th of June, feast of the Prince of the Apostles, and patron of "this fervent religious who," said he, "had inspired the Work of Reparation and the touching devotion, which for so many years, has been practiced in this holy spot." At the same time he established the confraternity in Reparation for Blasphemy and the Profanation of the Sunday, affiliated to that of St. Dizier; but taking advantage of the clause giving full liberty to the director to modify the minor rules, he gave it a distinctive character, making it in reality a confraternity of the Holy Face properly speaking, which was, as we have seen, the primitive object of Sister St. Peter. Finally, this most worthy successor of St. Martin founded a society of regulars, under the title of "Priests of the Holy Face" to attend to the new chapel and look after all the necessities of the pilgrimage which had commenced even during the lifetime of M. Dupont.

They live in community in the house of M. Dupont, binding themselves to follow in his steps under his protection, and to devote themselves to all the reparatory works of the epoch. Thus the work of the pious Carmelite and that of the "Holy man of Tours," has been canonically recognized and consolidated.

The diocese of St. Martin thus recovered the glory of which it had been accidentally deprived, it re-entered into the right which belonged originally to it, that of being considered the hearth on which the sacred fire of Reparation was first enkindled. From that time, the work, under the auspices and in the very dwelling of M. Dupont, has received a marvelous development, and is today spreading in other lands. The oratory of the Holy Face has become in a few years the center of prayers and "expiation," toward which turn all hearts from the different points of France, and we may say, from the entire Church.

The pious invocations composed by Sister Mary St. Peter, and improperly called Litanies of the Holy Face, have been authorized by a number of bishops; Pius IX himself, without giving them a liturgical approbation, has blessed and enriched them with an indulgence; they are at present translated into English, Spanish, Italian, and German, to satisfy the many demands of the faithful. Confraternities of the Holy Face, like the one founded at Tours by Mgr. Colet, are established in many cities, notably at Versailles, Reims, Laval, Perpignan; and St. Brieuc. We even behold it passing over to other lands, to Belgium, Holland and even to America.

From all sides the people demand the "Holy Face" this faithful copy of the veil of Veronica, identical to that venerated by M. Dupont. It would be impossible to calculate the number of these sacred effigies, exposed for pious veneration in thousands of places, and nearly always having a lamp burning before them. They are to be found in private houses, in oratories, in asylums and in communities, in public chapels, in parishes and in cathedrals. Even in the time of M. Dupont there were pictures of the Holy Face venerated in the hospital of Vincennes, at the Visitation of Paray-le-Monial, and at the Benedictines of Arras.

In our day, Notre-Daine de Paris, the cathedral of Perpignan, the Basilica of Lourdes, and the provisory chapel of the Sacred Heart at Montmartre also contain a copy of this picture.

The Priests of the "Holy Face," undertake to have them expedited from Borne, to facilitate their propagation, or rather the propagation goes on of itself, so natural, so necessary does this idea of Reparation seem to the faithful.

This Reparation is urgent, every Catholic heart feels its necessity; pious souls greet it with transports of joy. Now. if it be true that France, God's privileged nation, the Eldest Daughter of the Church, if it be true that among all peoples she is the most guilty, she is therefore the most deserving of punishment, for "Much shall be required of him to whom much has been given." If it be true that here more than elsewhere, the profanation of the Sunday is the acknowledged evil, that blasphemy is unblushingly tolerated, and that both the one and the other engender more crime, produce more ruin and ravage society more than any other evil, is it not then just that we should look up to generous Christians (whose number is infinite in our dear France) for the accomplishment and for the propagation of a work so repeatedly besought by Sister Mary St. Peter in the Name of the Lord? And since the cradle of the Work has been providentially placed in the very heart of the country, in this city of Tours, which has the happy privilege of possessing the tomb of the great protector of the nation, together with the house in which the pious devotee of the Holy Face died in the odor of sanctity, what more natural, what more just than to make it the center of our affections, of our prayers, of our hopes? What more patriotic, what more Catholic than to unite to re-establish and to repair, even as we behold impiety, aye infidelity itself, rally its votaries to ravage, to destroy.

The work revealed to this noble religious, is, as she has remarked, "a crying necessity and a pledge of mercy." Let us then have but one heart and one soul in uniting to appease divine justice, and we shall experience the effects of His mercy, which shall be the more gracious and abundant as our reparation shall have been prompter and more fervent.

FINIS.